GARBAGE AND OTHER POLLUTION

ISSN 1538-6651

GARBAGE AND OTHER POLLUTION

Sandra Alters

INFORMATION PLUS® REFERENCE SERIES
Formerly published by Information Plus, Wylie, Texas

GALE GROUP
*
THOMSON LEARNING

Detroit • New York • San Diego • San Francisco
Boston • New Haven, Conn. • Waterville, Maine
London • Munich

GARBAGE AND OTHER POLLUTION

Sandra Alters, *Author*

The Gale Group Staff:

Coordinating Editors: Ellice Engdahl, *Series Editor*; Charles B. Montney, *Series Graphics Editor*

Managing Editor: Debra M. Kirby

Contributing Editors: Elizabeth Manar, Kathleen Meek

Contributing Associate Editors: Paula Cutcher-Jackson, Nancy Franklin, Prindle LaBarge, Sharon M. McGilvray, Heather Price, Michael T. Reade

Imaging and Multimedia Content: Barbara J. Yarrow, *Manager, Imaging and Multimedia Content*; Dean Dauphinais, *Imaging and Multimedia Content Editor*; Kelly A. Quin, *Imaging and Multimedia Content Editor*; Robyn Young, *Imaging and Multimedia Content Editor*; Leitha Etheridge-Sims, *Image Cataloger*; Mary K. Grimes, *Image Cataloger*; David G. Oblender, *Image Cataloger*; Lezlie Light, *Imaging Coordinator*; Randy Bassett, *Imaging Supervisor*; Robert Duncan, *Imaging Specialist*; Dan Newell, *Imaging Specialist*; Luke Rademacher, *Imaging Specialist*; Christine O'Bryan, *Graphic Specialist*

Indexing: Susan Kelsch, *Indexing Supervisor*

Permissions: Kim Davis, *Permissions Associate*; Maria Franklin, *Permissions Manager*

Product Design: Michelle DiMercurio, *Senior Art Director and Product Design Manager*; Michael Logusz, *Graphic Artist*

Production: Evi Seoud, *Assistant Manager, Composition Purchasing and Electronic Prepress*; Keith Helmling, *Buyer*; Dorothy Maki, *Manufacturing Manager*

Cover photo © PhotoDisc.

ISBN 0-7876-5103-6 (set)
ISBN 0-7876-6057-4 (this volume)
ISSN 1538-6651 (this volume)
Printed in the United States of America
10 9 8 7 6 5 4 3 2 1

TABLE OF CONTENTS

CHAPTER 1

This chapter describes the history of waste management from ancient to modern times. Early efforts at recycling, the modern-day American "throwaway society," total amounts of waste generated, and federal laws concerning waste are also explained.

CHAPTER 2

Chapter 2 defines municipal solid waste (MSW) and examines how it is generated and dealt with. A substantial section details landfills, into which a majority of MSW goes. Also covered are alternative treatments for MSW, including combustion and recycling; packaging as MSW; and recent trends and future projections about waste management.

CHAPTER 3

Recycling and composting are two ways to reduce the amount of waste that has to be disposed. Types of recycling programs and facilities are looked at, and recycling rates of specific wastes are analyzed. Also included are brief accounts of recycling around the world and projections for future waste recovery.

CHAPTER 4

Conveyed in this chapter are facts about pollution that exists in the air. Smog and the health effects of air pollution are covered, and there is detailed treatment of the major air pollutants. Also described are the effects of automobiles on air pollution, national and international laws and treaties on the topic, and the quality of air indoors.

CHAPTER 5

This chapter explains why water pollution is such a serious issue, detailing health risks for humans and whole ecosystems. The Clean Water Act is covered, and the current state of pollution in oceans, estuaries, lakes, reservoirs, ponds, rivers, streams, and wetlands in the United States is explored in depth.

CHAPTER 6

Ground water is distinct from surface water in that it is found only below the earth's surface; however, it may still become polluted. In this chapter are found the factors that affect ground pollution, sources and types of such pollution, and strategies for protecting or cleaning up ground water.

CHAPTER 7

Solid waste that can be considered dangerous is classified as hazardous waste. Information on the management and government regulation of hazardous waste is included in this chapter, and the topics of Brownfields, environmental justice, and ground water contamination are also tackled. The latter two-thirds of the chapter describes various aspects of radioactive waste, including what it is, how it is disposed of, how it is transported, and how other countries deal with its disposal.

CHAPTER 8

Various polls discussed in this chapter display how Americans feel about waste management issues. Poll results presented include how sympathetic people feel to the environmental movement, what Americans' major environmental concerns are, how well the public feels the government is addressing these concerns, how much environmental knowledge people have, and how the importance of environmental protection compares to that of economic growth.

PREFACE

Garbage and Other Pollution is one of the latest volumes in the Information Plus Reference Series. Previously published by the Information Plus company of Wylie, Texas, the Information Plus Reference Series (and its companion set, the Information Plus Compact Series) became a Gale Group product when Gale and Information Plus merged in early 2000. Those of you familiar with the series as published by Information Plus will notice a few changes from the 2000 edition. Gale has adopted a new layout and style that we hope you will find easy to use. Other improvements include greatly expanded indexes in each book, and more descriptive tables of contents.

While some changes have been made to the design, the purpose of the Information Plus Reference Series remains the same. Each volume of the series presents the latest facts on a topic of pressing concern in modern American life. These topics include today's most controversial and most studied social issues: abortion, capital punishment, care for the elderly, crime, health care, the environment, immigration, minorities, social welfare, women, youth, and many more. Although written especially for the high school and undergraduate student, this series is an excellent resource for anyone in need of factual information on current affairs.

By presenting the facts, it is Gale's intention to provide its readers with everything they need to reach an informed opinion on current issues. To that end, there is a particular emphasis in this series on the presentation of scientific studies, surveys, and statistics. These data are generally presented in the form of tables, charts, and other graphics placed within the text of each book. Every graphic is directly referred to and carefully explained in the text. The source of each graphic is presented within the graphic itself. The data used in these graphics is drawn from the most reputable and reliable sources, in particular the various branches of the U.S. government and major independent polling organizations. Every effort has been made to secure the most recent information available. The reader should bear in mind that many major studies take years to conduct, and that additional years often pass before the data from these studies are made available to the public. Therefore, in many cases the most recent information available in 2002 dated from 1999 or 2000. Older statistics are sometimes presented as well, if they are of particular interest and no more recent information exists.

Although statistics are a major focus of the Information Plus Reference Series, they are by no means its only content. Each book also presents the widely held positions and important ideas that shape how the book's subject is discussed in the United States. These positions are explained in detail and, where possible, in the words of their proponents. Some of the other material to be found in these books includes: historical background; descriptions of major events related to the subject; relevant laws and court cases; and examples of how these issues play out in American life. Some books also feature primary documents, or have pro and con debate sections giving the words and opinions of prominent Americans on both sides of a controversial topic. All material is presented in an even-handed and unbiased manner; the reader will never be encouraged to accept one view of an issue over another.

HOW TO USE THIS BOOK

Modern American society is consumption-driven, which means that goods and materials are produced and discarded. The production and consumption of goods, though, results in pollution and waste. This book provides a snapshot of the current condition of garbage and other pollution in the United States. Included is information on the makeup of solid waste, including ways in which it is disposed and/or recycled; the pollution found in air and water; hazardous waste; and the opinions of Americans on various environmental concerns.

Garbage and Other Pollution consists of eight chapters and three appendices. Each of the chapters is devoted to a particular aspect of garbage and pollution. For a summary of the information covered in each chapter, please see the synopses provided in the Table of Contents at the front of the book. Chapters generally begin with an overview of the basic facts and background information on the chapter's topic, then proceed to examine sub-topics of particular interest. For example, Chapter Six: Pollution of Ground Water begins with a definition of ground water, an explanation of the water cycle, and a list of factors that can affect the pollution of ground water. It then goes on to provide in-depth coverage of the major sources of ground water contamination, including underground storage tanks; septic systems and sewage disposal; landfills and hazardous waste sites; pesticides, herbicides, and fertilizers; and surface impoundments. Also included is a section on the treatment and prevention of ground water pollution. Readers can find their way through a chapter by looking for the section and sub-section headings, which are clearly set off from the text. Or, they can refer to the book's extensive index if they already know what they are looking for.

Statistical Information

The tables and figures featured throughout *Garbage and Other Pollution* will be of particular use to the reader in learning about this issue. These tables and figures represent an extensive collection of the most recent and important statistics on garbage and pollution, as well as related issues—for example, graphics in the book cover waste generation rates, materials recovery facility processing equipment, glass generation and recovery, nitrogen dioxide emissions by source category, characteristics of alternative transportation fuels, beach closings and advisories over a 12-year period, the nuclear fuel cycle, and public attitudes concerning the priority of various environmental problems. Gale believes that making this information available to the reader is the most important way in which we fulfill the goal of this book: to help readers understand the issues and controversies surrounding garbage and other pollution in the United States and reach their own conclusions.

Each table or figure has a unique identifier appearing above it, for ease of identification and reference. Titles for the tables and figures explain their purpose. At the end of each table or figure, the original source of the data is provided.

In order to help readers understand these often complicated statistics, all tables and figures are explained in the text. References in the text direct the reader to the relevant statistics. Furthermore, the contents of all tables and figures are fully indexed. Please see the opening section of the index at the back of this volume for a description of how to find tables and figures within it.

In addition to the main body text and images, *Garbage and Other Pollution* has three appendices. The first is the Important Names and Addresses directory. Here the reader will find contact information for a number of government and private organizations that can provide information on garbage and/or pollution. The second appendix is the Resources section, which can also assist the reader in conducting his or her own research. In this section, the author and editors of *Garbage and Other Pollution* describe some of the sources that were most useful during the compilation of this book. The final appendix is the index. It has been greatly expanded from previous editions, and should make it even easier to find specific topics in this book.

COMMENTS AND SUGGESTIONS

The editors of the Information Plus Reference Series welcome your feedback on *Garbage and Other Pollution*. Please direct all correspondence to:

Editors
Information Plus Reference Series
27500 Drake Rd.
Farmington Hills, MI 48331-3535

ACKNOWLEDGEMENTS

The editors wish to thank the copyright holders of material included in this volume and the permissions managers of many book and magazine publishing companies for assisting us in securing reproduction rights. We are also grateful to the staffs of the Detroit Public Library, the Library of Congress, the University of Detroit Mercy Library, Wayne State University Purdy/Kresge Library Complex, and the University of Michigan Libraries for making their resources available to us.

Following is a list of the copyright holders who have granted us permission to reproduce material in Information Plus: Garbage and Other Pollution. *Every effort has been made to trace copyright, but if omissions have been made, please let us know.*

Acknowledgements are listed in the order the tables and figures appear in the text of Garbage and Other Pollution. *For more detailed citations, please see the sources listed under each table and figure.*

Figure 1.1. "Garbage Then & Now." Environmental Industry Associations, Washington, DC. Reproduced by permission.

Table 1.1. Ryan, John C. and Alan Thein Durning. From "Per Capita Resource Consumption, Mid 1990s," in *Stuff: The Secret Lives of Everyday Things*. Northwest Environment Watch, Seattle, WA, 1997. Reproduced by permission.

Figure 1.2. "Figure ES-1: Waste Generation Rates From 1960 to 1999," from *Municipal Solid Waste in the United States: 1999 Facts and Figures*. U.S. Environmental Protection Agency, Washington, DC, 2000.

Figure 1.3. "Distribution of Solid Waste, 1992," from *Solid Waste: State and Federal Efforts to Manage Nonhazardous Waste*. U.S. General Accounting Office, Washington, DC, 1995.

Table 2.1. "Table ES-1," "Table ES-2," and "Table ES-3," from *Municipal Solid Waste in the United States: 1999 Facts and Figures*. U.S. Environmental Protection Agency, Washington, DC, 2000. Data from Franklin Associates.

Figure 2.1. "Figure ES-3: 1999 Total Waste Generation - 230 Million Tons (Before Recycling)," from *Municipal Solid Waste in the United States: 1999 Facts and Figures*. U.S. Environmental Protection Agency, Washington, DC, 2000.

Table 2.2. "Table 19. Products Generated in the Municipal Waste Stream, 1960 to 1999 (With Detail on Containers and Packaging)," from *Municipal Solid Waste in the United States: 1999 Facts and Figures*. U.S. Environmental Protection Agency, Washington, DC, 2000. Data from Franklin Associates.

Table 2.3. Goldstein, Nora and Celeste Madtes. "Table 2. Municipal Solid Waste (MSW) generation (unless noted), recycling and disposal methods by state (1999 data unless noted)" in "The State of Garbage in America, Part II," from *Biocycle*, November 2000. Reprinted with permission from *Biocycle* magazine. For more information, visit www.biocycle.net.

Figure 2.3. "Figure 26. Municipal solid waste management, 1960 to 1999," from *Municipal Solid Waste in the United States: 1999 Facts and Figures*. U.S. Environmental Protection Agency, Washington, DC, 2000.

Figure 2.4. "'Bathtub' Model of Modern Sanitary Landfill," from *Let's Reduce and Recycle: Curriculum for Solid Waste Man-agement*. U.S. Environmental Protection Agency, Washington, DC, 1990.

Table 2.4. Goldstein, Nora. "Table 2. Number of municipal solid waste landfills and incinerators, average tip fees, and capacity by state for 1999," in "The State of Garbage in America: Part I" from *Biocycle*, April 2000. Reprinted with permission from *Biocycle* magazine. For more information, visit www.biocycle.net.

Table 2.5. "Table 1. Municipal solid waste generation, waste imports and exports by state for 1999" in "The State of Garbage in America: Part I," from *Biocycle*, April 2000. Reprinted with permission from *Biocycle* magazine. For more information, visit www.biocycle.net.

Figure 2.5. "States with Operational Landfill Gas-to-Energy Facilities, May 2001." U.S. Environmental Protection Agency, Landfill Methane Outreach Program, May 2001.

Table 2.6. "Sources of Lead in MSW," from *MSW Factbook*. U.S. Environmental Protection Agency, Washington, DC, 1997.

Figure 2.6. "Fresh Kills Municipal Landfill," from *Hazardous Substances and Public Health*, v. 8, Winter, 1998. Agency for Toxic Substances and Disease Registry. Reproduced by permission.

Figure 2.7. "Waste Combustion Plant with Pollution Control System," from *Let's Reduce and Recycle: Curriculum for Solid Waste Management*. U.S. Environmental Protection Agency, Washington, DC, 1990.

Table 2.7. Goldstein, Nora and Celeste Madtes. From "Table 3. Residential curbside recycling and yard trimmings composting sites by state" in "The State of Garbage in America, Part II," from *Biocycle*, November 2000. Reprinted with permission from *Biocycle* magazine. For more information, visit www.biocycle.net.

Figure 2.8. "Figure 8. Plastics products generated in MSW, 1999," from *Municipal Solid Waste in the United States: 1999 Facts and Figures*. U.S. Environmental Protection Agency, Washington, DC, 2000.

Figure 2.9. "Figure 17. Diagram of solid waste management," from *Municipal Solid Waste in the United States: 1999 Facts and Figures*. U.S. Environmental Protection Agency, Washington, DC, 2000. Data from Franklin Associates.

Table 2.8. "Table 24: Selected Examples of Source Reduction Practices," from *Municipal Solid Waste in the United States: 1999 Facts and Figures*. U.S. Environmental Protection Agency, Washington, DC, 2000. Data from Franklin Associates.

Table 2.9. McCarthy, James E. "Table 1. Federal Regulations on Solid Waste Management," from *Solid Waste Issues in the 106th Congress*. Congressional Research Service, The Library of Congress, Washington, DC, April 27, 2000.

Table 2.10. "Projections of materials generated in the municipal waste stream: 2000 and 2005," from *Characterization of Municipal Solid Waste in the United States: 1998 Update*. U.S. Environmental Protection Agency, Washington, DC, 1999.

Figure 2.10. "Historical and projected generation of municipal solid waste, 1960–2005," from *Characterization of Municipal Solid Waste in the United States: 1998 Update*. U.S. Environmental Protection Agency, Washington, DC, 1999.

Figure 3.1. "Figure 11. Recovery and discards of MSW, 1960 to 1999," from *Municipal Solid Waste in the United States: 1999 Facts and Figures*. U.S. Environmental Protection Agency, Washington, DC, 2000.

Figure 3.2. "The International Recycling Symbols," from *Talkin' Trash!: A Guide to Solid Waste Disposal and Recycling in Bay County, Florida*. Bay County Solid Waste Management Department. Reproduced by permission.

Table 3.1. Goldstein, Nora and Celeste Madtes. "Table 6. State diversion goals and recovery rates" in "The State of Garbage in America, Part II" in *Biocycle*, November 2000. Reprinted with permission from *Biocycle* magazine. For more information, visit www.biocycle.net.

Table 3.2. "MRF Processing Equipment," from *The Cost to Recycle at a Materials Recovery Facility*. National Solid Wastes Management Association, Washington, DC, 1992. Reproduced by permission.

Table 3.3. "Table 29: Generation, Materials Recovery, Composting, Combustion, and Discards of Municipal Solid Waste, 1960 to 1999," from *Municipal Solid Waste in the United States: 1999 Facts and Figures*. U.S. Environmental Protection Agency, Washington, DC, 2000. Data from Franklin Associates.

Table 3.4. "Table ES-4: Generation and Recovery of Materials in MSW, 1999 (In millions of tons and percent of generation of each material)," from *Municipal Solid Waste in the United States: 1999 Facts and Figures*. U.S. Environmental Protection Agency, Washington, DC, 2000.

Figure 3.3. "Figure 12. Materials recovery, 1999," from *Municipal Solid Waste in the United States: 1999 Facts and Figures*. U.S. Environmental Protection Agency, Washington, DC, 2000.

Figure 3.4. "Figure 13. Materials Generated and Discarded in Municipal Solid Waste, 1999 (in percent of total generation and discards)," from *Municipal Solid Waste in the United States: 1999 Facts and Figures*. U.S. Environmental Protection Agency, Washington, DC, 2000.

Figure 3.5. "Recycling Types of Containers," from *Recycle Glass for the Earth's Future*. Mid-America Glass Recycling Program, Tulsa, OK, 1993. Reproduced by permission.

Figure 3.6. "Figure 3. Paper generation and recovery, 1960 to 1999," from *Municipal Solid Waste in the United States: 1999 Facts and Figures*. U.S. Environmental Protection Agency, Washington, DC, 2000.

Figure 3.7. "Figure 5. Glass Generation and Recovery, 1960 to 1999," from *Municipal Solid Waste in the United States: 1999 Facts and Figures*. U.S. Environmental Protection Agency, Washington, DC, 2000.

Figure 3.8. "Glass recycling process," from *Recycle Glass for the Earth's Future*. Mid-America Glass Recycling Program, Tulsa, OK, 1993. Reproduced by permission.

Figure 3.9. "Figure 7. Metals generation and recovery, 1960 to 1999," from *Municipal Solid Waste in the United States: 1999 Facts and Figures*. U.S. Environmental Protection Agency, Washington, DC, 2000.

Figure 3.10. "Figure 9. Plastics generation and recovery, 1960 to 1999," from *Municipal Solid Waste in the United States: 1999 Facts and Figures*. U.S. Environmental Protection Agency, Washington, DC, 2000.

Table 3.5. "Table 21: Recovery of Products in Municipal Solid Waste, 1960 to 1999 (With Detail on Containers and Packaging. In percent of generation of each product)," from *Municipal Solid Waste in the United States: 1999 Facts and Figures*. U.S. Environmental Protection Agency, Washington, DC, 2000. Data from Franklin Associates.

Table 3.6. "NCL packaging study, selected statistics" in "Great Taste, Less Landfilling," from *The ULS Report*, v. 6, April/May/June 1999. Reproduced by permission.

Figure 3.11. "How Product Design Affects Materials Flows," from *Characterization of Municipal Solid Waste in the United States: 1998 Update*. U.S. Environmental Protection Agency, Washington, DC, 1999.

Figure 3.12. "Historical and projected recovery rates," from *Characterization of Municipal Solid Waste in the United States: 1998 Update*. U.S. Environmental Protection Agency, Washington, DC, 1999.

Table 3.7. "Generation, Recovery, Combustion, and Disposal of Municipal Solid Waste: 1997, 2000, and 2005," from *Characterization of Municipal Solid Waste in the United States: 1998 Update*. U.S. Environmental Protection Agency, Washington, DC, 1999.

Figure 3.13. "Municipal solid waste management, 1980 to 2005," from *Characterization of Municipal Solid Waste in the United States: 1998 Update*. U.S. Environmental Protection Agency, Washington, DC, 1999.

Table 4.1. "Common Air Pollutants (Criteria Air Pollutants)," from *The Plain English Guide to the Clean Air Act*. U.S. Environmental Protection Agency, Washington, DC, 1993.

Table 4.2. "Table 4-3. Nonattainment Status," from *National Air Quality Trends Report, 1998*, and "Table 4-1. Areas Redesignated Between September 1999 and September 2000," from *National Air Quality and Emissions Trends Report, 1999*. U.S. Environmental Protection Agency, Office of Air Quality Planning and Standards, Emissions Monitoring and Analysis Division, Air Quality Trends Analysis Group, Research Triangle Park, NC.

Table 4.3. "Air pollutants, in order of harm to plants," from *Agriculture and the Environment*. U.S. Department of Agriculture, Washington, DC, 1992.

Table 4.4. "Percent change in air quality and emissions, 1980–1999," from *Latest Findings on National Air Quality: 1999 Status and Trends*. U.S. Environmental Protection Agency, Washington, DC, August 2000.

Figure 4.1. "Figure 4-2. Classified ozone nonattainment areas," from *National Air Quality and Emissions Trends Report, 1999*. U.S. Environmental Protection Agency, Office of Air Quality Planning and Standards, Emissions Monitoring and Analysis Division, Air Quality Trends Analysis Group, Research Triangle Park, NC, March 2001.

Figure 4.2. "Figure 2-33. Anthropogenic VOC emissions by source category, 1999," from *National Air Quality and Emissions Trends Report, 1999*. U.S. Environmental

Protection Agency, Office of Air Quality Planning and Standards, Emissions Monitoring and Analysis Division, Air Quality Trends Analysis Group, Research Triangle Park, NC, March 2001.

Figure 4.3. "Figure 2-19. NO$_x$ Emissions by Source Category, 1999," from *National Air Quality and Emissions Trends Report, 1999*. U.S. Environmental Protection Agency, Office of Air Quality Planning and Standards, Emissions Monitoring and Analysis Division, Air Quality Trends Analysis Group, Research Triangle Park, NC, March 2001.

Figure 4.4. "Figure 2-16. Trend in annual mean NO$_2$ concentrations by type of location, 1980–1999," from *National Air Quality and Emissions Trends Report, 1999*. U.S. Environmental Protection Agency, Office of Air Quality Planning and Standards, Emissions Monitoring and Analysis Division, Air Quality Trends Analysis Group, Research Triangle Park, NC, March 2001.

Figure 4.5. "Figure 2-4. CO emissions by source category, 1999," from *National Air Quality and Emissions Trends Report, 1999*. U.S. Environmental Protection Agency, Office of Air Quality Planning and Standards, Emissions Monitoring and Analysis Division, Air Quality Trends Analysis Group, Research Triangle Park, NC, March 2001.

Figure 4.6. "Figure 2-6. Trend in national total CO emissions, 1980–1999," from *National Air Quality and Emissions Trends Report, 1999*. U.S. Environmental Protection Agency, Office of Air Quality Planning and Standards, Emissions Monitoring and Analysis Division, Air Quality Trends Analysis Group, Research Triangle Park, NC, March 2001.

Figure 4.7. "Figure 2-41. Total PM^{10} emissions by source category, 1999," from *National Air Quality and Emissions Trends Report, 1999*. U.S. Environmental Protection Agency, Office of Air Quality Planning and Standards, Emissions Monitoring and Analysis Division, Air Quality Trends Analysis Group, Research Triangle Park, NC, March 2001.

Figure 4.8. "Figure 2-39. National PM^{10} emissions trend, 1980–1999 (traditionally inventoried sources only)," from *National Air Quality and Emissions Trends Report, 1999*. U.S. Environmental Protection Agency, Office of Air Quality Planning and Standards, Emissions Monitoring and Analysis Division, Air Quality Trends Analysis Group, Research Triangle Park, NC, March 2001.

Figure 4.9. "Figure 2-67. SO$_2$ emissions by source category, 1999," from *National Air Quality and Emissions Trends Report, 1999*. U.S. Environmental Protection Agency, Office of Air Quality Planning and Standards, Emissions Monitoring and Analysis

Division, Air Quality Trends Analysis Group, Research Triangle Park, NC, March 2001.

Figure 4.10. "Figure 2-66. National total SO$_2$ emissions trend, 1980–1999," from *National Air Quality and Emissions Trends Report, 1999*. U.S. Environmental Protection Agency, Office of Air Quality Planning and Standards, Emissions Monitoring and Analysis Division, Air Quality Trends Analysis Group, Research Triangle Park, NC, March 2001.

Figure 4.11. "Figure 2-12. Pb emissions by source category, 1999," from *National Air Quality and Emissions Trends Report, 1999*. U.S. Environmental Protection Agency, Office of Air Quality Planning and Standards, Emissions Monitoring and Analysis Division, Air Quality Trends Analysis Group, Research Triangle Park, NC, March 2001.

Figure 4.12. "Figure 2-9. Pb maximum quarterly mean concentration trends by location (excluding point-source oriented sites), 1980–1999," from *National Air Quality and Emissions Trends Report, 1999*. U.S. Environmental Protection Agency, Office of Air Quality Planning and Standards, Emissions Monitoring and Analysis Division, Air Quality Trends Analysis Group, Research Triangle Park, NC, March 2001.

Figure 4.13. Johnson, Susan. "States with Lead Disclosure Laws" in "Lead Hazard Disclosures in Real Estate Transactions," from *NCSL Legisbrief*, v. 5, February 1997. National Conference of State Legislatures, Denver, CO. Copyright National Conference of State Legislatures. Updated September 2001 by personal communication with Doug Farquhar of the NCSL.

Table 4.5. "Table E-2. TRI Total Releases by State, Original and New Industries, 1999," in "Toxics Release Inventory 1999 Executive Summary," from *1999 Toxics Release Inventory*. U.S. Environmental Protection Agency, Washington, DC, April 2001.

Figure 4.14. "Figure 5-3. National contribution by emission source type for individual urban HAPs and diesel particulate matter, 1996," from *National Air Quality and Emissions Trends Report, 1999*. U.S. Environmental Protection Agency, Office of Air Quality Planning and Standards, Emissions Monitoring and Analysis Division, Air Quality Trends Analysis Group, Research Triangle Park, NC, March 2001.

Figure 4.15. "Comparison of Growth Areas and Emission Trends," from *Latest Findings on National Air Quality: 1999 Status and Trends*. U.S. Environmental Protection Agency, Washington, DC, August 2000.

Table 4.6. "What are the current characteristics of the alternative fuels?" from *Alternative Fuels Data Center: Frequently Asked Questions*. U.S. Department of Energy,

Office of Transportation Technology, Alternative Fuels Data Center, Washington, DC.

Table 4.7. Table 1. Estimated Number of Alternative-Fueled Vehicles in Use in the United States, by Fuel, 1992–2001," from *Alternatives to Traditional Transportation Fuels 1999*. U.S. Department of Energy, Energy Information Administration, Washington, DC, 1999.

Table 4.8. "Percentage of new fleet light duty vehicle acquisitions that must be AFVs (Alternative Fuel Vehicles), 1997–2006," from *EPAct/Clean Fuel Fleet Program Fact Sheet*. U.S. Department of Energy, Office of Transportation Technologies, September 1998.

Figure 4.16. "Figure 3.1: Total Federal Expenditures for Indoor Pollution Research by Category, Fiscal Years 1987 Through 1999," from *Indoor Pollution: Status of Federal Research Activities*. U.S. General Accounting Office, Washington, DC, 1999.

Figure 4.17. "Figure 3.2. Total Federal Expenditures for Indoor Pollution Research, by Agencies, Fiscal Years 1987 Through 1999," from *Indoor Pollution: Status of Federal Research Activities*. U.S. General Accounting Office, Washington, DC, 1999.

Table 5.1. "Table 1-1. Pollution Source Categories Used in This Report," from *National Water Quality Inventory: 1998 Report to Congress*. U.S. Environmental Protection Agency, Washington, DC, 2000.

Figure 5.1. "Bioaccumulation of pollutants in the food chain," from *National Water Quality Inventory: 1998 Report to Congress*. U.S. Environmental Protection Agency, Washington, DC, 2000.

Table 5.2. Dorfman, Mark. "Table 4: Pathogens and Swimming-Related Illnesses," from *Testing the Waters XI: A Guide to Beach Water Quality at Vacation Beaches*. Natural Resources Defense Council, New York, NY, August 2001.

Figure 5.2. "Figure 8-1. Fish and Wildlife Consumption Advisories in the United States," from *National Water Quality Inventory: 1998 Report to Congress*. U.S. Environmental Protection Agency, Washington, DC, 2000.

Figure 5.3. "Figure 8-2. Pollutants Causing Fish and Wildlife Consumption Advisories in Effect in 1998," from *National Water Quality Inventory: 1998 Report to Congress*. U.S. Environmental Protection Agency, Washington, DC, 2000.

Table 5.3. "Table 8-1. Shellfish Harvesting Restrictions Reported by the States," from *National Water Quality Inventory: 1998 Report to Congress*. U.S. Environmental Protection Agency, Washington, DC, 2000.

Table 5.4. Dorfman, Mark. "Table 2: U.S. Ocean, Bay, and Great Lakes Beach Closings and Advisories, 1988–2000," from *Testing the Waters XI: A Guide to Beach Water Quality at Vacation Beaches*. Natural Resources Defense Council, New York, NY, August 2001.

Figure 5.4. "Transmitted Air Pollutants: Emissions to Effects," from *Acid Rain and Transported Air Pollutants: Implications for Public Policy*. Office of Technology Assessment, 1984.

Figure 5.5. "The Potential Hydrogen (pH) Scale)," from *Acid Rain*. U.S. Environmental Protection Agency, 1980.

Table 5.5. "Effects of pH on aquatic life," from *National Water Quality Inventory: 1996 Report to Congress*. U.S. Environmental Protection Agency, Washington, DC, 1998.

Table 5.6. "Table 8. Properties and effects of metals of primary concern in marine environments," from *Wastes in Marine Environments*. U.S. Congress, Office of Technology Assessment, Washington, DC, 1987.

Figure 5.6. "Summary of Use Support," from *National Water Quality Inventory: 1998 Report to Congress*. U.S. Environmental Protection Agency, Washington, DC, 2000.

Table 5.7. "2000 international coastal cleanup—United States dirty dozen," from *The International Coastal Cleanup*. The Ocean Conservancy, Washington, DC.

Figure 5.7. "Figure 5-12. Leading POLLUTANTS In Impaired Ocean Shoreline Waters" and "Figure 5-13. Leading SOURCES of Ocean Shoreline Impairment," from *National Water Quality Inventory: 1998 Report to Congress*. U.S. Environmental Protection Agency, Washington, DC, 2000.

Figure 5.8. "Potential physical, chemical, and biological results of marine oil spills," from *Bioremediation for Marine Oil Spills*. Office of Technology Assessment, Washington, DC, 1991.

Figure 5.9. "Oil spill boundary defining the area affected by the Exxon Valdez oil spill and federal lands located within the boundary," from *Natural Resources Restoration: Status of Payments and Use of Exxon Valdez Oil Spill Settlement Funds*. U.S. General Accounting Office, Washington, DC, 1998.

Table 5.8. "Potential Advantages and Disadvantages of Bioremediation," from *Bioremediation for Marine Oil Spills*. U.S. Congress, Office of Technology Assessment, Washington, DC, 1991. Reproduced by permission.

Figure 5.10. "Figure 5-3. Leading POLLUTANTS in Impaired Estuaries" and "Figure 5-4. Leading SOURCES of Estuary Impairment," from *National Water Quality Inventory: 1998 Report to Congress*. U.S. Environmental Protection Agency, Washington, DC, 2000.

Figure 5.11. "Figure 4-2. Summary of Use Support in Assessed Lakes, Ponds, and Reservoirs," from *National Water Quality Inventory: 1998 Report to Congress*. U.S. Environmental Protection Agency, Washington, DC, 2000.

Figure 5.12. "Leading POLLUTANTS in Impaired Lakes" and "Figure 4-3. Leading SOURCES of Lake Impairment," from *National Water Quality Inventory: 1998 Report to Congress*. U.S. Environmental Protection Agency, Washington, DC, 2000.

Figure 5.13. "Figure 3-2. Summary of Use Support in Assessed Rivers and Streams," from *National Water Quality Inventory: 1998 Report to Congress*. U.S. Environmental Protection Agency, Washington, DC, 2000.

Figure 5.14. "Figure 3-4. Leading POLLUTANTS in Impaired Rivers and Streams" and "Figure 3-5. Leading SOURCES of River and Stream Impairment," from *National Water Quality Inventory: 1998 Report to Congress*. U.S. Environmental Protection Agency, Washington, DC, 2000.

Figure 6.1. "Distribution of Water on Earth's Surface," from *The National Water Quarterly Inventory: 1996 Report to Congress*. U.S. Environmental Protection Agency, Washington, DC, 1998.

Figure 6.2. "The Water Cycle," from *National Water Quality Inventory: 1998 Report to Congress*. U.S. Environmental Protection Agency, Washington, DC, 2000.

Figure 6.3. "Figure 1-1. Ground Water," from *National Water Quality Inventory: 1998 Report to Congress*. U.S. Environmental Protection Agency, Washington, DC, 2000.

Table 6.1. "Table 1. Activities that can cause groundwater contamination," from *Citizen's Guide to Groundwater Protection*. U.S. Environmental Protection Agency, Washington, DC, 1990, updated 1999.

Figure 6.4. "Figure 7-1. National Ground Water Use," from *National Water Quality Inventory: 1998 Report to Congress*. U.S. Environmental Protection Agency, Washington, DC, 2000.

Figure 6.5. "Figure 7-5. Sources of Ground Water Contamination," from *National Water Quality Inventory: 1998 Report to Congress*. U.S. Environmental Protection Agency, Washington, DC, 2000.

Figure 6.6. "Figure 7-6. Major Sources of Ground Water Contamination," from *National Water Quality Inventory: 1998 Report to Congress*. U.S. Environmental Protection Agency, Washington, DC, 2000.

Figure 6.7. "Figure 7-7. Ground Water Contamination as a Result of Leaking Underground Storage Tanks," from *National Water Quality Inventory: 1998 Report to Congress*. U.S. Environmental Protection Agency, Washington, DC, 2000.

Figure 6.8. "Underground Storage Tank leak detection methods," from *Operating and Maintaining Underground Storage Tank Systems: Practical Help and Checklists*. U.S. Environmental Protection Agency, Washington, DC, 2000.

Figure 6.9. "Primary Treatment," from *How Wastewater Treatment Works...The Basics*. U.S. Environmental Protection Agency, Washington, DC, 1998.

Figure 6.10. "Secondary Treatment," from *How Wastewater Treatment Works...The Basics*. U.S. Environmental Protection Agency, Washington, DC, 1998.

Figure 6.11. "Generation, treatment, and disposal of municipal effluent and sludge," from *National Water Quality Inventory: 1996 Report to Congress*. U.S. Environmental Protection Agency, Washington, DC, 1998.

Figure 6.12. "Cross section of a minimal groundwater monitoring system," from *Hazardous Waste: Compliance with Groundwater Monitoring Requirements at Land Disposal Facilities*. U.S. General Accounting Office, 1995.

Figure 6.13. "Figure 2. Percentage of potentially eligible sites with groundwater contamination," from *Hazardous Waste—Unaddressed Risks at Many Potential Superfund Sites*. U.S. General Accounting Office, Washington, DC, 1998.

Figure 6.14. Barbash, Jack E., et al. From *Distribution of Major Herbicides in Ground Water of the United States*. U.S. Geological Survey and U.S. Environmental Protection Agency, Sacramento, CA, 1999.

Figure 6.15. Barbash, Jack E., et al. "Frequencies of herbicide detection in ground water during the NAWQA (1993–1995) investigations," from *Distribution of Major Herbicides in Ground Water of the United States*. U.S. Geological Survey and U.S. Environmental Protection Agency, Sacramento, CA, 1999.

Table 6.2. "Red meat, poultry, and fish (boneless, trimmed equivalent): Per capita consumption." Retrieved from Per Capita Food Consumption Data System http://www.ers.usda.gov/Data/FoodConsumption/Spreadsheets/mtpcc.xls, October 15, 2001. U.S. Department of Agriculture, Economic Research Service, Washington, DC, 1999.

Figure 6.16. "Proportions of Financial and Technical Assistance for Animal Waste

Management, by Federal Agency, Fiscal Years 1996–98," from *Animal Agriculture—Waste Management Practices*. U.S. General Accounting Office, Washington, DC, 1999.

Figure 6.17. "Figure 1. Representation of fate and transport analysis," from *Guide for Industrial Waste Management*. U.S. Environmental Protection Agency, Washington, DC, 1999.

Figure 6.18. "Status of Comprehensive State Ground Water Protection Programs (CSGW-PP)." Retrieved from http://www.epa.gov/safewater/csgwpp.html, October 16, 2001. U.S. Environmental Protection Agency, Office of Ground Water and Drinking Water, Washington, DC.

Table 6.3. "Federal Laws Administered by EPA Affecting Ground Water," from *Safe Drinking Water Act, Section 1429 Ground Water Report to Congress*. U.S. Environmental Protection Agency, Office of Water, Washington, DC, 1999.

Figure 7.1. "What kinds of hazardous waste are there?" from *Fast Flash 1: Hazardous Substances and Hazardous Waste*. Retrieved from http://www.epa.gov/superfund/students/clas_act/haz-ed/ff_01.htm, October 16, 2001. U.S. Environmental Protection Agency, Washington, DC.

Figure 7.2. "Types of Environmental and Public Health Risks Addressed at Superfund Sites," from *Superfund: Program Management*. U.S. General Accounting Office, Washington, DC, 1992.

Table 7.1. "Percentage of Potentially Eligible Sites Contributing to Specified Adverse Conditions and Percentage of Sites for Which Conditions' Presence is Uncertain," from *Hazardous Waste: Unaddressed Risks at Many Potential Superfund Sites*. U.S. General Accounting Office, Washington, DC, 1998.

Table 7.2. "Assessments of States' Financial Capabilities to Clean Up Potentially Eligible Sites," from *Hazardous Waste: Unaddressed Risks at Many Potential Superfund Sites*. U.S. General Accounting Office, Washington, DC, 1998.

Figure 7.3. "Figure 1. Measuring the Progress of Site Remediation at NPL Sites," from *Superfund Cleanup Figures*. Retrieved from http://www.epa.gov/superfund/action/process/mgmtrpt.htm, October 16, 2001. U.S. Environmental Protection Agency, Washington, DC.

Figure 7.4. "Expected Completion Dates for Construction of Remedies," from *Superfund: Half the Sites Have All Cleanup Remedies in Place or Completed*. U.S. General Accounting Office, Washington, DC, 1999.

Figure 7.5. "Figure 2. GAO's Estimate of Site Completions, by Year," from *Superfund: Information on the Program's Funding and Status*. U.S. General Accounting Office, Washington, DC, 1999.

Table 7.3. "Table 1. EPA Major Appropriations Accounts: FY1999, FY2000, FY2001 and FY2002 Actions," from *Environmental Protection Agency: FY 2002 Budget Issues*. Congressional Research Service, Washington, DC, 2001.

Figure 7.6. "Environmental Protection Agency funding by appropriations accounts, 1983–2002," from *Environmental Protection Agency: FY 2002 Budget Issues*. Congressional Research Service, Washington, DC, 2001.

Figure 7.7. "Poverty Rate Within 1 Mile of Metropolitan Landfills Compared With Rate in Rest of Host County or Nation," from *Hazardous and Nonhazardous Wastes: Demographics of People Living Near Waste Facilities*. U.S. General Accounting Office, Washington, DC, 1995.

Figure 7.8. "Median Household Income Within 1 Mile of Metropolitan Landfills Compared With Income in Rest of Host County or Nation," from *Hazardous and Nonhazardous Wastes: Demographics of People Living Near Waste Facilities*. U.S. General Accounting Office, Washington, DC, 1995.

Table 7.4. "New Developments in Environmental Justice," from *NCSL Legisbrief*, August/September 1999. National Conference of State Legislatures, Denver, CO. Copyright National Conference of State Legislatures. Updated September 2001 by personal communication with Sia Davis of the NCSL. Reproduced by permission.

Figure 7.9. "Releases to the Groundwater at Hazardous Waste Facilities," from *Hazardous Waste: Compliance with Groundwater Monitoring Requirements at Land Disposal Facilities*. U.S. General Accounting Office, Washington, DC, 1995.

Figure 7.10. "Frequency of Monitoring Violations Cited Since October 1, 1989," from *Hazardous Waste: Compliance with Groundwater Monitoring Requirements at Land Disposal Facilities*. U.S. General Accounting Office, Washington, DC, 1995.

Figure 7.11. Mahoney, Katherine A. and Linda K. Murakam. "Sources of Radiation," from *Farewell to Arms: Cleaning Up Nuclear Weapons Facilities*. National Conference of State Legislatures, Denver, CO, 1993. Reproduced by permission.

Figure 7.12. "Nuclear Chain Reaction," from *NRC Regulator of Nuclear Safety*. U.S. Nuclear Regulatory Commission, June 1993.

Figure 7.13. "Figure 2. The Nuclear Fuel Cycle," from *Nuclear Nonproliferation: Implications of the U.S. Purchase of Russian Highly Enriched Uranium*. U.S. General Accounting Office, Washington, DC, 2000.

Figure 7.14. "Figure 2. DOE's Major Low-Level and Mixed Waste-Generating Sites and Disposal Facilities," from *Low-Level Radioactive Wastes: Department of Energy Has Opportunities to Reduce Disposal Costs*. U.S. General Accounting Office, Washington, DC, 2000.

Table 7.5. "Table 3. Past and Future Disposal Volumes of Low-Level and Mixed Wastes for DOE's 20 Major Waste-Generating Sites," from *Low-Level Radioactive Wastes: Department of Energy Has Opportunities to Reduce Disposal Costs*. U.S. General Accounting Office, Washington, DC, 2000.

Figure 7.15. "Figure 1.1. States' Memberships in Compacts," from *Low-Level Radioactive Wastes: States Are Not Developing Disposal Facilities*. U.S. General Accounting Office, Washington, DC, September 1999.

Figure 7.16. "Figure ES-1. Map Showing Current Locations of Waste Destined for Geologic Disposal," from *Yucca Mountain Science and Engineering Report*. U.S. Department of Energy, Washington, DC, May 2001.

Figure 7.17. "Waste Isolation Pilot Plant Site." U.S. Department of Energy.

Figure 7.18. "Defense transuranic waste generating and storage sites," from *The Waste Isolation Pilot Plant: Pioneering Nuclear Waste Disposal*. U.S. Department of Energy, Carlsbad Area Office, February 2000.

Figure 7.19. "Figure 1-5. Map Showing the Location of Yucca Mountain in Relation to Major Highways; Surrounding Counties, Cities, and Towns in Nevada and California; the Nevada Test Site; and Death Valley National Park," from *Yucca Mountain Science and Engineering Report*. U.S. Department of Energy, Washington, DC, May 2001.

Table 8.1. Dunlap, Riley E. and Lydia Saad. "Levels of participation in and sympathy for the environmental movement, 2000–01," from *Only One in Four Americans Are Anxious About the Environment*. Retrieved from http://www.gallup.com/poll/releases/pr010416.asp, October 2, 2001. The Gallup Organization, Princeton, NJ, April 16, 2001. Reproduced by permission.

Table 8.2. Dunlap, Riley E. and Lydia Saad. "Opinion on progress in dealing with environmental problems, selected years 1990–2001," from *Only One in Four Americans Are Anxious About the Environment*. Retrieved from http://www.gallup.com/poll/releases/pr010416.asp, October 2, 2001. The Gallup Organization,

Princeton, NJ, April 16, 2001. Reproduced by permission.

Table 8.3. Dunlap, Riley E. and Lydia Saad. From "Opinion on amount of effort put into protecting the environment, March 2001," in *Only One in Four Americans Are Anxious About the Environment.* Retrieved from http://www.gallup.com/poll/releases/pr0104 16.asp, October 2, 2001. The Gallup Organization, Princeton, NJ, April 16, 2001. Reproduced by permission.

Table 8.4. "Priority of Environmental Problems," from *The Wirthlin Report: Current Trends in Public Opinion From Wirthlin Worldwide*, v. 10, November 2000. Wirthlin Worldwide, McLean, VA. Reproduced by permission.

Table 8.5. Dunlap, Riley E. and Lydia Saad. "Degree of worry about environmental problems, 1989, 2000, and 2001," in *Only One in Four Americans Are Anxious About the Environment.* Retrieved from http://www.gallup.com/poll/releases/pr0104 16.asp, October 2, 2001. The Gallup Organization, Princeton, NJ, April 16, 2001. Reproduced by permission.

Table 8.6. "Industry Environmental Scorecard," from *The Wirthlin Report: Current Trends in Public Opinion From Wirthlin Worldwide*, v. 10, November 2000. Wirthlin Worldwide, McLean, VA. Reproduced by permission.

Table 8.7. "Reliability of Sources About Environmental Health Risks," from *The Wirthlin Report: Current Trends in Public Opinion From Wirthlin Worldwide*, v. 9, November 1999. Wirthlin Worldwide, McLean, VA. Reproduced by permission.

Table 8.8. "Figure 18: National Environmental Report Card," from *The Ninth Annual National Report Card on Environmental Attitudes, Knowledge, and Behaviors.* The National Environmental Education & Training Foundation and Roper Starch Worldwide, Washington, DC, May 2001. Reproduced by permission.

Table 8.9. "Figure 19: Percentage Answering Knowledge Questions Correctly," from *The Ninth Annual National Report Card on Environmental Attitudes, Knowledge, and Behaviors.* The National Environmental Education & Training Foundation and Roper Starch Worldwide, Washington, DC, May 2001. Reproduced by permission.

Figure 8.1. "Figure 14: Current Regulation of Specific Environmental Issues," from *The Ninth Annual National Report Card on Environmental Attitudes, Knowledge, and Behaviors.* The National Environmental Education & Training Foundation and Roper Starch Worldwide, Washington, DC, May 2001. Reproduced by permission.

Figure 8.2. "Figure 20: Environmental Activities Performed Frequently in Day-to-Day Life," from *The Ninth Annual National Report Card on Environmental Attitudes, Knowledge, and Behaviors.* The National Environmental Education & Training Foundation and Roper Starch Worldwide, Washington, DC, May 2001. Reproduced by permission.

Table 8.10. "Figure 1: Awareness and Opinion of Environmental Education in Schools," from *The Ninth Annual National Report Card on Environmental Attitudes, Knowledge, and Behaviors.* The National Environmental Education & Training Foundation and Roper Starch Worldwide, Washington, DC, May 2001. Reproduced by permission.

Figure 8.3. "Figure 10: Will Technology Save the Environment?" from *The Ninth Annual National Report Card on Environmental Attitudes, Knowledge, and Behaviors.* The National Environmental Education & Training Foundation and Roper Starch Worldwide, Washington, DC, May 2001. Reproduced by permission.

Figure 8.4. "Figure 7: When Compromise Is Impossible, Environment Favored Over Economic Development," from *The Ninth Annual National Report Card on Environmental Attitudes, Knowledge, and Behaviors.* The National Environmental Education & Training Foundation and Roper Starch Worldwide, Washington, DC, May 2001. Reproduced by permission.

Table 8.11. Dunlap, Riley E. and Lydia Saad. "Opinion about priority level of the environment and the economy, selected years, 1984–2001," from *Only One in Four Americans Are Anxious About the Environment.* Retrieved from http://www.gallup.com/poll/releases/pr0104 16.asp, October 2, 2001. The Gallup Organization, Princeton, NJ, April 16, 2001. Reproduced by permission.

Figure 8.5. "Environmentalism Barometer," from *The Wirthlin Report: Current Trends in Public Opinion From Wirthlin Worldwide*, v. 10, November 2000. Wirthlin Worldwide, McLean, VA. Reproduced by permission.

Table 8.12. Dunlap, Riley E. and Lydia Saad. "Opinion on President Bush's decision for the U.S. not to adhere to the Kyoto treaty, April 2001," from *Only One in Four Americans Are Anxious About the Environment.* Retrieved from http://www.gallup.com/poll/releases/pr010416.asp, October 2, 2001. The Gallup Organization, Princeton, NJ, April 16, 2001. Reproduced by permission.

CHAPTER 1
HISTORICAL PERSPECTIVE—GARBAGE THEN AND NOW

Garbage, trash, refuse, rubbish, and waste—these terms are often used interchangeably. What do they mean? Are they all the same thing?

Garbage is "wet" discarded matter that is generally edible by animals. Food remains and yard clippings are examples of garbage. Trash is "dry" discarded matter that is generally inedible. Newspapers, bottles, and cans are examples of trash. Refuse refers to both garbage and trash, while rubbish is refuse plus construction and demolition debris. Waste, which is more properly termed solid waste, includes rubbish along with semisolids, liquids, and gases from mining, agricultural, commercial, and industrial activities. All animals produce garbage when they eat food and then cast aside the remains. However, only humans produce trash, refuse, rubbish, and solid waste.

THE FIRST GARBAGE DUMPS

The earliest humans did not have garbage disposal problems. They lived in nomadic tribes, wandering the countryside and following herds of wild animals that they hunted and killed for food and clothing. Scavengers and insects ate their discarded food remains, and what was left decomposed. More recently, about 10,000 years ago, people began to form villages and become farmers. For the first time, they had to live with their garbage, which smelled bad and attracted wild animals. Therefore, some villagers dug pits into which they tossed garbage. One of the best ways scientists learn about such prehistoric communities is by studying their garbage pits.

CLEANING UP ANCIENT CITIES

About 4,500 years ago, one of the world's first great civilizations began to develop in what is now Pakistan and northwestern India. Ruins show that the two major cities in this area were large and well planned. One of the cities, Mahenjo-Daro, was built using a design that called for homes to contain built-in rubbish chutes and trash bins. A few hundred years after that, in the ancient Egyptian city of Heracleopolis, religious leaders and the wealthy had their refuse collected and then dumped into the Nile River. At about the same time in Crete, the bathrooms of the kings were connected to sewers.

About 1,300 years later, Jerusalem developed a sewer system that served the entire city—not just the rich or powerful. A few hundred years later (approximately 2,500 years ago), the city of Athens, Greece, passed the first garbage dump law in the Western world, requiring that garbage be dumped at least one mile outside the city walls. Figure 1.1, a historical timeline of waste management practices, begins at about this time (500 B.C.), with its first entry denoting the organization of Athens's municipal dumping ground. About 500 years later, major cities of the Roman Empire had sewage and water systems, although the refuse collection systems were not always adequate.

In Europe during the Middle Ages (approximately 400 to 1500 A.D.), refuse collection and disposal took a step backward. These systems were not considered important and people threw their garbage and trash into the streets and rivers. Disease spread quickly, and in 1388 the English Parliament made it illegal to throw garbage into the rivers. However, by 1400, the piles of garbage outside the city gates of Paris were so high that it was hard to defend the city because the mounds of garbage were as tall as the city walls. (See Figure 1.1.)

THE COMING OF THE INDUSTRIAL REVOLUTION

From the 1700s through the early 1800s, the Western world was marked by the Industrial Revolution. The development of factories and the congestion of cities with factory workers characterized this period. People lived in crowded housing and the sanitation was poor, allowing raw sewage to get into water supplies in some cities. The

FIGURE 1.1

Timeline of waste management practices, B.C. 500–2001 A.D.

500 B.C.
Athens organizes the first municipal dump in the western world. Scavengers must dispose of waste at least one mile from city walls.

1400
Garbage piles up so high outside Paris gates that it interferes with the city's defenses.

1842
A report in England links disease to filthy environmental conditions and helps launch the "age of sanitation."

1874
In Nottingham, England, a new technology called "the destructor" provides the first systematic incineration of municipal refuse.

1885
The nations's first garbage incinerator is built on Governor's Island, N.Y.

1890s
750,000 watermelon rinds are discarded during the summer months in New York City.

1896
Waste reduction plants, which compress organic wastes to extract grease, oils and other by-products, are introduced to the U.S. from Vienna. The plants are later closed due to their noxious emissions.

1900s
In Milwaukee, 12,500 horses in the city leave an estimated 133 tons of manure and urine on the streets.

1902
Seventy-nine percent of 161 U.S. cities surveyed in a Massachusetts Institute of Technology study provide regular collection of refuse.

1911
In Manhattan, Brooklyn and the Bronx, citizens produce about 4.6 pounds of refuse each day. Yearly collections per capita include 141 pounds of wet garbage, 1,443 pounds of ash, and 88 pounds of dry rubbish.

1916
The U.S. produces 15,000 tons of paper a day, using 5,000 tons of old paper in the process, a 33 percent recycling rate. Cities begin switching from horse-drawn to motorized refuse collection equipment.

1942–45
Americans collect rubber, paper, scrap metal, fats and tin cans to help the war effort. The sudden surge of waste paper gluts markets, and prices drop from $9 to $3 per ton.

1965
The first federal solid waste management law, the Solid Waste Disposal Act (SWDA), authorizes research and provides for state grants.

1388
English Parliament bans waste disposal in public waterways and ditches

1690
Paper is made from recycled fibers (waste paper and old rags) at the Rittenhouse Mill near Philadelphia.

1860s
In Washington, D.C., citizens still dump garbage and slop in the street, while pigs, rats, and cockroaches run freely.

1880
New York City scavengers remove 15,000 horse carcasses. (City horses, many of which pulled street-cars, had a two-year life expectancy.)

1889
Washington, D.C., Health Officer reports that, "Appropriate places for [refuse] are becoming scarcer year by year, and the question as to some other method of disposal... must soon confront us. Already the inhabitants in proximity to the public dumps are beginning to complain...."

1894
Harper's Weekly reports that "...the garbage problem is the one question of sanitation that is uppermost in the minds of local authorities."

1899
Colonel Waring, New York City's Street Cleaning Commissioner, organizes the first rubbish sorting plant for recycling in the U.S.

1900s
Piggeries are developed in small-to medium-sized towns, whereby swine are fed fresh or cooked garbage. An expert estimates that 75 pigs could consume 1 ton of garbage refuse per day.

1904
The nation's first major aluminum recycling plants open in Cleveland and Chicago

1914
After a shaky start, incinerators catch on in North American cities. Approximately 300 plants operate in the U.S. and Canada.

1920s
Landfilling—reclaiming wet lands near cities with layers of garbage, ash and dirt—becomes a popular disposal method.

1959
The American Society of Civil Engineers publishes the standard guide to sanitary landfilling. To guard against rodents and odors, the guide suggests compacting the refuse and covering it with a layer of soil each day.

---

polluted water caused typhoid fever and other illnesses. Additionally, the burning of coal, which powered most factories and heated most city homes, filled the air of industrial cities with smoke and soot.

In 1842 an English government commission reported that the terrible sanitation conditions caused disease. (See Figure 1.1.) By 1869 England had created a Sanitary Commission to improve sanitation and garbage disposal in English cities.

FIGURE 1.1

Timeline of waste management practices, B.C. 500–2001 A.D. [CONTINUED]

1960
More than 33 percent of U.S. cities collect waste that is separated in some manner.

President Johnson commissions the "National Survey of Community Solid Waste Practices," providing the first comprehensive data on solid waste since the 1800s.

1971
Oregon passes the nation's first bottle bill.

1976
The Resource Conservation and Recovery Act (RCRA) creates the first significant role for federal government in waste management. The law emphasizes recycling and conserivng energy and other resources, and launches the nation's hazardous waste management program.

1979
EPA issues landfill criteria that prohibit open dumping.

1986
Rhode Island enacts the nation's first statewide madatory recycling law. Citizens and businesses must separate recyclables from trash.

Fresh Kills on Staten Island, N.Y., becomes the largest landfill in the world.

1988
EPA estimates that more than 14,000 landfills have closed since 1978, more than 70 percent of those operating at that time.

Lacking disposal capacity, New Jersey exports more than 50 percent of its solid waste to neighboring states.

1989
Arizona archeologist William Rathje recovers corn on the cob intact after 18 years in an Arizona landfill. His research indicates that biodegradability has minimal impact on landfill capacity.

1991
EPA releases RCRA Subtitle D landfill standards that include requirements for location, groundwater protection and monitoring and post-closure care.

1995
The number of landfills in the U.S. is approximately 2,800, down from an estimated 20,000 landfills in 1970. This significant decrease in the number of landfills in the U.S. is due to landfill closures forced by stricter regulatory programs.

1998
States average a landfill disposal capacity of at least 16 more years.

The national average landfill tipping fee is $31.81, compared to a national average incinerator tipping fee of nearly $60 per ton.

2001
New York City's Fresh Kills Landfill scheduled to close.

1970
The U.S. celebrates the first Earth Day April 22.

The Resource Recovery Act amends the SWDA and requires the federal government to issue waste disposal guidelines.

The Clean Air Act establishes federal authority to fight urban smog and air toxins. New regulations lead to incinerator shutdowns.

The U.S. Environmental Protection Agency (EPA) is created.

1975
All 50 states have some solid waste regulations, although content varies widely.

1978
The Public Utility Regulatory Policies Act is passed following the Arab oil embargo. The act guarantees a market for energy created by small power producers and encourages growth of the waste-to-energy industry and methane recovery from landfills.

The Supreme Court rules that garbage is protected by the Interstate Commerce Clause; therefore, New Jersey cannot ban shipments of waste from Philadelphia.

1984
During the Olympic Games in Los Angeles, athletes, trainers, coaches and spectators produce 6.5 million pounds of trash in 22 days, more than 6 pounds per person per day (versus the national average of 3.6 pounds per person per day).

1987
Mobro, the Islip, Long Island, garbage barge, is rejected by six states and three countries, drawing public attention to the landfill capacity shortage in the Northeast. The garbage is finally incinerated in Brooklyn and the ash brought to a landfill near Islip.

1989
Twenty-six states have comprehensive laws making recycling an integral part of waste management. Seven states require curbside separation of recyclables.

Between 1986 and mid-1989, 33 states consider or enact restrictions on out-of-state waste.

1989
Sudden growth in curbside collection of newspaper gluts the market; prices drop to zero, and some communities pay to have material taken away.

1994
The Supreme Court's decision in *C.A. Carbone v. Town of Clarkstown, N.Y.*, decalres that flow control requirements are unconstitutional.

1997
The U.S. recycled 22.4 percent of the municipal solid waste stream, compared to a 6.4 percent recycling rate in 1960. The U.S. composted 5.6 percent of the waste stream, incinerated 16.9 percent, and landfilled the remaining 55.1 percent.

1998
USA Waste Services, Inc., purchased Waste Management, Inc., increasing the size of the largest waste management company in the U.S. to one with more than $12 billion in annual revenues.

SOURCE: "Garbage Then & Now," Environmental Industry Associations, Washington, DC

IN THE UNITED STATES

During the 1600s and 1700s in colonial America, people dumped their refuse into the streets as they did in European cities. Pigs roamed the streets and ate the garbage. In 1657 New Amsterdam (now New York) became the first city to pass laws against street disposal. Nonetheless, as late as the 1860s, residents of Washington, D.C., still threw their garbage into the streets. (See Figure 1.1.)

When the United States became industrialized in the 1800s, most Americans did not think that what they were doing would hurt the environment. Factories often dumped their chemicals directly into rivers and lakes. Cities poured their sewage into the same rivers and lakes. Garbage was deposited into nearby garbage dumps without any concern that it might harm ground water. Ships dumped garbage overboard into rivers, lakes, and oceans.

The air became polluted, as did the land and the water. Postcards proudly showed factories pouring smoke into the air. By the early 1900s, air pollution problems became particularly serious; smoke and soot filled the air over many Eastern and Midwestern cities. In some industrial cities, the air frequently became so hazy that drivers needed streetlights and headlights to see during the day.

This lack of concern for the environment led to serious problems. New Orleans had typhoid epidemics because sewage was poured into streets and canals. Memphis lost nearly 10 percent of its population to yellow fever. Infant mortality was very high in large cities.

And it was not only people that produced waste. In New York, about 120,000 horses drew carriages, hauled wagons, and pulled streetcars, while in Chicago, 83,000 horses did such work. These animal workers produced thousands of tons of manure that dirtied the streets of U.S. cities. This waste had to be cleaned up and dumped elsewhere. (See the entry for 1900s in Figure 1.1.)

EARLY EFFORTS TO REUSE GARBAGE AND TRASH

Although pre-1900s refuse disposal practices were poor, most Americans produced much less garbage and trash than they do today. Food scraps were boiled to make soups or were fed to farm animals. Durable items were passed on to the next generation or to people in need. Objects that were of no further use to adults became toys for children. Broken items were repaired or dismantled for reuse. Things that could no longer be used were burned for fuel, especially in the homes of the poor. Even middle-class Americans traded rags to peddlers in exchange for buttons or teakettles. These ragmen worked the streets, begging for or buying at low prices items such as bones, paper, old iron, rags, and bottles. They then sold the junk to dealers who marketed it to manufacturers.

Using scraps and prolonging the useful lives of items saved money. In 1919 in the publication *Save and Have, A Book of 'Saving Graces' for American Homes* (New York), the University Society discussed habits of thrift. The Society recommended keeping cake fresh by storing it with an apple and "turning" worn sheets by tearing them down the middle and sewing up the good sides. Other suggestions included collecting grease to make soap, reusing flour sacks for dishtowels or clothing, using jars for drinking glasses, and keeping a can on the stove containing grease that was used over and over.

Besides giving away clothes, mending and remaking them, and using them as rags for work, women reworked textiles into useful household furnishings, such as quilts, rugs, and upholstery. In the American culture of the time, such activities demonstrated a woman's frugality and creative skill and came to represent an aspect of a woman's "virtue." A growing paper industry also made it profitable for thrifty housewives to save rags, which were used by paper mills to make paper.

A trade in used goods such as rags provided crucial resources for early industrialization. However, these early systems of recycling diminished in the early 1900s. Sanitary reformers and municipal trash collection did away with scavenging. Technology made available cheap and new alternatives. People made fewer things and bought more than had previous generations. They also saved and repaired less and threw out more. In *A Social History of Trash* (Henry Holt and Co., New York, 1999), Susan Strasser describes this change in the nation's mindset:

> The rhetoric of convenience, luxury, and cleanliness was potent. It sold a wide variety of products that transformed Americans' relationship to waste and, in general, to the material world. In a few decades, the ideal of the durable and reusable was displaced by aspirations of leisure and luxury, ease and cleanliness. The new ways were entrenched by 1929, in principle if not always in practice, and neither a depression nor the material shortages of a world war were enough to reverse what most people saw as progress.

Old-fashioned reuse and recycling did not cease overnight. During the first decades of the twentieth century, most people still threw away relatively little. Publications such as *Save and Have*, mentioned previously, were popular. Nonetheless, as the century progressed, middle-class people learned to discard things, attracted by convenience and a desire to avoid any association with scavenging and poverty. Success often meant that one did not have to use second-hand goods. As municipalities became responsible for collecting and disposing of refuse, Americans found it easier to throw things away.

PURSUING WASTE DISPOSAL

Throughout the 1800s, many cities passed anti-dumping ordinances, but they were often ignored. Some landowners and merchants resented ordinances, which they considered an infringement on their rights. Therefore, as cities grew, refuse piles grew, becoming not only public eyesores but also threats to public health.

By the end of the 1800s, city leaders began to recognize that they had to do something about proper refuse disposal. As a result, most major cities had set up refuse collection systems by the turn of the century. Many cities introduced incinerators to burn some of the refuse. When World War I began in 1914, about 300 incinerators were operating in the United States and Canada. By the 1920s, landfilling became a popular refuse disposal method. In this method, garbage and trash were dumped in wetlands near cities in an effort to reclaim these areas. In 1959 the American Society of Civil Engineers published the standard guide to sanitary landfilling, suggesting that refuse be compacted and covered daily to guard against rodents and odors. (See Figure 1.1.) In 1965 the United States government passed the Solid Waste Disposal Act, the first of many solid waste management laws.

A CONSUMER SOCIETY—A GLUT OF WASTE

The amount of refuse Americans create is at an all-time high. In 1999 Americans produced nearly 1,700 pounds of refuse per person for the year, or 4.62 pounds per person per day. Even after subtracting the amount of materials recovered for recycling, those figures only drop to about 1,200 pounds of refuse per person for the year, or 3.33 pounds per person per day. (*Municipal Solid Waste in the United States: 1999 Facts and Figures,* Environmental Protection Agency, Washington, DC, 2000.)

Not only do Americans collectively use and discard millions of tons of refuse each year (even when recycling is considered), they use and discard a variety of materials. In fact, the variety of materials used by people in the United States, Europe, Japan, and other industrialized countries dwarfs that of a century ago. Today's materials use draws from all 92 naturally occurring elements in the periodic table, compared with approximately 20 at the turn of the century. The United States Geological Survey (USGS) estimates that U.S. consumption of metal, glass, wood, cement, and chemicals has grown eighteen-fold since 1900. The United States alone uses one-third of the world's materials. Table 1.1 shows the per capita resource consumption of Americans in the mid-1990s.

Why do Americans produce so much refuse? First, approximately 285 million people live in this country. As the population has grown, so has the volume of waste produced. Second, many consumer goods are designed for short-term use. In fact, this concept has fostered one of America's nicknames—"the throwaway society." This situation contrasts sharply with the practices of earlier eras, when materials were reused or transformed for other uses.

TABLE 1.1

Per capita resource consumption, mid-1990s

Material	Pounds Per Day
Stone and cement	27
Coal	19
Miscellaneous minerals	17
Oil	16
Farm products	12
Wood	11
Range grass	10
Metals	8
Natural gas	1
Total	**121**

SOURCE: John C. Ryan and Alan Thein Durning, *Stuff: The Secret Lives of Everyday Things,* Northwest Environment Watch, Seattle, WA, 1997

Susan Strasser observed that tissues and cereal boxes—good examples of consumer "throwaways"—represent the new relationship between consumers and the products they buy. "More and more things were made and sold with the understanding that they would soon be worthless or obsolete," she reported.

In recent decades, interest in recycling has grown, and most states are making recycling an important part of waste collection and disposal. Nonetheless, the nation's landfills are becoming full, and new ones are being constructed. Many states send their refuse to other states or even to other countries, but some of these states and countries are no longer accepting other people's garbage.

HOW MUCH WASTE?

During the twentieth century, as the United States grew and became richer, the nation produced more garbage and trash, or municipal solid waste (MSW). Since 1960 America's population has grown nearly 53 percent (an increase of about half), from 178.5 million in 1960 to 272.7 million in 1999. However, the amount of MSW produced has more than doubled. Figure 1.2 shows this increase—from 88.1 million tons per year in 1960 to 229.9 million tons per year in 1999. Figure 1.2 also shows that each American produced 72 percent more waste in 1999 than in 1960. Despite these increases, MSW is only a fraction of all the waste generated in the U.S.

The United States Environmental Protection Agency (EPA) reported that Americans generated about 13 billion tons of nonhazardous solid waste in 1992 (*Solid Waste: State and Federal Efforts to Manage Nonhazardous Waste,* U.S. General Accounting Office, Washington, DC, 1995). Of this, only 200 million tons were municipal solid waste—the rubbish from households, businesses, and institutions. (As Figure 1.2 shows, this figure climbed to nearly 230 million tons in 1999.) However, most of the

FIGURE 1.2

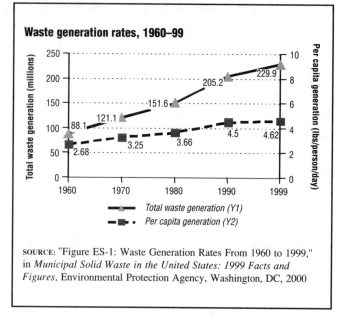

Waste generation rates, 1960–99

SOURCE: "Figure ES-1: Waste Generation Rates From 1960 to 1999," in *Municipal Solid Waste in the United States: 1999 Facts and Figures,* Environmental Protection Agency, Washington, DC, 2000

FIGURE 1.3

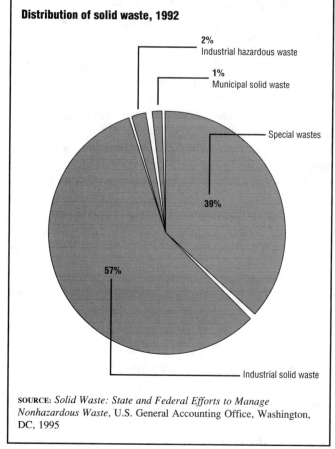

Distribution of solid waste, 1992

SOURCE: *Solid Waste: State and Federal Efforts to Manage Nonhazardous Waste,* U.S. General Accounting Office, Washington, DC, 1995

nonhazardous waste comprised special waste (5.2 billion tons) and nonhazardous industrial waste (7.6 billion tons). Special waste comes from mining, oil and gas production, electric utilities, and cement kilns, while nonhazardous industrial waste is produced during the processes of manufacturing. Manufacturing facilities dispose of their nonhazardous waste in landfills and waste piles, mix it with the soil, or store it in shallow ponds called surface impoundments.

Manufacturing produces huge amounts of waste. The paper industry, which uses many chemicals to produce paper, accounts for the largest proportion of manufacturing wastes—35 percent of the total. The iron and steel (20 percent) and chemical industries (14 percent) produce most of the rest. Many of the big manufacturing plants have sites on their own property where they can discard waste or treat it so it will not pollute the groundwater, rivers, or streams. Still others ship it to private disposal sites for dumping or for treatment. Smaller manufacturers often use private waste disposal companies or the city waste collection and disposal facilities.

Mining also produces much waste, most of it waste rock and tailings. In the mining process, waste rock is separated from ore. Ore is rock that contains enough metal to make it worth processing. Tailings are the "leftovers" after ore is processed to remove the metal. Chemicals are often used to remove metals from ore. After these chemicals have done their job, they become waste. Sometimes the chemical wastes are liquid, and sometimes they are solid.

Almost all (96 to 98 percent) of the waste from gas and oil drilling is wastewater that is pumped out of the ground before oil is found, or water that is mixed with oil. Wastewater must be separated from oil and gas before these crude products can be processed into refined oil or

gas for automobiles or home heating. The rest of the oil and gas waste comes from mud and rock that surfaces during drilling. Most oil and gas companies dispose of their own wastes.

Hazardous waste is that which burns readily, is explosive, is corrosive, or contains certain amounts of toxic chemicals. The EPA reported that the United States produced 40 million tons of hazardous waste in 1999 (*National Biennial RCRA Hazardous Waste Report: Based on 1999 Data,* Environmental Protection Agency, Washington, DC, 2001).

In summary, as Figure 1.3 shows, most of the solid waste produced in the United States is industrial solid waste and special wastes. Hazardous waste and municipal solid waste (our rubbish) comprises only a small fraction of the total. However, the "throwaway society" mindset supports industry and therefore the production of industrial solid waste, as does our reliance on oil, gas, and electric utilities—the producers of special wastes.

LAWS GOVERNING THE DISPOSAL OF WASTE

The Resource Conservation and Recovery Act (RCRA) was enacted by Congress in 1976, building on the Solid Waste Disposal Act (SWDA) of 1965 and a 1970 amendment of the SWDA called the Resource Recovery

Act. The scope of the RCWA was expanded by amendments in 1980, 1984, 1992, and 1996. The RCRA's primary goals are to:

(1) protect human health and the environment from the potential hazards of waste disposal,

(2) conserve energy and natural resources,

(3) reduce the amount of waste generated, and

(4) ensure that wastes are managed in an environmentally sound manner.

The RCRA regulates the management of solid waste, hazardous waste, and underground storage tanks holding petroleum products or certain chemicals.

Other federal laws indirectly regulate waste disposal by protecting against pollution that might result from improper waste disposal practices. For example, the Federal Water Pollution Control Act (Clean Water Act) was originally enacted in 1948 and totally revised by amendments in 1972 that gave the Clean Water Act its current form. The most recent set of amendments to this law is the Water Quality Act of 1987. These acts provide legislation to protect against the pollution of America's lakes, rivers, coastal areas, and aquifers (underground areas of water). The Safe Drinking Water Act, enacted in 1974, protects the quality of drinking water in the United States.

The Clean Air Act of 1990 establishes federal standards for autos and other mobile sources of air pollution, for sources of hazardous air pollutants, and for the emissions that cause acid rain. This legislation began as the Air Pollution Control Act of 1955 and the Clean Air Act of 1963, with a major revision of the legislation in 1970.

CHAPTER 2
MUNICIPAL SOLID WASTE (MSW)

As defined by the U.S. Environmental Protection Agency (EPA), municipal solid waste (MSW) includes durable goods (those with a lifespan of more than three years, such as tires, appliances, and furniture), nondurable goods (those with a life span of less than three years, such as paper, certain disposable products, and clothing), containers and packaging, food scraps, yard trimmings, and miscellaneous inorganic refuse from residential, institutional, and industrial sources. MSW does not include construction and demolition wastes, automobile bodies, municipal sludge, combustion ash, and industrial process wastes that generally are discarded in locations other than municipal landfills or incinerators.

HOW MUCH MSW IS THERE AND WHAT IS IN IT?

The EPA, in *Municipal Solid Waste in the United States: 1999 Facts and Figures* (2000), reported that Americans produced nearly 230 million tons of municipal solid waste in 1999, up from 223 million tons in 1998. Per capita, Americans generated 4.62 pounds of waste per day in 1999, up from 4.52 pounds per person per day in 1998. That figure is also up from a relatively stable 4.4 to 4.5 pounds per person per day throughout the rest of the 1990s. (See Table 2.1.)

BioCycle Magazine, a waste industry publication, provides an annual nationwide survey, "The State of Garbage in America," compiled from state data. In its 2000 survey (Part I, April 2000, and Part II, November 2000), *BioCycle* reported that the total amount of MSW generated in 1999 was at a record high of 390 million tons. (The *BioCycle* survey included industrial waste, which was not counted in figures compiled by the EPA in *Municipal Solid Waste in the United States: 1999 Facts and Figures*.)

Figure 2.1 shows the categories of materials that are considered MSW. The category making up the largest proportion of MSW is paper and paperboard. In 1999,

38.1 percent of all MSW by weight was paper, followed by yard wastes (12.1 percent), food wastes (10.9 percent), plastics (10.5 percent), metals (7.8 percent), rubber, leather, and textiles (6.6 percent), glass (5.5 percent), wood (5.3 percent), and other (3.2 percent).

Table 2.2 categorizes MSW somewhat differently from Figure 2.1, focusing on containers and packaging and their share of total MSW. Table 2.2 shows that containers and packaging made up 33.1 percent of total MSW in 1999. Paper and paperboard packaging (17.9 percent) made up a bit more than half of this amount. The total proportion of paper and paperboard packaging in municipal solid waste has not increased much since 1960 (from 16 percent to 17.9 percent). Steel packaging and glass packaging have both decreased in proportion, but plastics packaging has increased from 0.1 percent in 1960 to 4.9 percent in 1999. The total proportion of containers and packaging in MSW increased by 2 percent during that same time.

WASTE DISPOSAL

The three primary methods of the disposal and recovery of waste are landfilling, combustion or incineration, and recycling and composting. (Composting is a method of decomposing yard waste for reuse as fertilizer.) According to the EPA, in 1999, 57 percent of all wastes went into landfills (down from 62 percent in 1993), 28 percent was recycled (up from 22 percent in 1993), and 15 percent was incinerated, roughly the same as in 1993. (See Figure 2.2.)

These data differ somewhat from those in the 2000 *BioCycle* study, which found that 60 percent of MSW went into landfills in 1999 (down from 71 percent in 1993 and 67 percent in 1995). Thirty-three percent was recycled (up from 19 percent in 1993 and 23 percent in 1995), and 7 percent was burned in incinerators (down from 11 percent in 1993 and 10 percent in 1995). (See Table 2.3.)

TABLE 2.1

Generation, materials recovery, composting, and discards of municipal solid waste, 1960–99

	Millions of tons								
	1960	**1970**	**1980**	**1990**	**1994**	**1995**	**1997**	**1998**	**1999**
Generation	88.1	121.1	151.6	205.2	214.4	211.4	219.1	223.0	229.9
Recovery for recycling	5.6	8.0	14.5	29.0	42.2	45.3	47.3	48.4	50.8
Recovery for composting*	Neg.	Neg.	Neg.	4.2	8.5	9.6	12.1	13.1	13.1
Total materials recovery	5.6	8.0	14.5	33.2	50.6	54.9	59.4	61.6	63.9
Discards after recovery	82.5	113.0	137.1	172.0	163.7	156.5	159.8	161.5	166

	Pounds per person per day								
	1960	**1970**	**1980**	**1990**	**1994**	**1995**	**1997**	**1998**	**1999**
Generation	2.68	3.25	3.66	4.50	4.51	4.40	4.49	4.52	4.62
Recovery for recycling	0.17	0.22	0.35	0.64	0.89	0.94	0.97	0.98	1.02
Recovery for composting*	Neg.	Neg.	Neg.	0.09	0.18	0.20	0.25	0.27	0.26
Total materials recovery	0.17	0.22	0.35	0.73	1.06	1.14	1.22	1.25	1.28
Discards after recovery	2.51	3.04	3.31	3.77	3.44	3.26	3.27	3.27	3.33
Population (thousands)	179,979	203,984	227,255	249,907	260,682	263,168	267,645	270,561	272,691

	Percent of total generation								
	1960	**1970**	**1980**	**1990**	**1994**	**1995**	**1997**	**1998**	**1999**
Generation	100.0%	100.0%	100.0%	100.0%	100.0%	100.0%	100.0%	100.0%	100.0%
Recovery for recycling	6.4%	6.6%	9.6%	14.2%	19.7%	21.5%	21.6%	21.7%	22.1%
Recovery for composting*	Neg.	Neg.	Neg.	2.0%	4.0%	4.5%	5.5%	5.9%	5.7%
Total materials recovery	6.4%	6.6%	9.6%	16.2%	23.6%	26.0%	27.1%	27.6%	27.8%
Discards after recovery	93.6%	93.4%	90.4%	83.8%	76.4%	74.0%	72.9%	72.4%	72.2%

*Composting of yard trimmings and food wastes. Does not include mixed MSW composting or backyard composting.
Details may not add to totals due to rounding.

SOURCE: "Table ES-1: Generation, Materials Recovery, Composting, and Discards of Municipal Solid Waste, 1960–1999 (In millions of tons)," "Table ES-2: Generation, Materials Recovery, Composting, and Discards of Municipal Solid Waste, 1960–1999 (In pounds per person per day)," and "Table ES-3: Generation, Materials Recovery, Composting, and Discards of Municipal Solid Waste, 1960–1999 (In percent of total generation)," in *Municipal Solid Waste in the United States: 1999 Facts and Figures,* Environmental Protection Agency, Washington, DC, 2000. Data from Franklin Associates.

FIGURE 2.1

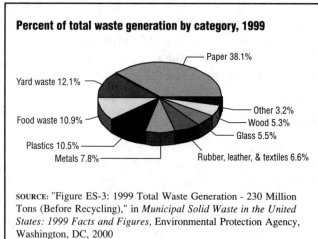

Percent of total waste generation by category, 1999

Paper 38.1%
Yard waste 12.1%
Food waste 10.9%
Plastics 10.5%
Metals 7.8%
Rubber, leather, & textiles 6.6%
Glass 5.5%
Wood 5.3%
Other 3.2%

SOURCE: "Figure ES-3: 1999 Total Waste Generation - 230 Million Tons (Before Recycling)," in *Municipal Solid Waste in the United States: 1999 Facts and Figures,* Environmental Protection Agency, Washington, DC, 2000

Incineration facilities burn MSW at a high temperature, reducing waste volume and generating electricity. Incineration is generally more costly than using landfills, and many people are concerned about incineration's risk to the environment and human health. These factors may be contributing to the slight decrease in use (proportionally) of incineration as a MSW disposal method, as shown in the *BioCycle* study.

Table 2.3 shows how each state disposed of its MSW in 1999. Some states, such as New Mexico (90 percent), Montana and Nevada (89 percent each), and Kansas (88 percent), disposed of most of their MSW in landfills. These states are less densely populated than many others, generate less MSW than many other states, and have more space for landfills than do more densely populated states. Conversely, many states in the Northeast, along with Minnesota, Hawaii, and the District of Columbia, discarded less than 50 percent of their waste in landfills.

According to *BioCycle*, recycling is becoming more important everywhere in the United States. Delaware (57 percent), Arkansas (45 percent), Maine, New York, and South Dakota (42 percent each), and New Jersey (40 percent) all recycled a significant portion of their MSW in 1999.

Figure 2.3 graphs landfill, combustion, and recycling data in millions of tons from 1960 to 1999. This graph shows how the proportion of MSW that is recovered through recycling and composting has grown over the decades, especially since the late 1980s. Additionally, landfill use declined from the late 1980s through 1996, but is now on the rise again.

TABLE 2.2

Products generated[1] in the municipal waste stream, with detail on containers and packaging, 1960–99

	Percent of total generation							
	1960	**1970**	**1980**	**1990**	**1995**	**1997**	**1998**	**1999**
Products								
Durable goods	11.3%	12.1%	14.4%	14.5%	14.7%	15.2%	15.4%	15.4%
Nondurable goods	19.7%	20.7%	22.7%	25.4%	27.1%	27.1%	27.0%	27.1%
Containers and packaging								
Glass packaging								
Beer and soft drink bottles	1.6%	4.6%	4.4%	2.7%	2.4%	2.3%	2.4%	2.4%
Wine and liquor bottles	1.2%	1.6%	1.6%	1.0%	0.8%	0.8%	0.8%	0.8%
Food and other bottles & jars	4.2%	3.7%	3.2%	2.0%	2.2%	1.7%	1.7%	1.6%
Total glass packaging	7.0%	9.8%	9.2%	5.8%	5.5%	4.8%	4.9%	4.8%
Steel packaging								
Beer and soft drink cans	0.7%	1.3%	0.3%	0.1%	neg.	Neg.	Neg.	Neg.
Food and other cans	4.3%	2.9%	1.9%	1.2%	1.3%	1.3%	1.2%	1.2%
Other steel packaging	0.3%	0.2%	0.2%	0.1%	0.1%	0.1%	0.1%	0.1%
Total steel packaging	5.3%	4.4%	2.4%	1.4%	1.4%	1.4%	1.3%	1.3%
Aluminum packaging								
Beer and soft drink cans	neg.	0.1%	0.6%	0.8%	0.8%	0.7%	0.7%	0.7%
Other cans	neg.	Neg.	Neg.	Neg.	Neg.	Neg.	Neg.	Neg.
Foil and closures	0.2%	0.3%	0.3%	0.2%	0.2%	0.2%	0.2%	0.2%
Total aluminum packaging	0.2%	0.5%	0.8%	0.9%	0.9%	0.9%	0.9%	0.9%
Paper & paperboard pkg								
Corrugated boxes	8.3%	10.5%	11.3%	11.7%	13.6%	13.5%	13.3%	13.6%
Milk cartons[2]			0.5%	0.2%	0.2%	0.2%	0.2%	0.2%
Folding cartons[2]			2.5%	2.1%	2.5%	2.5%	2.5%	2.5%
Other paperboard packaging	4.4%	4.0%	0.2%	0.1%	0.1%	0.1%	0.1%	0.1%
Bags and sacks[2]			2.2%	1.2%	0.9%	0.9%	0.8%	0.7%
Wrapping papers[2]			0.1%	0.1%	0.0%			
Other paper packaging	3.3%	3.1%	0.6%	0.5%	0.5%	0.6%	0.6%	0.7%
Total paper & board pkg	16.0%	17.7%	17.4%	15.9%	18.0%	17.7%	17.5%	17.9%
Plastics packaging								
Soft drink bottles[2]			0.2%	0.2%	0.3%	0.3%	0.4%	0.4%
Milk bottles[2]			0.2%	0.3%	0.3%	0.3%	0.3%	0.3%
Other containers	0.1%	0.8%	0.6%	0.7%	0.6%	0.7%	1.0%	1.1%
Bags and sacks[2]			0.3%	0.5%	0.6%	0.7%	0.7%	0.7%
Wraps[2]			0.6%	0.7%	0.8%	1.0%	0.9%	1.1%
Other plastics packaging	0.1%	1.0%	0.5%	1.0%	1.1%	1.3%	1.2%	1.2%
Total plastics packaging	0.1%	1.7%	2.2%	3.4%	3.6%	4.3%	4.4%	4.9%
Wood packaging	2.3%	1.7%	2.6%	4.0%	2.9%	3.2%	3.3%	3.3%
Other misc. Packaging	0.1%	0.1%	0.1%	0.1%	0.1%	0.1%	0.1%	0.1%
Total containers & pkg	31.1%	36.0%	34.7%	31.4%	32.4%	32.4%	32.5%	33.1%
Total product wastes[3]	62.0%	68.8%	71.8%	71.4%	74.2%	74.6%	74.9%	75.5%
Other wastes								
Food wastes	13.8%	10.6%	8.6%	10.1%	10.3%	11.2%	11.2%	10.9%
Yard trimmings	22.7%	19.2%	18.1%	17.1%	14.0%	12.7%	12.4%	12.1%
Miscellaneous inorganic wastes	1.5%	1.5%	1.5%	1.4%	1.5%	1.5%	1.5%	1.5%
Total other wastes	38.0%	31.2%	28.2%	28.6%	25.8%	25.4%	25.1%	24.5%
Total MSW generated - %	100.0%	100.0%	100.0%	100.0%	100.0%	100.0%	100.0%	100.0%

Note: Details may not add to totals due to rounding.
Neg. = Less than 5,000 tons or 0.05 percent.
[1]Generation before materials recovery or combustion.
[2]Not estimated separately prior to 1980. Paper wraps not reported separately after 1996.
[3]Other than food products.

SOURCE: "Table 19. Products Generated in the Municipal Waste Stream, 1960 to 1999 (With Detail on Containers and Packaging)," in *Municipal Solid Waste in the United States: 1999 Facts and Figures,* Environmental Protection Agency, Washington, DC, 2000. Data from Franklin Associates.

LANDFILLS

Prior to using landfills, cities used open dumps, areas in which garbage and trash were simply discarded in huge piles. However, open dumps produced unpleasant odors and attracted animals. In 1979, as part of the Resource Conservation and Recovery Act (RCRA), the EPA designated conditions under which solid waste disposal facilities and practices would not pose adverse effects to human health and the environment. As a result of the implementation of these criteria, open dumps had to be closed or upgraded to meet the criteria for landfills.

Landfills are areas where waste is placed into the land. They usually have liner systems and other safeguards to prevent groundwater contamination. MSW is

FIGURE 2.2

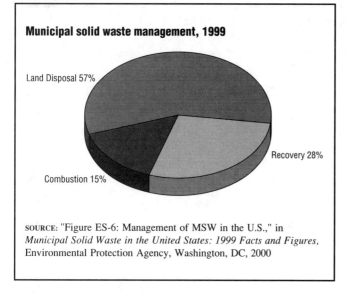

Municipal solid waste management, 1999

Land Disposal 57%

Recovery 28%

Combustion 15%

SOURCE: "Figure ES-6: Management of MSW in the U.S.," in *Municipal Solid Waste in the United States: 1999 Facts and Figures*, Environmental Protection Agency, Washington, DC, 2000

TABLE 2.3

Municipal Solid Waste (MSW) generation (unless noted), recycling and disposal methods by state

(1999 data unless noted)

State	Solid Waste (tons/year)	Recycled[1] (%)	Incinerated (%)	Landfilled (%)
Alabama	5,710,000[2]	23	5	72
Alaska	675,000	7	11	82
Arizona	5,187,000	26	<1	74
Arkansas	4,063,000	45	1	54
California	60,000,000[2]	37	0	63
Colorado	6,455,000[3]	n/a	n/a	n/a
Connecticut[4]	3,168,000	24	65	11
Delaware[5]	2,000,000	57	9	34
Dist. of Columbia	220,000[6]	15	70	15
Florida[7]	24,858,000[8,9]	28	16	56
Georgia	11,420,000[10]	n/a	n/a	n/a
Hawaii	1,884,000[3]	28	35	37
Idaho	794,000[7]	n/a	n/a	n/a
Illinois	13,515,000[8,11]	23	2	75
Indiana	6,798,000[10]	32	5	63
Iowa	3,500,000[8]	37[12]	<1	63
Kansas	3,000,000	12	<1	88
Kentucky	4,077,000[3,10]	33	<1	67
Louisiana	4,800,000	17	0	83
Maine[13]	1,635,000[8]	42	40	18
Maryland	6,000,000	36	23	41
Massachusetts	8,142,000	38	43	19
Michigan	19,500,000[10]	n/a	n/a	n/a
Minnesota[14]	5,445,000	41	25	34
Mississippi	2,264,000[7]	14	2	84
Missouri[15]	9,560,000[3]	36[12]	<1	64
Montana	1,082,000[7,8]	11	0	89
Nebraska	1,820,000[2]	29	0	71
Nevada	3,153,000	11	0	89
New Hampshire[7]	1,284,000[16]	24	22	54
New Jersey[7]	7,800,000	40	21	39
New Mexico	2,966,000[8]	10	0	90
New York	29,650,000[3]	42	12	46
North Carolina[17]	13,000,000[2]	29	1	70
North Dakota	498,000[8]	20	0	80
Ohio	12,015,000	20	<1	80
Oklahoma	3,545,000[3,18]	n/a	n/a	n/a
Oregon	4,415,000[8]	30	11	59
Pennsylvania	98,000,000[8]	33	17	50
Rhode Island	421,000[19]	28[20]	0	72
South Carolina[21]	9,409,000[2]	31	2	67
South Dakota	514,000	42	0	58
Tennessee	9,213,000[7]	n/a	n/a	n/a
Texas	34,023,000[3,22]	35	<1	65
Utah	2,362,000[10]	20	4	76
Vermont	367,000	35	6	59
Virginia[7]	8,136,000	35	9	56

often compacted before it is placed in a landfill, and it is covered with soil. In the United States, 57 to 60 percent of MSW was disposed of in landfills in 1999. (See Figure 2.2 and Table 2.3.)

Decreasing Numbers of Landfills

The number of landfills available for MSW disposal has decreased over the past few decades. In the early 1970s the number of operating landfills in the United States was estimated at about 20,000. However, after the 1979 RCRA legislation, many open dumps closed, decreasing the number of operating "landfills." Additionally, many more landfills closed in the early 1990s because they could not conform to the new standards that took effect in 1993 under the 1992 RCRA amendment. Other landfills closed because they were full. In 1995, 2,893 landfills were operating, and by 1999, according to the 2000 *BioCycle* study, only 2,216 landfills were still open. (See Table 2.4.)

The trend is toward fewer, but larger, landfills, so a decrease in the number of landfills may continue. Table 2.4 shows the estimated years of landfill capacity remaining for each state as of 1999. Notice that Montana reports a remaining capacity of 1,546 years. The Montana Department of Environmental Quality bases this estimate on the amount currently disposed in its landfills and on licenses for expansion of existing sites.

Although the United States is one of the least crowded industrialized nations in the world in terms of population density per acre, population density and available landfill space varies widely across the country. New areas for landfills are becoming increasingly hard to find in some areas of the country (such as the Northeast), while other states have plenty of landfill space available. A few states (Connecticut, Massachusetts, New Jersey, and

Rhode Island) have insufficient land with suitable soil and water conditions for landfills. Since landfills are not welcome in most neighborhoods, useable land must be found away from residential areas.

Landfill Regulation

The new RCRA standards require landfill operators to do several things to lessen the chance of polluting the ground water below, since landfills contain a number of pollutants. In fact, municipal landfills comprise about one-fifth of the hazardous waste sites on the National Priority List for cleanup by Superfund.

The RCRA requirements to lessen the chance of pollution from landfills are as follows:

TABLE 2.3

Municipal Solid Waste (MSW) generation (unless noted), recycling and disposal methods by state [CONTINUED]

(1999 data unless noted)

State	Solid Waste (tons/year)	Recycled[1] (%)	Incinerated (%)	Landfilled (%)
Washington	6,638,000	33	0	67
West Virginia	1,300,000[10]	25	0	75
Wisconsin	4,000,000	n/a	n/a	n/a
Wyoming	53,000[7]	n/a	n/a	n/a
Total	382,594,000	33	7	60

n/a - information not available.

[1] includes yard trimmings composting and wood chipping.
[2] Includes industrial and agricultural wastes as well as C&D debris.
[3] Includes industrial waste and C&D debris.
[4] Of total MSW generated, 9% is exported. State estimates that 6% is landfilled out of state and 3% is incinerated (those amounts were added to final percentages).
[5] Calculations based on state's 1999 Delaware Recycling Report.
[6] All waste is exported. Number is only residential waste collected by District of Columbia.
[7] 1998 data.
[8] Includes C&D debris.
[9] Total amount of MSW collected.
[10] Total disposed, not generated.
[11] Generation calculated from county solid waste management plans dated 1988 to 1996.
[12] 37% is diversion rate that includes MSW recycled, composted, reused (i.e. not disposed or incinerated).
[13] 1997 data.
[14] Landfilling and incineration percentages include estimate for MSW burned or buried on-site and problem materials (e.g. appliances, tires, etc.) not recycled.
[15] MSW generation and 36% diversion calculated using a variable generation rate method based on personal consumption expenditures.
[16] Of total MSW generated, 7% is exported. State estimates one-third to one-half is incinerated and rest is landfilled (those amounts were added to final percentages).
[17] Recycled/composted and landfilled percentages based on newer disposal data and older recycled/composted data. FY 99-00 saw considerable rise in disposal, but state estimates no comparable rise in MSW recycled/composted, leading to 3% drop in recycling rate from 1999 State of Garbage in America survey.
[18] 1996 data.
[19] 421,000 tons is MSW generated. Total solid waste generated is 1,001,000 tons and includes municipal, commercial and industral waste.
[20] Includes alternative daily cover material.
[21] Based on BioCycle calculations using data in South Carolina Solid Waste Management Annual Report, FY 1999.
[22] Recycled rate difference between landfilled rate and MSW generated. Texas has not assessed its statewide recycling rate since 1997.

Notes: Eight states did not report a recycling, incineration and landfilling percentage. Wyoming did not respond to the Part II survey; the seven other states had no data available. Six states gave different generation totals than ones printed in the April, 2000 Part I report, resulting in 7.3 million ton decline in total U.S. tonnage. MSW includes residential, commercial, institutional streams. Additional fractions noted if included in number provided.

SOURCE: Nora Goldstein and Celeste Madtes, "Table 2. Municipal Solid Waste (MSW) generation (unless noted), recycling and disposal methods by state (1999 data unless noted)," in "The State of Garbage in America, Part II," in *BioCycle*, November 2000. Reprinted with permission from *BioCycle* magazine. For more information, visit www.biocycle.net.

FIGURE 2.3

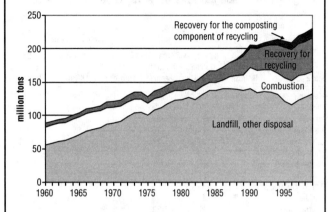

Municipal solid waste management, 1960–99

SOURCE: "Figure 26. Municipal solid waste management, 1960 to 1999," in *Municipal Solid Waste in the United States: 1999 Facts and Figures,* Environmental Protection Agency, Washington, DC, 2000

FIGURE 2.4

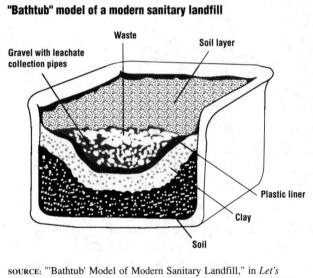

"Bathtub" model of a modern sanitary landfill

SOURCE: "'Bathtub' Model of Modern Sanitary Landfill," in *Let's Reduce and Recycle: Curriculum for Solid Waste Management,* U.S. Environmental Protection Agency, Washington, DC, 1990

• Landfill operators must monitor the ground water for pollutants, which is usually accomplished with a ground water monitoring well.

• Landfills must have plastic liners and a minimum of two feet of compacted soil, as well as a leachate collection system. (See Figure 2.4. Leachate is formed when rainwater filters through waste and draws out, or leaches, chemicals from those wastes.)

• Debris must be covered daily with soil to prevent odors and stop refuse from being blown away.

• Methane gas (a byproduct of decomposition) must be monitored, which is usually accomplished with an explosive gas monitoring well.

• Landfill owners are responsible for cleanup of any contamination.

Imports and Exports of Garbage

Due to the drop in the number of landfills in the United States and the problem some states have with finding appropriate landfill space, many cities and towns send their garbage to other states. In 1992, even before the new RCRA regulations enacted that year went into effect,

TABLE 2.4

Number of municipal solid waste landfills and incinerators, average tip fees, and capacity by state, 1999

State	Landfills			Incinerators		
	Number	Average tip fee ($/ton)	Remaining capacity (years)	Number	Average tip fee ($/ton)	Daily capacity (tons/day)
Alabama	29	33	10+	1	40	700
Alaska	239	70	n/a	4	80	210
Arizona	47	22	n/a	0	–	–
Arkansas	23	24	30	1	15	30
California	184	39	28	3	n/a	4,940
Colorado	115	n/a	n/a	1	n/a	n/a
Connecticut	1	n/a	n/a	6	n/a	7,360
Delaware	3	59	30	0	–	–
Dist. of Columbia	0	–	–	0	–	–
Florida	57	43	n/a	13	55	19,200
Georgia	70	27	23	1	59	500
Hawaii	10	47	3-50	1	81	2,000
Idaho	29	n/a	n/a	0	–	–
Illinois	58	28	17	1	n/a	1,400[1]
Indiana	37	n/a	12	2	n/a	2,175
Iowa	61	32	25	1	47	n/a
Kansas	54	23	n/a	1	50	15
Kentucky	35	n/a	n/a	0	–	–
Louisiana	23	25	n/a	0	–	–
Maine	8	55	7-10	4	55	2,850
Maryland	22	58	10+	4	n/a[2]	3,650
Massachusetts	43	n/a	1.8	9	n/a	8,600
Michigan	53	n/a	17	4	n/a	n/a
Minnesota	22	45	7.5	9	50	4,680
Mississippi	19	18	15	1	30	150
Missouri	26	27	5-10	2	n/a	n/a
Montana	33	13	1,546	0	–	–
Nebraska	24	27	n/a	0	–	–
Nevada	26	23	50+	0	–	–
New Hampshire	4	60	10	2	55	700
New Jersey	12	60	n/a[3]	5	51	6,490
New Mexico	77	25	50	0	–	–
New York	28	n/a	n/a[4]	10	n/a	12,000[5]
North Carolina	39	31	n/a	1	34	380
North Dakota	14	25	40+	0	–	–
Ohio	49	30	20	0	–	–
Oklahoma	41	18	20+	1	44	1,125
Oregon	29	25	40+	2	67	600

TABLE 2.4

Number of municipal solid waste landfills and incinerators, average tip fees, and capacity by state, 1999 [CONTINUED]

State	Landfills			Incinerators		
	Number	Average tip fee ($/ton)	Remaining capacity (years)	Number	Average tip fee ($/ton)	Daily capacity (tons/day)
Pennsylvania	49	n/a	12	5	n/a	8,950
Rhode Island	4	40	10	0	–	–
South Carolina	19	32	n/a[6]	1	60	700
South Dakota	15	32	n/a	0	–	–
Tennessee	51	30	5-10	2	38	1,250
Texas	184	25	31	9	n/a	n/a
Utah	36	n/a	25+	1	n/a	420[7]
Vermont	5	70	12.5[8]	0	–	–
Virginia	65	n/a	n/a	6	n/a	n/a
Washington	21	n/a	34	5	n/a	n/a
West Virginia	19	45	n/a	0	–	–
Wisconsin	46	30	6+	2	46	350
Wyoming	58	n/a	n/a	1	n/a	20
Total	2,216			122		

[1] Average ton/day capacity based on total of 422,000 tons received in 1999 at state's only incinerator. Of total received, 261,000 tons processed—118,000 tons recycled and 43,000 tons landfilled.

[2] Tipping fee range in state is $35 to $67.50/ton.

[3] 30 million tons of capacity remaining with 660,000 tons being added.

[4] 50 million tons of capacity remaining with 62 million tons being added.

[5] Average ton/day capacity based on total of 3.6 million tons/year of capacity.

[6] 76.3 million tons of capacity remaining with about 1.2 million tons being added.

[7] Average ton/day capacity based on total of 125,000 tons/year of capacity.

[8] 12.5 years remaining capacity if landfill at permitted rate (6.1 years if all municipal solid waste went only to Vermont landfills—currently 30% goes out of state.

SOURCE: Nora Goldstein, "Table 2. Number of municipal solid waste landfills and incinerators, average tip fees, and capacity by state for 1999," in "The State of Garbage in America: Part I," *BioCycle*, April 2000. Reprinted with permission from *BioCycle* magazine. For more information, visit www.biocycle.net.

about 19 million tons (9 percent of all MSW created) were sent out of state. By 1995, 25.1 million tons of waste passed over state lines for disposal. Some states must ship their MSW to far away states; some are even shipping their MSW to Africa and Latin America.

In 1999 most states imported and/or exported solid waste. (See Table 2.5.) Nearly 390 million tons were imported to the states reporting in the 2000 *Biocycle* survey and 16.1 million tons were exported from them.

Illinois is by far the largest waste importer, followed by Pennsylvania, Indiana, and Michigan. (See Table 2.5.) New York is by far the largest waste exporter, followed by New Jersey, Missouri, Maryland, and North Carolina. Each of these states exported more than 1 million tons of waste to other states in 1999. (Note: The New York data is from 1997.) New York's large amount of exported waste is dominated by New York City's commercial waste. Furthermore, waste exports from New York are expected to grow rapidly because Fresh Kills landfill (the

city's only landfill) closed on March 22, 2001. It reopened on September 13, 2001, after the September 11, 2001 terrorist attack on the World Trade Center, in order to receive the debris from the cleanup, but it is not accepting other MSW.

In addition to states importing and exporting solid waste, other countries import and export MSW, primarily paper, glass, plastic, or rubber. Canada and Mexico send and receive large amounts of solid waste to and from the United States. Imports to and exports from these countries reflect regional shipments of MSW (as if they were nearby states rather than neighboring countries).

Several states have tried to ban the importing of garbage into their states, but the Supreme Court, in *Chemical Waste Management, Inc. v. Hunt* (504 U.S. 334, 1992), ruled that the constitutional right to conduct commerce across state borders protects such shipments. Experts point out that newer, state-of-the-art landfills, which have multiple liners to prevent leaks and equipment to treat emissions, will have to accept waste from a wide region to be financially viable. According to industry representatives, these landfills cost as much as $400,000 an acre to build.

TABLE 2.5

Municipal solid waste generation, waste imports and exports by state, 1999

(unless noted)

State	Generation (unless noted) (tons/year)	Imported (tons/year)	Exported (tons/year)
Alabama	5,700,000[1]	210,000	n/a
Alaska	675,000[2]	0	20,000
Arizona	5,187,000	422,400	<1,000
Arkansas	1,643,000[2]	n/a	n/a
California	59,700,000	12,700	791,500
Colorado	6,455,000[3]	n/a	n/a
Connecticut	3,157,000[2]	234,000	267,100
Delaware	823,000[1]	0	n/a
Dist. of Columbia	220,000[4]	n/a	800,000
Florida	28,585,000[2,5,6]	n/a	n/a
Georgia	11,420,000[7]	453,900	n/a
Hawaii	1,873,000[3]	0	0
Idaho	794,000[2]	0	65,500[2]
Illinois	13,515,000[6,8]	15,978,000	n/a
Indiana	12,000,000[1,2]	2,185,000	220,000
Iowa	3,500,000[6]	425,000	100,000
Kansas	3,000,000	500,000-700,000	17,000
Kentucky	4,077,000[3,7]	475,400	n/a
Louisiana	4,600,000	n/a	n/a
Maine	1,635,000[6,9]	n/a	n/a
Maryland	6,300,000[2]	46,300	1,304,500
Massachusetts	7,936,000[2]	55,500[2]	945,700[2]
Michigan	19,500,000[7]	2,116,600	n/a
Minnesota	5,298,000[2]	n/a	450,000
Mississippi	2,264,000[2]	799,900	0
Missouri	8,013,000[2,3]	143,400	1,551,400
Montana	1,082,000[2,6]	30,000	n/a
Nebraska	2,200,000[1,2]	125,000	20,000
Nevada	3,389,000[2]	513,000	0
New Hampshire	1,284,000[2]	742,000[9]	93,700[9]
New Jersey	7,800,000[2]	600,000	1,600,000
New Mexico	2,732,000[2,6]	n/a	n/a
New York	29,900,000[3,9]	300,000[2]	4,600,000[9]
North Carolina	13,000,000[1]	91,000	1,200,000
North Dakota	498,000[6]	54,800	5,500
Ohio	12,428,000[10]	n/a	n/a
Oklahoma	3,545,000[3,10]	n/a	n/a
Oregon	4,302,000[2,6]	1,248,500	19,900
Pennsylvania	10,337,000[6]	7,974,500	300,000
Rhode Island	421,000[11]	0	0
South Carolina	9,409,000[1]	862,900	57,400
South Dakota	514,000	n/a	n/a
Tennessee	9,213,000[2]	297,100[2]	64,000[2]
Texas	36,401,000[2,12]	35,700[2]	395,000[2]
Utah	2,188,000[2]	11,400	n/a
Vermont	598,000[2,13]	n/a	n/a
Virginia	8,136,000[2]	n/a	n/a

How Garbage Decomposes in Landfills

Organic material (material that was once alive, such as paper and wood products, food scraps, and clothing made of natural fibers) decomposes in the following way: First, aerobic (oxygen-using) bacteria use the material as food and begin the decomposition process. Principal by-products of this aerobic stage are water, carbon dioxide, nitrates, and heat. This stage lasts about two weeks. However, in compacted, layered, and covered landfills, the availability of oxygen may be low.

After the available oxygen is used, anaerobic bacteria (those that do not use oxygen) continue the decomposition. They generally produce carbon dioxide and organic acids. This stage lasts one to two years.

TABLE 2.5

Municipal solid waste generation, waste imports and exports by state, 1999 [CONTINUED]

(unless noted)

State	Generation (unless noted) (tons/year)	Imported (tons/year)	Exported (tons/year)
Washington	6,212,000[2]	307,900	986,800
West Virginia	1,800,000[14]	250,000	215,000
Wisconsin	3,800,000[2,15]	1,200,000[2]	n/a
Wyoming	530,000[2]	0	0
Total	389,939,000		

Note: Municipal solid waste is residential, commercial, institutional streams. Additional fractions of waste stream are noted if included in number provided.

[1] Includes industrial, agricultural waste and construction and demolition (C&D) debris.
[2] 1998 data.
[3] Includes industrial waste and C&D debris.
[4] All waste is exported. Number provided is only residential waste collected by District of Columbia.
[5] Total amount of MSW collected.
[6] Includes C&D debris.
[7] Total amount disposed—not generated.
[8] Generation calculated from county solid waste management plans dated 1988 to 1996. That is used as basis for calculating state recycling rate.
[9] 1997 data.
[10] 1996 data.
[11] Includes industrial waste and small amount of C&D debris.
[12] Includes 5% industrial waste and 18% C&D debris.
[13] Includes C&D if mixed in with MSW .
[14] Includes agricultural waste, C&D debris.
[15] Includes only MSW disposed in landfills from Wisconsin generators.

SOURCE: Nora Goldstein, "Table 1. Municipal solid waste generation, waste imports and exports by state for 1999," in "The State of Garbage in America: Part I," in *Biocycle,* April 2000

During a final anaerobic stage of decomposition lasting several years or decades, methane gas is formed along with carbon dioxide. The duration of this stage and the amount of decomposition depend on landfill conditions, including temperature, soil permeability, and water levels.

In July 1992 *The Smithsonian* reported on a 20-year study called the Garbage Project. Conceived in 1971 and officially established at the University of Arizona in 1973, the Garbage Project was an attempt to apply archaeological principles to the study of solid waste. About 750 people processed more than 250,000 pounds of waste, excavating 14 tons of it from landfills.

Among the Garbage Project's findings was the discovery that although some degradation takes place initially (sufficient to produce large amounts of methane and other gases), it then slows to a virtual standstill. Study results revealed that an astonishingly high volume of old organic matter remained largely intact. Even after two decades, one-third to one-half of supposedly degradable organics remained in recognizable condition. The Smithsonian Institution concluded that well-designed and well-managed landfills, in particular, seemed more likely to preserve their contents than to transform them into humus or mulch.

FIGURE 2.5

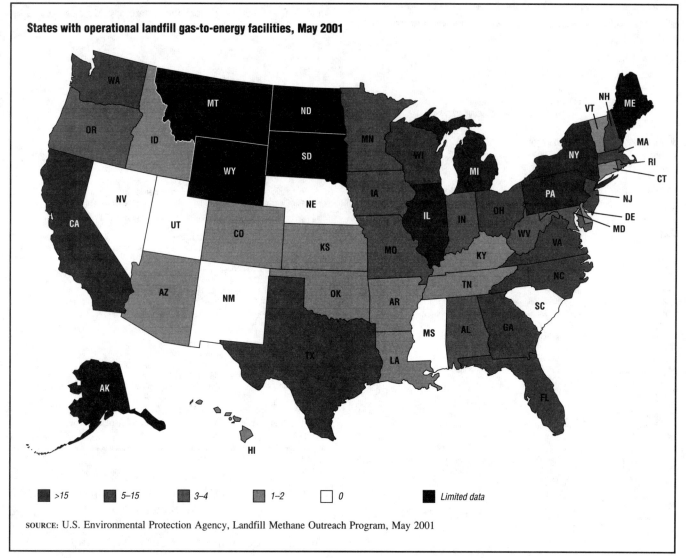

States with operational landfill gas-to-energy facilities, May 2001

Legend: >15 | 5–15 | 3–4 | 1–2 | 0 | ■ Limited data

SOURCE: U.S. Environmental Protection Agency, Landfill Methane Outreach Program, May 2001

Special Wastes

Certain types of municipal solid waste are particularly challenging for waste management facilities to process, either because of their volume or because they are more toxic than most materials.

SCRAP TIRES. The latest data from the Scrap Tire Management Council estimate that in 1996, 266 million tires were discarded in the United States. The majority of the tires, 66 percent, were from cars, while 19 percent were from scrapped vehicles, 10 percent were from light trucks, 4 percent were from medium and heavy trucks, and 1 percent was from farm vehicles (*Scrap Tire Use/Disposal Study, 1996 Update*, Washington, DC, 1997).

In 1996, 57 percent of scrap tires (152.5 million) were combusted for energy recovery. Twenty-four percent (64 million) were landfilled, stockpiled, or illegally dumped. Nine percent (24.5 million) were recycled for such uses as ground rubber in products and in asphalt highways. Six percent (15 million) were exported, and four percent (10

million) were used in civil engineering (The Scrap Tire Management Council, *Scrap Tire Use/Disposal Study, 1996 Update*, Washington, DC, 1997).

The 2 to 4 billion tires that have accumulated in landfills or uncontrolled tire dumps can pose health and fire hazards. Scrap tires are highly combustible, do not compost, and do not degrade easily. The material, primarily hydrocarbons, burns easily, producing toxic, bad-smelling air pollutants and toxic runoff when burned in the open. Health effects that can result from exposure to an open tire fire include irritation of the skin, eyes, and mucous membranes; respiratory effects; central nervous system depression; and cancer. (The controlled combustion of scrap tires in special incinerators does not produce these toxic emissions.) Scrap tires do not compress in landfills and provide breeding grounds for a variety of pests. In fact, some states ban the disposal of tires in landfills.

USED MOTOR OIL. Used oil is generated by large manufacturing facilities, industrial operations, service stations, quick-lube shops, and do-it-yourselfers who change the oil in their cars at home. Approximately 1.4 billion gallons of used oil is discarded by these sources per year (*RCRA Orientation Manual*, Environmental Protection Agency, Washington DC, 1998).

In 1980 Congress passed the Used Oil Recycling Act, and in 1992 developed a more comprehensive used oil recycling program. The Act and associated program include used oil management standards for all facilities that handle used oil.

The problem with used oil disposal is primarily with do-it-yourselfers. About 90 percent of the used oil they generate, about 200 million gallons annually, is discarded rather than recycled via a community program. That amount of discarded oil is equivalent to 18 *Exxon Valdez* spills dumped on the ground, poured down the sewers, or thrown in the trash where it will likely end up in landfills. All these disposal methods are likely to result in the used oil tainting water supplies. A small volume of motor oil can contaminate a large volume of water. One gallon of motor oil from a single oil change can pollute 1 million gallons of fresh water. Contaminants often found in used motor oil add to its toxicity.

Landfills and the Environment

METHANE. Methane, a flammable gas, is produced when organic matter decomposes in the absence of oxygen. If not properly vented or controlled, it can cause explosions and underground fires that smolder for years. Methane is also deadly to breathe. The RCRA requires landfill operators to monitor methane gas.

The Smithsonian Garbage Project found that for 15 or 20 years after a landfill stops accepting garbage, the wells still vent methane in fairly substantial amounts. Thereafter, methane production drops off rapidly, indicating that the landfill has stabilized.

Methane gas can be recovered through pipes inserted into landfills, and the gas can be used to generate energy. The Environmental Protection Agency (EPA) reported that as of May 2001, over 325 landfill gas-to-energy projects were operational in the United States. Additionally, the EPA estimated that about 700 other landfill sites present attractive opportunities for project development. Figure 2.5 shows the number of current landfill gas recovery and utilization projects in each state.

CADMIUM. Cadmium is a natural element in the earth's crust that is frequently found in municipal waste. It has uses in many products, including batteries, pigments, plastics, and metal coatings. The EPA estimates that 2,680 tons of cadmium had been deposited in MSW by 2000. Most cadmium in MSW comes from the disposal of batteries. The remainder comes from plastics, consumer electronics, pigments, appliances, glass, and ceramics.

TABLE 2.6

Sources of lead in MSW (Municiple Solid Waste), 1970–2000

(in tons)

Product	1970	1986	2000
Lead-acid batteries	83,525	138,043	181,546
Consumer electronics	12,233	58,536	85,032
Glass & ceramics	3,365	7,956	8,910
Plastics	1,613	3,577	3,228
Soldered cans	24,117	2,052	787
Pigments	27,020	1,131	682
All others	12,567	2,537	1,701
Total	**164,440**	**213,832**	**281,886**

SOURCE: "Sources of Lead in MSW," in *MSW Factbook*, U.S. Environmental Protection Agency, Washington, DC, 1997

When ingested by humans in polluted air or water, cadmium can build up in the human body over years, damaging the lungs, kidneys, nervous system, and stomach. It is also associated with the development of lung cancer.

LEAD. Lead is an environmental contaminant found in municipal waste that can damage virtually every human organ system. A naturally occurring metal found in small amounts in the earth's surface, lead is used in many products including lead-acid batteries, consumer electronics, glass and ceramics, plastics, cans, and pigments. Table 2.6 shows the amount of lead in MSW from each of these types of products for 1970, 1986, and 2000.

MERCURY. Another component of MSW is mercury. Mercury is a naturally occurring metal that is found both in liquid and gas form. It is used to produce chlorine gas and is used in the manufacture of many products. Once in ground and surface water, it accumulates in fish that humans may eat. It harms the human nervous system and other body organs. The EPA estimates that 172.7 tons of mercury was discarded in waste in 2000. Most of that came from household batteries, thermometers, electronics, paint residues, and pigments.

Landfill Financing

LANDFILL TIP FEES. Landfills charge disposal or "tip fees" to use their facilities. Tip fees range from a low of $13 per ton in Montana to a high of $70 per ton in Alaska and Vermont. In general, the highest tip fees are in the Northeast, and the lowest are in the Midwest and Southwest.

PAY-AS-YOU-THROW. Rather than pay for waste collection services through a flat tax or monthly fee, some communities have instituted "unit pricing," a fee for the amount of waste set on the curb. These programs are called Pay-As-You-Throw (PAYT) and encourage recycling. According to the EPA, the agency that instituted PAYT

FIGURE 2.6

Fresh Kills municipal landfill

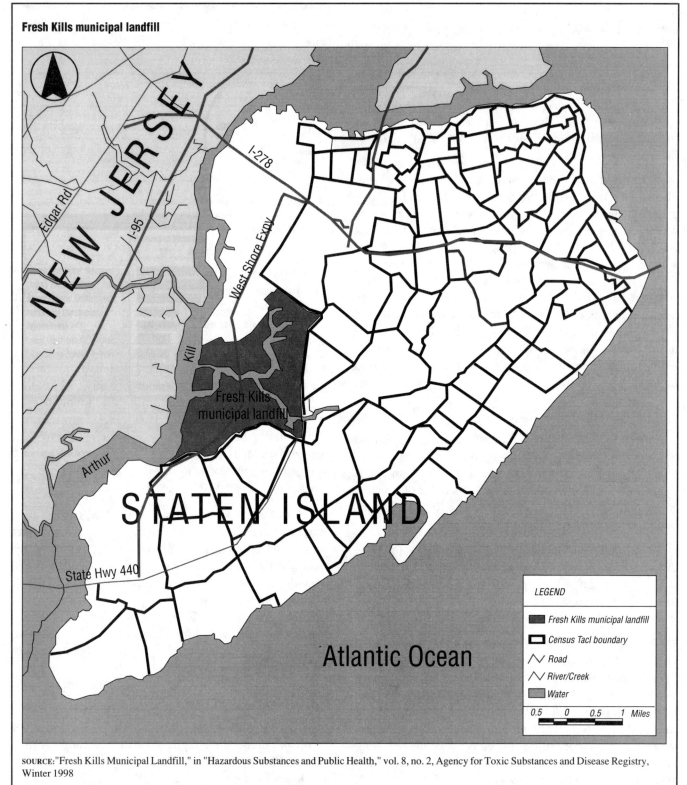

SOURCE:"Fresh Kills Municipal Landfill," in "Hazardous Substances and Public Health," vol. 8, no. 2, Agency for Toxic Substances and Disease Registry, Winter 1998

programs, PAYT communities reduce their waste by 14 to 27 percent and increase recycling by 32 to 59 percent.

According to a survey conducted by the Solid Waste Association of North America and the American Plastics Council, and another conducted by Duke University, more than 3,800 PAYT communities existed in the United States in 1998.

Illegal Dumping

Illegal dumping is a growing problem. One major reason for illegal dumping is the cost of legally disposing of

FIGURE 2.7

Waste combustion plant with pollution control system

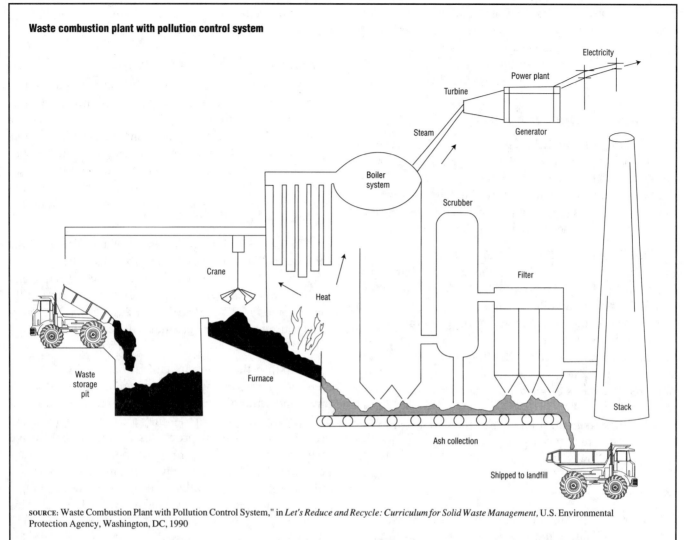

SOURCE: Waste Combustion Plant with Pollution Control System," in *Let's Reduce and Recycle: Curriculum for Solid Waste Management*, U.S. Environmental Protection Agency, Washington, DC, 1990

waste in landfills. In addition, the declining number of landfills, with those remaining often sited at a distance, has led to increased illegal dumping. Illegal dumping endangers human health and the environment because the dump sites become breeding grounds for animal and insect pests, present safety hazards for children, are sources of pollutants, and disrupt wildlife habitats.

The Largest Landfill in the World

Fresh Kills landfill in Staten Island, New York, is the largest landfill in the world, according to the *Guinness Book of World Records*. (See Figure 2.6.) The 53-year-old landfill had been closed for 172 days prior to September 11, 2001, when terrorist attacks felled the World Trade Center towers. Although Fresh Kills was supposed to be closed permanently, within two days of the attack debris from the wreckage was being ferried across the harbor.

Fresh Kills was New York's only remaining landfill and is as massive as the largest of the Egyptian pyramids in height and volume. It is now more than 500 feet tall and

rivals the Great Wall of China as the largest man-made structure in the world. The landfill covers approximately 2,200 acres.

When this site was actively collecting MSW, more than 500 people worked onsite 24 hours a day, six days a week. Every day 18 barges, carrying a total of 10,000 tons of garbage, transported municipal waste from the city's marine transfer stations to the landfill. Approximately 75,000 people live within one mile of the site.

Trends in Landfill Development

In the coming decades, it will be economically prohibitive to develop and maintain small-scale, local landfills. There will likely be fewer, larger, and more regional operations. Most waste will move away from its point of generation, resulting in increased interdependence among communities and states in waste disposal. More waste will cross state lines.

Landfilling is expected to continue to be the single most predominant MSW management method. Landfills will provide more diverse services—burial of waste, bioremediation, reuse facilities, leachate (fluid drainage) collection, and gas recovery. To make landfills more acceptable to neighborhoods, operators will likely establish larger buffer zones, use more green space, and show more sensitivity to land-use compatibility and landscaping.

COMBUSTION (INCINERATION)

According to the EPA, approximately 15 percent of MSW was incinerated in 1999. (See Figure 2.2.) A *BioCycle* report, "The State of Garbage in America—2000," compiled from data provided by the states, reports an incineration rate of 7 percent in 1999. (See Table 2.3.) *BioCycle* reports this rate as down from 10 percent in 1997.

Data from the EPA document 102 incinerators in the United States in 1999, with the ability to burn up to 96,000 tons of MSW per day. The *BioCycle* data document 122 incinerators in the United States in 1999, with Florida having the greatest number of incinerators (13), followed by New York (10), and Massachusetts, Minnesota, and Texas (9 each). (See Table 2.4.) Incinerators vary greatly in size, however. Smaller ones may burn only about 25 tons of garbage a day, while larger ones may burn up to 4,000 tons of garbage per day. Along with having the greatest number of incinerators, Florida has the greatest incineration capacity at 19,200 tons/day, followed by New York (12,000 tons/day), Pennsylvania (8,950 tons/day), and Massachusetts (8,600 tons/day).

Some experts think that incinerators are the best alternative to landfills, and many believe that they are good additions to landfills. In past years, it was common to burn MSW in incinerators to reduce volume. In the 1980s, however, MSW combustion began to incorporate energy recovery systems (steam or electricity). Such waste-to-energy (WTE) facilities help provide an alternative energy source, and the sale of the energy they recover helps offset the cost of operating the facility.

Figure 2.7 shows a typical waste-to-energy system. At this incinerator, the trucks dump waste into a pit. The waste is moved to the furnace by a crane. The furnace burns the waste at a very high temperature, heating a boiler that produces steam for generating electricity and heat. Ash collects at the bottom of the furnace where it is later removed and taken to a landfill for disposal.

Incinerators are very expensive to build. The country's largest incinerator, located in Detroit, cost $438 million. This huge incinerator produces enough steam to heat half of the city's central business district and enough electricity to supply 40,000 homes. However, most experts agree that energy recovery from MSW has only a limited potential for contributing to the nation's overall energy production. Although waste-derived energy production is currently less than one-half of 1 percent of the nation's total energy supply, the Department of Energy has set a goal for energy from waste at 2 percent of the total supply by 2010.

The Problem with Dioxins and Mercury

Mercury is released as a gaseous vapor as paints, fluorescent lights, batteries, electronics, and medical wastes are incinerated, and accumulates in fish after it enters ground and surface water. It harms the human nervous system and other body organs. Concentrations of mercury in fish result not only from human activities such as incineration in the United States, but also from mercury from natural sources as well as emissions from countries other than the United States.

The Office of Pollution Prevention and Toxics of the EPA states that it is taking steps to reduce the levels of mercury emissions from municipal waste combustors and medical waste incinerators. Once these actions are fully implemented in 2002, the EPA states that mercury emissions caused by human activities will be cut by 50 percent from 1990 levels.

Dioxin is the common name for a family of several hundred toxic compounds with similar chemical structures and biological characteristics. Dioxins are not deliberately manufactured—they are the unintended by-products of industrial processes that involve chlorine (such as chlorine bleaching of pulp and paper) or processes that burn chlorine with organic matter. Dioxins are also released in small amounts when sewage sludge, medical waste, hazardous waste, MSW, or fuels, such as wood, oil, and coal, are burned. Even car exhaust and cigarette smoke contain dioxins.

Dioxins are stable compounds that accumulate in the human body over a lifetime. In 1997 the International Agency for Research on Cancer listed dioxin as a "known" carcinogen (cancer-causing substance). The EPA calculates the average level of dioxin in the body of a middle-aged person to be 9 nanograms (one nanogram is one-billionth of a gram) per kilogram (ng/kg). The EPA believes the minimum level for causing harm in humans is 14 ng/kg. Human exposure occurs principally through eating food, especially animals (including fish) that have ingested dioxin.

In the United States, municipal waste incineration, the manufacture and use of certain herbicides (weed killers), and the chlorine bleaching of pulp and paper result in the major releases of dioxins to air and water. Over the past decade, the EPA and industry have worked together to reduce dioxin emissions. New regulations require that scrubbers, which pull pollutants out of smoke, be put on smokestacks to catch the dioxin. Currently in the United States, the largest sources of dioxin emissions to the environment appear to be the uncontrolled burning of residential waste and accidental fires at landfills.

RECYCLING

The proportion of municipal waste handled by recycling has been increasing, rising from 6.7 percent in 1960 to about 28 percent in 1997. Researchers from the *BioCycle* survey estimate that 33 percent of MSW was recycled in 1999, including composting of yard waste.

Before recyclable materials can be refashioned into new products, they must be collected. Most residential recycling involves curbside collection, drop-off programs, buy-back operations, and/or container deposit systems. In 1999 every state responding to the *BioCycle* survey except Alaska and Hawaii had at least one curbside recycling program. That year, there were 9,247 curbside programs in the United States, up from 7,375 in 1995. Those programs served about 133.2 million Americans, representing 61 percent of the U.S. population at that time. New York leads the nation with 1,472 curbside recycling programs, while California leads the nation in number of people served: 19.1 million. New York's programs serve 17.2 million people. (See Table 2.7.)

Processing recyclable materials is performed at materials recovery facilities (MRFs). As reported in *Municipal Solid Waste in the United States: 1999 Facts and Figures* (Environmental Protection Agency, Washington, DC, 2000), 480 MRFs were established in the United States by 1999 in order to process the collected materials. These MRFs processed an estimated 55,000 tons per day. The most extensive use of MRFs was in the Northeast. MRFs vary widely across the nation, depending on the incoming materials and the technology used to sort the materials. The majority of MRFs are classified as low technology, meaning the materials are sorted manually.

PACKAGING AS MSW

The EPA reports that containers and packaging accounted for 33.1 percent of all municipal waste in 1999. (See Table 2.2.) Containers and packaging are made of a number of materials: paper and paperboard, glass, steel, aluminum, plastics, wood, and small amounts of other materials.

Three-quarters of all products require a package, and 90 percent of those products requiring packaging are in the food and drink industry. Additional items requiring packaging are automotive products, hardware, housewares, and tobacco products.

For any product, from one to three types of packaging may be required depending on its purpose and the way in which it is shipped. The container that directly holds the product, such as a can, bottle, tube, or carton, is the primary packaging. Outer wrappings such as a decorated carton or gift box are secondary packaging. Tertiary packaging, such as divided cartons or shrink-wrapping of multiple products on a pallet, is used with products that are grouped for shipping and storage.

TABLE 2.7

Residential curbside recycling and yard trimmings composting sites by state

(1999 data unless noted)

State	Curbside Programs[1]	Curbside Population Served[2]	Percentage of Population Served	Yard Trimmings Sites
Alabama	39	1,100,000	24	20
Alaska	0	0	0	1
Arizona	25	2,250,000[3]	47	40
Arkansas	59	1,450,000	60	24
California	521	19,100,000	56	170
Colorado	n/a	n/a	n/a	n/a
Connecticut	169	3,274,000[4]	100	88
Delaware	2	n/a	n/a	n/a
Dist. of Columbia	1	315,000[5]	61	0
Florida[6]	372	12,046,000	80	22
Georgia	194	5,844,000	76	38
Hawaii	0[7]	0	0	9
Idaho	n/a	n/a	n/a	6
Illinois[8]	474	8,051,000	66	46
Indiana[6]	169	2,187,000	39	89
Iowa	583	1,500,000	50	70
Kansas	99	1,680,000	63	79
Kentucky	35	n/a	n/a	41
Louisiana	23	n/a	n/a	21
Maine	100	441,000	35	40
Maryland	100	3,627,000	70	17
Massachusetts	159	4,814,000	78	285
Michigan[9]	264	n/a	n/a	173
Minnesota	758	3,600,000	76	447
Mississippi	15	339,000	13	10
Missouri[6]	199	2,000,000	40	100
Montana	2	n/a	n/a	38
Nebraska	11	500,000	32	2
Nevada	3[10]	1,720,000	87	3
New Hampshire	38	436,000	36	63
New Jersey[6]	510	7,300,000	90	173
New Mexico	5	635,000	34	2
New York[11]	1,472	17,230,000	95	80
North Carolina	279	3,500,000	45	120
North Dakota	50	100,000	15	25
Ohio	372	n/a[12]	n/a	501
Oklahoma	9	969,000	29	4
Oregon	123	1,850,000	56	32
Pennsylvania	892	8,800,000	90	313
Rhode Island	25	865,000	86	16
South Carolina[13]	n/a	1,876,000	48	119
South Dakota	3	n/a	n/a	116
Tennessee	n/a	n/a	n/a	n/a
Texas[6]	186	5,300,000	27	166
Utah	n/a	n/a	n/a	13
Vermont[6]	94	322,000	54	25
Virginia[14]	62	1,144,000[15]	20	13

The cost of packaging as a percentage of total selling price varies greatly among products, from 1.4 to 40 percent. However, the average cost of packaging is 9 percent—in other words, the consumer pays an average of $1.00 for every $11.00 spent on packaged products.

Aluminum

According to the U.S. Department of Agriculture's Economic Research Service, soft-drink consumption has risen in the past few decades, from 24.3 gallons per person in 1970 to twice that, 50.8 gallons per person, in 1999. Additionally, the population has grown from about 205.1 million persons in 1970 to about 272.7 million persons in 1999. Therefore, can and plastic container use has

TABLE 2.7

Residential curbside recycling and yard trimmings composting sites by state [CONTINUED]

(1999 data unless noted)

State	Curbside Programs[1]	Curbside Population Served[2]	Percentage of Population Served	Yard Trimmings Sites
Washington	100	4,000,000	83	n/a
West Virginia	51	n/a	m/a	23
Wisconsin[16]	600	3,000,000	60	121
Wyoming	n/a	n/a	n/a	n/a
Total	9,247	133,165,000	61	3,804

n/a - Information not available.
[1] Municipal, county and other curbside programs available to residents.
[2] Conversion of 2.86 people/household used to determine population served by curbside when state provided number of households.
[3] 788,000 households.
[4] All residents have access to curbside recycling if choose.
[5] 110,000 households.
[6] 1998 data.
[7] Hawaii has one curbside program for yard trimmings only.
[8] Data based on survey by Illinois Recycling Association conducted in 1999, reflecting 1998 data. 38 counties responded to survey. Population served based on 2.7 million households.
[9] Based on survey by Michigan Recycling Coalition. Does not include communities with access to private sector subscription-based curbside services.
[10] 3 programs service 8 cities.
[11] 1996 data.
[12] Not known because private haulers do not provide numbers.
[13] Total of 174 curbside programs, including those collecting only MSW. State has data on number of households receiving curbside recycling services (656,000) out of the 174 total number.
[14] 1993 data.
[15] 4,000,000+ households.
[16] State reports no change in data since 1999. Mandatory for communities with population over 5,000 to have curbside service and no programs stopped in 1999.

SOURCE: Nora Goldstein and Celeste Madtes, "Table 3. Residential curbside recycling and yard trimmings composting sites by state," in "The State of Garbage in America, Part II," in *BioCycle*, November 2000. Reprinted with permission from *BioCycle* magazine. For more information, visit www.biocycle.net.

increased even beyond what soft drink per capita consumption figures predicted.

Beverage cans are made out of aluminum. In fact, beverage cans are currently the largest single use of aluminum. The Aluminum Association reports that aluminum cans are recycled at a higher rate than any other packaging material; the aluminum can recycling rate is presently about 62 percent, and the average aluminum can contains about 51 percent recycled content. Additionally, the manufacturers of aluminum cans have reduced can weight by 52 percent since 1972 and continue to find methods to reduce the weight further.

Plastics

The word "plastics" comes from the Greek word "plastikos," which means "to form." Today, the term refers to a wide range of flexible materials that can be molded or shaped into products such as fast-food packages, compact discs, contact lenses, and surgical sutures.

The advent of low-priced petrochemicals ushered in the age of plastics. Petrochemicals are substances derived from petroleum or natural gas. Plastics are made primarily from petroleum.

The plastics industry in the United States dates from the work of researcher John Wesley Hyatt in the 1860s. In 1939 nylon stockings were introduced at the World's Fair, and in 1940 plastic ornaments decorated the Christmas tree in Rockefeller Center. World War II spurred the development of new kinds of plastics and major growth in the industry. The 1955 Corvette was the first car to use plastic parts, and in 1982, Dr. Robert Jarvik designed the first artificial heart made largely of plastic.

Today, more plastics are produced in the United States than aluminum and all other nonferrous (non-iron) metals combined. Most of these plastics (a family of more than 45 types) are non-biodegradable and, once discarded, remain relatively intact for many years. The EPA predicts that the amount of plastic thrown away will continue to increase.

Figure 2.8 shows, in millions of tons, the plastics products generated as MSW in 1999. The bottom four bars measure the tonnage of various types of packaging, and together comprise about 11 million tons of MSW. Durable and nondurable goods together comprise about 13 million tons.

Plastics represented 10.5 percent of MSW by weight in 1999. (See Figure 2.1.) Plastics packaging represented 4.9 percent of MSW this same year. One way to reduce the quantity of plastics waste is to trim the amount of packaging. Manufacturers have already taken steps to reduce the weight of plastic containers. Other packaging design changes may help reduce plastics waste as well.

The Positive Side of Packaging

No one ever buys just a package. The package is a conveyor, a piece of the distribution system that protects, preserves, and holds the product on its journey from the manufacturer to the store and, ultimately, the consumer. In developing countries where product packaging is poor or nonexistent, 30 to 50 percent of food is lost between producer and consumer. For example, approximately 20 percent of China's food supplies spoil before reaching the consumer. The United Nations estimates that improved packaging would reduce crop losses by 5 percent.

Packaging also helps reduce disease. Packaging helps prevent contamination of food by bacteria and ensures that medical supplies reach hospitals undamaged. While packaging represents 9 percent of the price of food and beverages, without the protection of packaging, food and beverages would cost even more due to spoilage and damage, perhaps as much as 20 percent more. Packaging reduces the amount of inedible food waste in the

FIGURE 2.8

Plastics products generated in MSW (Municipal Solid Waste), 1999

SOURCE: "Figure 8. Plastics products generated in MSW, 1999," in *Municipal Solid Waste in the United States: 1999 Facts and Figures,* U.S. Environmental Protection Agency, Washington, DC, 2000

municipal waste stream and makes "seasonal" produce available nearly year-round.

Packaging protects against tampering of medications and foods, provides convenience in preparing meals, and enables the fast-food industry to give Americans the precious commodity of time. Latchkey children, single adults, and the elderly all benefit from single-serve, small-quantity packages. In addition, the packaging industry employs 2 million people in the United States, a $75 to $80 billion a year business.

Distribution Packaging

Part of the packaging and distribution system is largely unseen. About one-half of all packaging is primary and secondary consumer packaging—the familiar bottles, jars, cartons, wraps, and other containers found on a typical store shelf. The other half of packaging is distribution or tertiary packaging, which is used to transport products from manufacturers to retailers and consumers.

Distribution packaging can take many forms, such as corrugated boxes and trays, wood or plastic pallets, stretch-film ("shrink-wrap"), molded plastic foam, or plastic and paper bags. The primary purpose of distribution packaging is to ensure that products arrive at their destination safely

and securely, unharmed by hazards in transport and warehousing—such as temperature changes, vibration, compression, puncturing, biological contamination, and pilferage.

The fresh meat industry reflects recent changes in the packaging and distribution system in the United States. Beef is no longer shipped from processors to stores as sides of beef on hooks swinging in refrigerated trucks or railcars, as it was until the 1960s. Since fresh meat is sensitive to dehydration, oxygen, and bacterial contamination, its shelf life was about one week, and maintaining a large inventory was impossible. Today, beef is vacuum-packed in thin multi-layer plastic bags with an oxygen barrier. Packaging beef at the processor, instead of at the store, lowers transportation and processing costs since less waste—bones, fat, etc.—is shipped and rail cars can be packed more efficiently. The shelf life for vacuum-packaged beef is four to six weeks. About 95 percent of beef is now shipped in vacuum barrier bags. Although the use of tertiary packaging in the beef industry has increased, the quality of the product and its shelf life has increased as well.

About 48 percent of products sold in grocery stores in the United States are non-perishables packed in cans, bottles, boxes, and jars. To ensure that packages arrive undamaged at the stores, manufacturers use corrugated

FIGURE 2.9

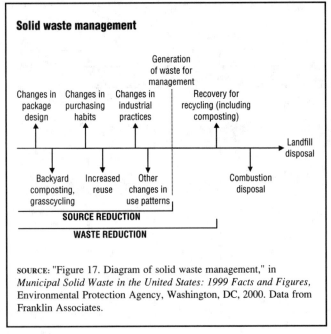

Solid waste management

SOURCE: "Figure 17. Diagram of solid waste management," in *Municipal Solid Waste in the United States: 1999 Facts and Figures,* Environmental Protection Agency, Washington, DC, 2000. Data from Franklin Associates.

boxing and wood pallets. While packaging is absolutely essential in getting food to the table, manufacturers of non-perishables are reassessing their delivery systems to see if some packaging can be modified, or even eliminated, to cut down on waste.

SOURCE REDUCTION

Source reduction is gaining more attention as an important option in solid waste management. Often called "waste prevention," source reduction activities lessen the amount of MSW before wastes are generated. (See Figure 2.9.)

Source reduction measures include:

• redesigning products or packages to reduce the quantity of materials or the toxicity of materials used, substituting lighter materials for heavier ones, and lengthening the life of products to postpone disposal.

• using packaging that reduces damage or spoilage to a product.

• reusing packages or products already manufactured.

• managing non-product organic wastes (food wastes, yard trimmings) through composting or other on-site alternatives to disposal.

Table 2.8 shows examples of source reduction practices.

TRENDS IN SOLID WASTE MANAGEMENT

In recent decades, the management of solid waste has become a major public concern. Municipalities nationwide have upgraded waste management programs and attempted to deal with public concern over waste issues. In most areas of the country, state and

local governments have played the lead role in transforming solid waste management. Private waste management firms have also been involved, often under contract or franchise agreements with local governments. Private firms manage most of the commercial waste, which comprises about 40 percent of MSW. Increasingly, they also collect residential waste, the remaining 60 percent of MSW.

The Federal Role in MSW Management

The federal government plays a key role in waste management. Its legislation has set landfill standards under the RCRA and incinerator and landfill emission standards under The Clean Air Act. Table 2.9 lists and describes federal regulations involving waste management.

Some waste management laws have been controversial, resulting in legal challenges. Consequently, the federal government has also had an effect on waste management programs through federal court rulings. In a series of recent rulings, including Supreme Court decisions such as *Chemical Waste Management, Inc. v. Hunt* [504 U.S. 334, 1992], federal courts have held that shipments of waste are protected under the interstate commerce clause of the U.S. Constitution. As a result, state and local governments may not prohibit landfills from accepting waste from other states, nor may they impose fees on waste disposal that discriminate on the basis of origin.

FLOW CONTROL LAWS. Flow control laws require private waste collectors to dispose of their waste in specific landfills. State and/or local governments institute these laws to guarantee that any new landfill they build will be used. That way, when they sell bonds to get the money to build a new landfill, the bond purchasers will not worry that they will not be repaid. Since 1980 about $10 billion in municipal bonds have been issued to pay for the construction of solid waste facilities. In many of those cases, flow control authority was used to guarantee the investment. Flow control also benefits recycling plants where recycling is financed by fees collected at incinerators or landfills. In the process, however, a monopoly is created, prohibiting facilities outside a jurisdiction from offering competitive services. As a result, there have been a number of court challenges to flow control laws.

In 1994 the Supreme Court, in *C & A Carbone v. Clarkstown* (511 US 383), held that flow control violates the interstate commerce clause. In response, however, many local governments have strongly pushed for the restoration of flow control authority. They have appealed to Congress, with its authority to regulate interstate commerce, to restore the use of flow control. Thus far, bills proposed to address flow control have failed.

In 1997 a federal district court, in *Atlantic Coast Demolition and Recycling Inc. v. Atlantic County* (112 F 3d 652), overturned New Jersey's flow control requirements.

TABLE 2.8

Selected examples of source reduction practices

Source reduction practice	MSW product categories			
	Durable goods	Nondurable goods	Containers & packaging	Organics
Redesign				
Materials reduction	• Downgauge metals in appliances	• Paperless purchase orders	• Concentrates	• Xeriscaping
Materials substitution	• Use of composites in appliances and electronic circuitry		• Cereal in bags • Coffee brick • Multi-use products	
Lengthen life	• High mileage tires • Electronic components reduce moving parts	• Regular servicing • Look at warranties • Extend warranties	• Design for secondary uses	
Consumer practices				
	• Purchase long lived products	• Repair • Duplexing • Sharing • Reduce unwanted mail	• Purchasing: products in bulk, concentrates	
Reuse				
By design	• Modular design	• Envelopes	• Pallets • Returnable secondary packaging	
Secondary	• Borrow or rent for temporary use • Give to charity • Buy or sell at garage sales	• Clothing • Waste paper scratch pads	• Loosefill • Grocery sacks • Dairy containers • Glass and plastic jars	
Reduce/eliminate toxins				
	• Eliminate PCBs	• Soy ink, waterbased • Waterbased solvents • Reduce mercury	• Replace lead foil on wine bottles	
Reduce organics				
Food wastes				• Backyard composting • Vermi-composting
Yard trimmings				• Backyard composting • Grasscycling

SOURCE: "Table 24: Selected Examples of Source Reduction Practices," in *Municipal Solid Waste in the United States: 1999 Facts and Figures,* Environmental Protection Agency, Washington, DC, 2000. Data from Franklin Associates.

As a result, much of New Jersey's waste leaves the state for cheaper disposal elsewhere.

In Minnesota, a federal district court, in *Ben Oehrleins, Inc. v. Hennepin County* (GA8 N.96-2120, 1997), ruled in favor of waste haulers who claimed that the county was liable for damages resulting from enforcement of flow control ordinances. The jury awarded the plaintiffs $7.1 million as compensation for the higher costs they were forced to pay as a result of flow control programs. In March 1998 Hennepin County agreed to pay $3.45 million to settle the suit and agreed to lift its garbage delivery restrictions for the next five years.

RECYCLING ISSUES. In 1995 Congress passed the National Highway System Designation Act. This legislation repealed federal requirements that up to 20 percent of the asphalt pavement used in federal highway projects had to contain rubber-modified asphalt made from scrap tires or other recovered materials. The goal of repealing of the requirements was to enable federal transportation officials to focus on the most useful and cost-effective ways of achieving important safety aims and to increase states' discretion to implement their highway programs in ways best suited to their own circumstances.

In 1996 Congress passed the Mercury-Containing and Rechargeable Battery Management Act (known as the "battery recycling bill"). This law phased out the use of mercury in batteries and provided for the efficient and cost-effective collection and recycling or proper disposal of used nickel cadmium batteries, small sealed lead-acid batteries, and certain other batteries. It also exempted certain battery collection and recycling programs from some hazardous waste requirements.

PROJECTIONS OF MUNICIPAL SOLID WASTE GENERATION

Based on 1998 data, the EPA expected Americans to produce 223 million tons of MSW in 2000 and predicts they will produce 240 million tons in 2005. Generation of waste paper and paperboard, plastics, metals, wood, and other materials, such as rubber and textiles, is projected to

TABLE 2.9

Federal regulations on solid waste management

Authority	Regulation	Status	EPA Annual Cost Estimate
RCRA Subtitle D	Municipal Solid Waste Landfill Criteria: location, design, and operating groundwater monitoring, and corrective action closure and post-closure care financial assurance criteria	Promulgated 10/9/91, with some subsequent modifications effective 10/9/93 for large landfills, 4/9/94 for others requirements phased in; final compliance deadline 10/9/97 effective 10/9/93 for large landfills, 4/9/94 for others effective 4/97	$330,000,000
RCRA Subtitle D	Non-Municipal Solid Waste Landfill Criteria	Promulgated 7/1/96; requirements took effect 18 months to 2 years after promulgation	$12,650,000 - 51,000,000
Clean Air Act, Section 111	Air Emissions from Municipal Solid Waste Landfills	Promulgated 3/12/96; effective immediately for new landfills	$94,000,000
Clean Air Act, Sections 111 and 129	Emissions from Municipal Solid Waste Combustors (Incinerators):		
	combustion practices, carbon monoxide, dioxins/furans, particulates, acid gases, nitrogen oxides; applied only to combustors with capacity of 250 tons per day or more	Promulgated 2/11/91; effective 8/12/91	$472,000,000
	maximum achievable control technology for carbon monoxide, dioxins, particulate matter, cadmium, lead, mercury, sulfur dioxide, hydrogen chloride, nitrogen oxides; applies to incinerators with capacity of 35 tons per day or more	Originally promulgated 12/19/95; as the result of a court decision, EPA repromulgated the standards for combustors with capacity >250 tons per day 8/25/97; regulations for smaller combustors were reproposed 8/30/99. Effective date of requirements varies.	$405,000,000
RCRA Sections 3001 - 3005	Management of Ash from Municipal Waste Combustors (Incinerators)	Supreme Court ruled May 2, 1994, that ash was not exempt from hazardous waste management regulations, despite EPA guidance to the contrary. Hazardous waste testing and management regulations were promulgated 5/19/80, with many subsequent amendments.	not available
Executive Orders 12873 and 13101; RCRA Section 6002	Federal Procurement of Recycled Products	Procurement guidelines for paper, retread tires, used oil and insulation materials took effect in 1988. Executive Orders 12873 (10/20/93) and 13101 (9/14/98) strengthened paper requirements. EPA designated an additional 19 recycled content product categories for procurement preferences 5/1/95; 12 product categories were added 11/13/97; and 19 more were proposed for addition 8/26/98.	not available

SOURCE: James E. McCarthy, "Table 1. Regulations on Solid Waste Management," in *Solid Waste Issues in the 106th Congress,* Congressional Research Service, The Library of Congress, Washington, DC, April 27, 2000

increase. Only the generation of waste glass is expected to decline. (See Table 2.10.) Food waste is projected to increase at the same rate as the population. Generation of yard trimmings per capita has been decreasing due to legislation regulating their disposal. Many municipalities will not take yard trimmings. Overall, based on 1998 data, the EPA projected municipal solid waste generation to increase at a rate of 1 percent per year from 1998 through 2000, then to increase 1.4 percent annually from 2000 through 2005. (See Figure 2.10.)

TABLE 2.10

Projections of materials generated* in the municipal waste stream, 2000 and 2005

	Million tons		% of total	
Materials	**2000**	**2005**	**2000**	**2005**
Paper and Paperboard	87.7	94.8	39.3%	39.6%
Glass	11.9	11.2	5.3%	4.7%
Metals	17.6	18.7	7.9%	7.8%
Plastics	23.4	26.7	10.5%	11.2%
Wood	14.0	15.8	6.3%	6.6%
Others	19.7	22.2	8.8%	9.3%
Total Materials in Products	174.3	189.4	78.1%	79.1%
Other Wastes				
Food Wastes	22.5	23.5	10.1%	9.8%
Yard Trimmings	23.0	23.0	10.3%	9.6%
Miscellaneous Inorganic Wastes	3.4	3.6	1.5%	1.5%
Total Other Wastes	48.9	50.1	21.9%	20.9%
Total MSW Generated	223.2	239.5	100.0%	100.0%

* Generation before materials recovery or combustion.
  Details may not add to totals due to rounding.

SOURCE: "Projections of materials generated* in the municipal waste stream: 2000 and 2005," in *Characterization of Municipal Solid Waste in the United States: 1998 Update,* U.S. Environmental Protection Agency, Washington, DC, 1999

FIGURE 2.10

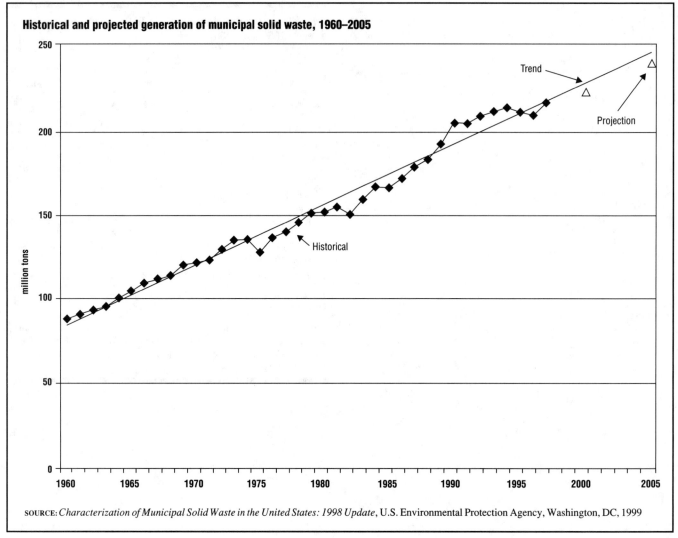

Historical and projected generation of municipal solid waste, 1960–2005

SOURCE: *Characterization of Municipal Solid Waste in the United States: 1998 Update*, U.S. Environmental Protection Agency, Washington, DC, 1999

CHAPTER 3
MATERIALS RECOVERY—RECYCLING AND COMPOSTING

Materials recovery is the removal of municipal solid waste (MSW) from the waste stream for recycling and composting. (See Figure 2.9.) Recycling is the sorting, collecting, and processing of wastes such as paper, glass, plastic, and metals, which are then refashioned or incorporated into new products that are sold and bought. Composting is the decomposition of organic wastes, such as food scraps and yard trimmings, in a manner that produces a humus-like substance generally used as fertilizer.

Recycling MSW can offer many advantages. It conserves energy otherwise used to incinerate the waste; reduces the amount of landfill space needed for disposal of waste; reduces possible environmental pollution due to its disposal; generates jobs and small-scale enterprise; reduces dependence on foreign imports of metals; and replaces some chemical fertilizers with composting material, which further lessens possible environmental pollution.

Recycling has become an important factor in waste management in the United States in recent decades. (See Figure 2.3.) State and local governments see recycling as a way to save money and prolong the life of landfill space. Many Americans believe that recycling is also a way to aid the environment. For example, if paper is recycled, fewer trees have to be cut down to make paper. However, others claim that recycling does not justify its cost in many instances.

Nevertheless, recycling generally continues to be considered a highly effective waste management technique. Many analysts claim that more than half of consumer waste can be economically recycled. In 1999 recycling (including composting) recovered 28 percent of MSW, up from 25 percent in 1994 and just 6.4 percent in 1960. (See Figure 2.2 and Figure 3.1.) Figure 3.2 shows the international

FIGURE 3.1

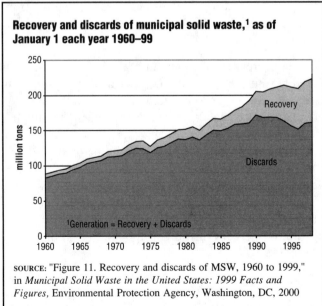

Recovery and discards of municipal solid waste,[1] as of January 1 each year 1960–99

SOURCE: "Figure 11. Recovery and discards of MSW, 1960 to 1999," in *Municipal Solid Waste in the United States: 1999 Facts and Figures,* Environmental Protection Agency, Washington, DC, 2000

FIGURE 3.2

The International Recycling Symbols

As the three arrows of the international recycling symbol show, recycling involves three distinct steps:

1. The seperation and collection of recyclable materials,
2. The processing and manufacturing of these materials into new products and,
3. The purchase and use of recyled products.

SOURCE: "The International Recycling Symbols," in *Talkin' Trash!: A Guide to Solid Waste Disposal and Recycling in Bay County, Florida* Bay County Solid Waste Management Department. [Online] http://recycle.co.bay.fl.us/recycling_symbols.html [Accessed 8/30/2001]

recycling symbols affixed to products that are made from recycled materials or that are recyclable.

THE ROLE OF OBSOLESCENCE IN MSW GENERATION

At one time, goods were scarce and were made to last a long time. That was considered part of their inherent workmanship. Henry Ford believed that "a Ford was forever." He insisted that his Model T and Model A cars were "so strong and so well-made that no one ought ever to have to buy a second one." Soon, however, it became evident that there was a substantial resale market for second-hand cars. Furthermore, it was quickly recognized that the industry could be more profitable if a person bought nine or ten cars over his or her lifetime rather than one or two.

By the 1920s technological and stylistic obsolescence began to characterize a growing number of American consumer products. American society has become based on consumerism, in which goods are manufactured with the knowledge that they will become obsolete in a relatively short time.

THE ROLE OF STATES AND CITIES IN RECYCLING EFFORTS

The oldest recycling law in the United States is the Oregon Recycling Opportunity Act, which was passed in 1983 and went into effect in 1986. Today, most states have some type of recycling program. (See Table 2.7.)

BioCycle magazine's "The State of Garbage in America" report (November 2000) revealed that Americans recycled 33 percent of the total tonnage of MSW generated in 1999, which is a record amount, up from 8 percent in 1990. Additionally in 1999, Americans produced more waste than ever before—382.6 million tons. Regionally, the highest recycling rate was reported by the Mid-Atlantic states (40 percent), followed by the West and Midwest (35 percent each), New England (34 percent), the Great Lakes (26 percent), and the Rocky Mountain states (19 percent). In 1999 Delaware recycled the greatest proportion of its waste (57 percent), followed by Arkansas (45 percent), Maine, New York, and South Dakota (42 percent each). (See Table 2.3.)

A growing number of states require that many consumer goods sold must be made from recycled products. In addition, many states have set recycling/recovery goals ranging from 25 percent to 70 percent. Rhode Island and New Jersey have the highest recycling goals of all the states, at 70 percent and 65 percent respectively. Alabama, Georgia, Louisiana, Mississippi, Montana, Nevada, Ohio, and Virginia have the lowest (25 percent). Arkansas and Virginia have exceeded their goals. Alabama, Florida, Missouri, Pennsylvania, and South Carolina are 4 percent or less away from meeting their goals. (See Table 3.1.)

The most common method of funding state recycling and composting programs is solid waste disposal fees/landfill surcharges, followed by budget appropriations.

For recycling programs to work, there must be markets for recycled products. To help create demand, some states require that newspaper publishers use a minimum proportion of recycled paper. Many states require that recycled materials be used in making products such as telephone directories, trash bags, glass, and plastic containers. All states have some kind of "buy recycled" program that requires them to purchase recycled products when possible.

The federal government also helps create a market for recycled goods. Executive Order 12873 (1999) requires federal agencies to purchase recyclable goods, and Executive Order 13101 (1998) raises the recycled content of copier paper purchased by federal agencies from 20 percent to 30 percent. Additionally, almost all books and pamphlets released by the U.S. Government Printing Office (GPO) are printed on recycled paper.

The states also use other incentives for recycling. Most states have introduced curbside collection or public drop-off sites for recyclables. Some states provide financial assistance, incentive money, or tax credits or exemptions for recycling businesses. And almost all states bar certain recyclable materials (such as car and boat batteries, grass cuttings, tires, used motor oil, glass, plastic containers, and newspapers) from entering their landfills.

METHODS OF COLLECTING RECYCLABLE MATERIALS

Curbside Programs

Before recyclable materials can be processed and made into new products, they must be collected. Most residential recycling involves curbside collection, drop-off programs, buy-back operations, and/or container deposit systems.

The increase in the amount of recycling can be measured by the growth in the number of people receiving curbside recycling service, in which items to be recycled are placed in special containers for pickup at their homes. In 1988, when *BioCycle* began its survey, only 1,042 curbside programs were operating in the United States. *BioCycle*'s 2000 "The State of Garbage in America" survey reported 9,247 curbside recycling programs in the United States in 1999, up from 7,375 in 1995. The 1999 programs served about 133.2 million Americans, representing 61 percent of the U.S. population at that time. (See Table 2.7.)

In 1999 the extent of curbside recycling programs varied greatly by geographic region. The Mid-Atlantic served 89 percent of its population with curbside programs, followed by New England (75 percent), the Great Lakes (61 percent), the West (60 percent), the South (55 percent), the Rocky Mountain region (43 percent), and the Midwest (35 percent).

Drop-Off Centers

Drop-off centers typically collect residential waste, although some accept commercial waste. They are found in grocery stores, charitable organizations, city-sponsored sites, and apartment complexes. The types of materials accepted vary, although drop-off centers generally accept a greater variety of materials than do curbside collection services. States reporting over 100 dropoff centers in 1999 (*BioCycle,* November 2000) include Pennsylvania (533), Georgia (382), Maine (375), Iowa (368), South Carolina (348), New Hampshire (196), Missouri (194), Texas (174), Massachusetts (173), North Carolina (121), and North Dakota (100 to 120).

Commercial Recyclables Collection

The largest quantity of recovered materials comes from the commercial sector. Old corrugated containers and office papers are widely collected from businesses. Grocery stores and other retail outlets that use corrugated packaging return large amounts of recovered materials.

Buy-Back and Deposit Centers

A buy-back center is usually a commercial operation that pays individuals for recovered materials, such as scrap metal, aluminum cans, or paper. In addition, as of November 2000, 10 states—California, Connecticut, Delaware, Iowa, Maine, Massachusetts, Michigan, New York, Oregon, and Vermont—had introduced container deposit systems. In these programs, the consumer pays a deposit on beverage containers when purchased, which is redeemed on return of the empty containers.

Composting

About 20 percent of MSW is food and yard waste. (See Table 2.10.) All plant-based materials in these categories can be recycled by means of composting. The substances most commonly composted are grass cuttings, garden clippings, leaves, and coffee grounds, but well-chopped plant-based food wastes are suitable as well. Using meat-based food scraps is usually discouraged because they are likely to attract animals.

To prepare a compost heap or pile, plant wastes are layered with manure or soil to speed decomposition (decay). Each six inches or so of plant material is layered with about an inch of soil. Watering the mixture and aerating it (turning it) also speeds decomposition. The compost should decay for five to seven months before it is used.

Gardeners mix compost with the soil to loosen the structure of the soil and provide it with nutrients, or

TABLE 3.1

State diversion goals and recovery rates

State	Goal (%)	Rate (%)	Dead-line	Is Goal Mandatory?
Alabama	25	23	none	No
Arkansas	40	45	2000	No
California	50	37	2000	Yes
Connecticut	40	24	2000	No
Dist. of Columbia	45	15	2000	Yes
Florida	30	28	1994	Yes
Georgia [1]	25	n/a	1996	No
Hawaii	50	28	2000	No
Indiana	50	32	2001	No
Iowa	50	37	2000	No
Louisiana	25	17	1992	No
Maine [2]	50	42	n/a	No
Maryland [3]	35/40	36	2005	No
Massachusetts [4]	46	38	2000	No
Minnesota	50/35 [5]	41	1996	No
Mississippi	25	14	1996	No
Missouri	40	36	1998	No
Montana	25	11	1996	No
Nebraska	50	29	2002	No
Nevada	25	11	1995	No
New Hampshire [6]	40	24	2000	No
New Jersey	65	40	2000	Yes
New Mexico	50	10	2000	No
New York [7]	50	42	1997	No
North Carolina	40	29	2001	No
North Dakota	40	20	2000	No
Ohio	25	20	2000	No
Oregon [8]	50	30	2000	Yes
Pennsylvania	35	33	2003	No
Rhode Island	70	28	none	No
South Carolina [9]	35	31	2005	No
South Dakota	50	42	2000	No
Texas	40	35	1994	No
Vermont [10]	50	35	2005	No
Virginia	25	35	1997	Yes
Washington	50	33	1995	No
West Virginia	50	25	2010	No

[1] Per capita waste disposal reduction of 25%.
[2] Deadline for meeting goal, as well as goal itself, is being changed.
[3] Legislation passed in 1999 established a 40% voluntary statewide waste diversion rate composed of a 35% recycling goal and up to 5% credit (based on activities, not measured tonages) for source reduction. Mandated goals of 15% and 20% (minimum) for counties still apply .
[4] State also has 88% non-MSW reduction, 60% MSW reduction, with 70% average to be achieved by 2010.
[5] 50% in Metro Twin Cities counties, 35% in greater Minnesota.
[6] Goal changed from waste reduction to diversion.
[7] 50% goal comprised of 40 to 42% recycling and 8 to 10% waste reduction.
[8] State has "recovery" goal of 50%.
[9] 35% recycling of MSW. Goal also amended in October, 2000 to include 25% recycling of total waste stream and 30% reduction of solid waste sent to MSW landfills and MSW incinerators.
[10] Goal changed from 40% to 50% by 2005.

SOURCE: Nora Goldstein and Celeste Madtes, "Table 6. State diversion goals and recovery rates," in "The State of Garbage in America, Part II," in *BioCycle,* November 2000. Reprinted with permission from *BioCycle* magazine. For more information, visit www.biocycle.net.

spread it on top of the soil as a mulch to keep in moisture. Since compost adds nutrients to the soil, slows soil erosion, and improves water retention, it is an alternative to the use of chemical fertilizers. Compost created on a large scale is often used in landscaping, land reclamation, and landfill cover, and to provide high-nutrient soil for farms and nurseries.

TABLE 3.2

MRF (Materials Recovery Facilitiy) processing equipment

Type of Equipment	Description	Purpose
Infeed Conveyors	Z-shaped moving conveyor belts, which usually start below floor level and elevate materials to a certain height above floor level. Usually of steel, apron-pan construction; may also be either chain-driven rubber belts or rubber slider belts.	Move mixed paper and non-paper material from tipping floor into process area, and deposit it onto sorting conveyors or into sorting equipment. Also used to feed sorted materials into the baler(s).
Sorting Conveyors	Horizontal moving rubber belts, of either slider or trough-pulley design. Usually mounted on elevated platforms, below which are storage bins, bunkers, or transfer conveyors.	Hand-sorters stand on one or both sides of the belt and pull specific materials, which are then dropped/tossed into storage bins or bunkers. Negatively-sorted materials are allowed to remain on the belt.
Transfer Conveyors	Moving rubber belts, of slider or trough-pulley design.	Transport loose, separated materials from the sorting area to processing equipment and processed materials from processing equipment to storage bunkers or trailers.
Baling Presses or "Balers"	Machines that compress loose material into dense rectangular blocks or "bales." Typical bale dimensions are 2.5 ft. x 4 ft. x 5 ft. long. The bale is formed by a moving pressure plate, mounted on a hydraulic cylinder or "ram," which packs the material together inside a closed chamber.	Densify recyclables for ease of handling and for more cost-effective shipping.
Magnetic Separator	Typically an electromagnet housed in a moving conveyor belt. The device is mounted above a conveyor carrying commingled recyclables. Ferrous metals, e.g., tin cans, are attracted by the magnet and shoveled onto a transfer conveyor by the moving belt.	Automatically remove ferrous metals from the commingled materials stream.
Eddy-current Separator	Consists of a short belt conveyor that surrounds the eddy current mechanism. The mechanism contains a rotor with rare earth magnets of alternating polarity. As the rotor spins, it creates a magnetic field, which induces eddy currents in non-ferrous metals passing over it. These currents in turn establish a repulsive magnetic force that hurls the metals off the belt at different trajectories than non-metallics. A splitter plate divides the two flows.	Automatically remove aluminum and non-ferrous metals from the commingled materials stream.
"Air Classifier" or "AirKnife"	Normally consists of a blower or suction fan and accompanying tubes and chutes. The air jet created by the blower or fan captures or diverts the lighter materials in the stream from the heavier ones.	Divide the commingled stream into "lights" (aluminum and plastics) and "heavies" (glass). Also may be used to extract paper labels during glass beneficiation processes.
Inclined Sorting Table	A proprietary device that consists of an inclined moving conveyor and a "curtain" of dangling chains that travels along the surface of the conceyor.	Used to separate the commingled stream into lights and heavies.
Trommel Screen	A cylindrical drum with holes of specific size that rotates about its central axis. "Undersize" material (material smaller in diameter than the holes) falls through the holes and is thus separated from "oversize" material.	Most often used to size-classify and remove caps from crushed glass after it is sorted. Also may be used to separate lights from heavies, although this application usually results in unacceptably high glass breakage.
Vibrating or Oscillating Screen	Flat plates, punched with holes, that are mechanically vibrated in one or two dimensions. A similar design is the "finger" screen, which instead of pierced plates employs parallel bars for the screening surface. Undersize materials fall through the holes or between the bars, while oversize material slides across the screening surface.	Separate mixed broken glass from the commingled stream. Also sometimes used to size-classify lights for easier sorting or eddy current separation.
Glass Crusher	Consists of a crushing chamber, with rotating hammers or drums. Many models are sold with attached transfer conveyors and magnetic head pulleys for removal of caps.	Increase density of sorted glass by breaking it into small pieces.
Can Flattener	Consists of one or two rotating drums or wheels mounted inside a crushing chamber. Most models come equipped with an attached blower and blow-tube, which shoot the crushed cans directly into a waiting trailer.	Densify aluminum and/or steel cans for more cost-effective shipping.
Can Densifier	Similar in principle to a baler, but produces small, dense blocks called "briquettes." The briquettes are bundled together with steel strapping prior to shipment.	Densify aluminum and/or steel cans for more cost-effective shipping.
Granulator	Machines which use rotating propeller-like blades to chop plastic bottles into small chips.	Densify plastic for more cost-effective shipping, and to prepare it for remanufacturing.
Plastic Bottle Perforator	A rotating drum upon which spikes are mounted. The spikes pierce the bottles in multiple locations, thus decreasing their resilience.	Make plastic bottles easier to bale. Especially effective on bottles whose caps have been screwed back on.

SOURCE: "MRF Processing Equipment," in *The Cost to Recycle at a Materials Recovery Facility*, National Solid Wastes Management Association, Washington, DC, 1992

TABLE 3.3

Generation, materials recovery, composting, combustion, and discards of municipal solid waste, 1960–99

	Pounds per person per day								
	1960	**1970**	**1980**	**1990**	**1994**	**1995**	**1997**	**1998**	**1999**
Generation	2.68	3.25	3.66	4.50	4.51	4.40	4.49	4.52	4.62
Recovery for recycling	0.17	0.22	0.35	0.64	0.89	0.94	0.97	0.98	1.02
Recovery for composting[1]	Neg.	Neg.	Neg.	0.09	0.18	0.20	0.25	0.27	0.26
Total Materials Recovery	0.17	0.22	0.35	0.73	1.06	1.14	1.22	1.25	1.28
Discards after recovery	2.51	3.04	3.31	3.77	3.44	3.26	3.27	3.27	3.33
Combustion[2]	0.82	0.67	0.33	0.70	0.68	0.74	0.75	0.70	0.68
Discards to landfill, other disposal[3]	1.69	2.36	2.98	3.07	2.76	2.52	2.52	2.57	2.65
Population (thousands)	179,979	203,984	227,255	249,907	260,682	263,168	267,645	270,561	272,691

Note: Details may not add to totals due to rounding.
[1] Composting of yard trimmings and food wastes. Does not include mixed MSW composting or backyard composting.
[2] Includes combustion of MSW in mass burn or refuse-derived fuel form, and combustion with energy recovery of source separated materials in MSW (e.g., wood pallets and tire-derived fuel).
[3] Discards after recovery minus combustion.

SOURCE: Adapted from "Table 29: Generation, Materials Recovery, Composting, Combustion, and Discards of Municipal Solid Waste, 1960 to 1999," in *Municipal Solid Waste in the United States: 1999 Facts and Figures,* Environmental Protection Agency, Washington, DC, 2000. Data from Franklin Associates.

Yard waste is especially suitable for composting due to its high moisture content. Over the past decade, composting yard trimmings has become an accepted waste management method in many U.S. locations. The practice got a huge boost beginning in the late 1980s when many states banned yard trimmings from disposal facilities. The 2000 *BioCycle* report revealed that in 1999 there were 3,804 public yard trimming composting sites in the United States.

MATERIALS RECOVERY FACILITIES (MRFS)

Materials recovery facilities (MRFs) process recyclable materials. An MRF sorts collected recyclables, processes them, and ships them to companies that use these processed materials. For example, an MRF may sort and crush various types of glass recovered from curbside programs and then ship the processed glass to a bottle factory where it will be used, along with other materials, to produce new bottles.

MRFs vary widely, depending on the materials they accept and the technology and labor used to sort and process the materials. Most MRFs are classified as low technology because most sorting is done manually. MRFs classified as high technology sort recyclables using eddy currents (swirling air or water), magnetic pulleys, optical sensors, and air classifiers.

Newspaper is the major paper commodity processed at MRFs, along with corrugated boxes, used telephone books, magazines, and mixed waste paper. Non-paper commingled recyclables consist of aluminum beverage containers, food cans, glass food and beverage containers, and certain plastics. Most MRFs have separate processing lines for paper and commingled container streams. The type of processing equipment found in a particular plant depends upon the markets for which the processed recyclables are destined and the distances they must be transported. Table 3.2 describes various pieces of MRF processing equipment and explains the purpose of each.

In 1999, 480 materials recovery facilities helped process approximately 55,000 tons of recyclables per day (*Municipal Solid Waste in the United States: 1999 Facts and Figures,* Environmental Protection Agency, Washington, DC, 2000). In 1997 approximately three-fourths of MRFs were private enterprises.

MATERIAL RECYCLING RATES

As the per capita rate of MSW generation rose from 2.68 pounds per person per day in 1960 to 4.62 pounds per person per day in 1999, the per capita rate of recovery rose from 0.17 pounds per day to 1.28 pounds per day. Of the remaining MSW in 1999, an estimated 0.68 pounds of discards per person per day were managed through incineration, and 2.65 pounds per person per day went to landfills or other disposal. (See Table 3.3.)

Figure 3.3 shows the materials recovered from MSW in 1999. Fifty-seven percent was paper and paperboard, followed by yard trimmings (20 percent), metals (10 percent), glass (5 percent), and plastics (2 percent). Of the total waste paper and paperboard generated in 1999, 41.9 percent was recovered. About 35 percent of all waste metals were recovered that year, while only 5.6 percent of plastics and 5.9 percent of waste wood were recovered. (See Table 3.4.)

Figure 3.4 shows how the rate of recovery of materials affected their proportion of MSW discards in 1999. For

TABLE 3.4

Generation and recovery of materials in municipal solid waste, 1999

	Weight Generated	Weight Recovered	Recovery as a Percent of Generation
Paper and paperboard	87.5	36.7	41.9%
Glass	12.6	2.9	23.4%
Metals			
Steel	13.3	4.5	33.6%
Aluminum	3.1	0.9	27.8%
Other nonferrous metals[1]	1.4	0.9	66.9%
Total metals	17.8	6.3	35.2%
Plastics	24.2	1.4	5.6%
Rubber and leather	6.2	0.8	12.7%
Textiles	9.1	1.2	12.9%
Wood	12.3	0.7	5.9%
Other materials	4.0	0.9	21.4%
Total Materials in Products	**173.6**	**50.8**	**29.3%**
Other wastes			
Food, other[2]	25.2	0.6	2.2%
Yard trimmings	27.7	12.6	45.3%
Miscellaneous inorganic wastes	3.4	Neg.	Neg.
Total Other Wastes	**56.3**	**13.1**	**23.3%**
TOTAL MUNICIPAL SOLID WASTE	**229.9**	**63.9**	**27.8%**

Note: Includes wastes from residential, commercial, and institutional sources.
Neg.= Less than 50,000 tons or 0.05 percent.
[1]Includes lead from lead-acid batteries.
[2]Includes recovery of paper for composting.

SOURCE: "Table ES-4: Generation and Recovery of Materials in MSW, 1999 (In millions of tons and percent of generation of each material)," in *Municipal Solid Waste in the United States: 1999 Facts and Figures*, Environmental Protection Agency, Washington, DC, 2000

FIGURE 3.3

Percent by weight of materials recovery by category, 1999

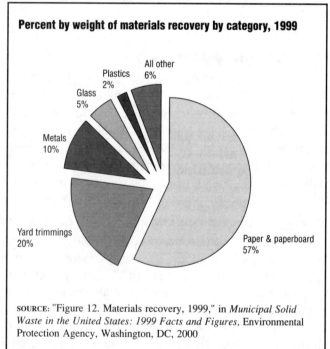

SOURCE: "Figure 12. Materials recovery, 1999," in *Municipal Solid Waste in the United States: 1999 Facts and Figures*, Environmental Protection Agency, Washington, DC, 2000

FIGURE 3.4

Percent of total generation and discards in municipal solid waste, 1999

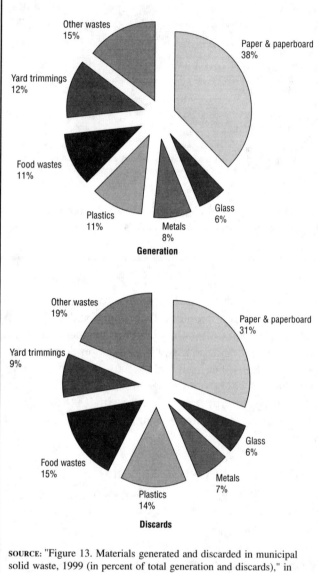

SOURCE: "Figure 13. Materials generated and discarded in municipal solid waste, 1999 (in percent of total generation and discards)," in *Municipal Solid Waste in the United States: 1999 Facts and Figures*, Environmental Protection Agency, Washington, DC, 2000

example, paper and paperboard accounted for 38 percent of the solid waste generated in 1999, but after recovery, paper made up only 31 percent of waste that was discarded. Categories of MSW with low recovery rates, such as plastics, increased in their proportion of MSW discards to MSW generation as those with high recovery rates, such as paper and yard wastes, decreased in proportion.

Paper

The paper industry has been at the leading edge of the dramatic expansion in recycling. Paper may be reused several times before the fibers are destroyed and it can no longer be used to make new paper. (See Figure 3.5.)

FIGURE 3.5

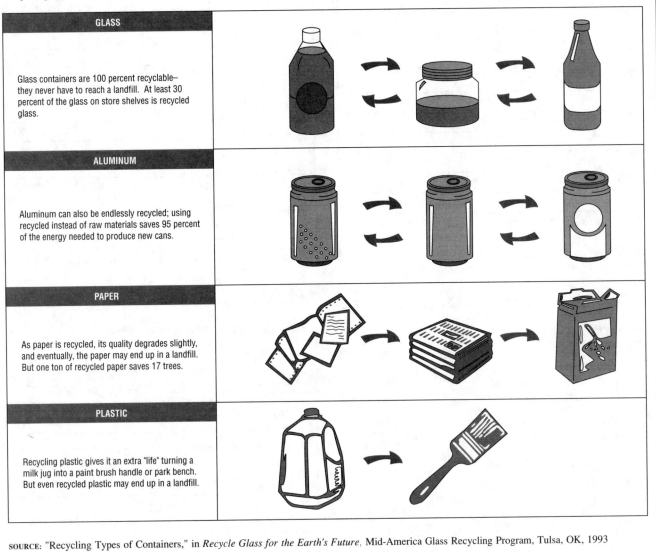

Recycling types of containers

GLASS	
Glass containers are 100 percent recyclable—they never have to reach a landfill. At least 30 percent of the glass on store shelves is recycled glass.	

ALUMINUM	
Aluminum can also be endlessly recycled; using recycled instead of raw materials saves 95 percent of the energy needed to produce new cans.	

PAPER	
As paper is recycled, its quality degrades slightly, and eventually, the paper may end up in a landfill. But one ton of recycled paper saves 17 trees.	

PLASTIC	
Recycling plastic gives it an extra "life" turning a milk jug into a paint brush handle or park bench. But even recycled plastic may end up in a landfill.	

SOURCE: "Recycling Types of Containers," in *Recycle Glass for the Earth's Future*, Mid-America Glass Recycling Program, Tulsa, OK, 1993

The EPA estimates that the amount of paper recovered from waste in the United States grew from 13 million tons in 1985 to 36.7 million tons in 1999. Figure 3.6 shows the growth of paper generation and recovery from 1960 to 1999. Even though paper and paperboard recovery is high, only about 10 percent of the paper used in printing and writing is recycled paper because it is slightly more costly to produce than "virgin" paper.

Glass

In 1999 glass made up 6 percent of municipal solid waste generated and 6 percent of MSW discards. (See Figure 3.4.) About 23 percent of all glass was recovered for recycling during that year. Figure 3.7 shows glass generation and recovery rates from 1960 to 1999.

Glass containers are 100 percent recyclable, and over 30 percent of the glass used in containers is made from recycled glass. (See Figure 3.5.) Figure 3.8 shows the glass-recycling loop. (Cullet, mentioned in Figure 3.8, is broken or crushed glass used in glass-making.)

Metals

Metal recycling is as old as metalworking. Coins and jewelry made of gold and silver were melted down in ancient times to make new coins with images of the latest ruler. Metal objects were generally considered valuable and were frequently sold or given away, rarely simply discarded. When metal objects could not be repaired, they could be melted down and fashioned into something else. With some metals this was particularly easy. For example, lead has a melting point so low that it can be heated over a wood fire and reworked. Tin melts at an even lower point.

Ferrous metals (iron and steel) are the largest category of metals in MSW. They are used in durable goods,

FIGURE 3.6

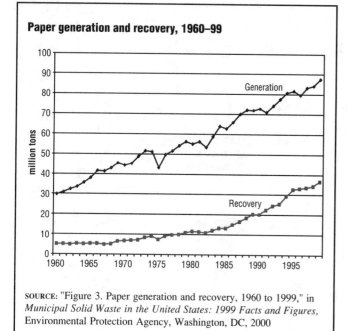

Paper generation and recovery, 1960–99

SOURCE: "Figure 3. Paper generation and recovery, 1960 to 1999," in *Municipal Solid Waste in the United States: 1999 Facts and Figures,* Environmental Protection Agency, Washington, DC, 2000

FIGURE 3.8

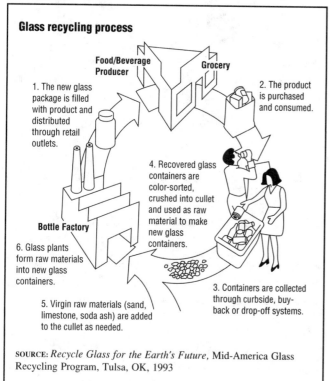

Glass recycling process

Food/Beverage Producer

Grocery

1. The new glass package is filled with product and distributed through retail outlets.

2. The product is purchased and consumed.

Bottle Factory

6. Glass plants form raw materials into new glass containers.

4. Recovered glass containers are color-sorted, crushed into cullet and used as raw material to make new glass containers.

5. Virgin raw materials (sand, limestone, soda ash) are added to the cullet as needed.

3. Containers are collected through curbside, buy-back or drop-off systems.

SOURCE: *Recycle Glass for the Earth's Future,* Mid-America Glass Recycling Program, Tulsa, OK, 1993

such as appliances, furniture, tires, and other long-lasting goods. Approximately 26.9 percent of ferrous metal MSW was recovered in 1999.

Aluminum and other nonferrous metals make up the remainder of metals recovered from MSW. Aluminum is found in cans and packaging. Lead, zinc, and copper are found in batteries, appliances, and consumer electronics.

FIGURE 3.7

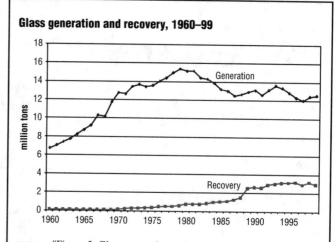

Glass generation and recovery, 1960–99

SOURCE: "Figure 5. Glass generation and recovery, 1960 to 1999," in *Municipal Solid Waste in the United States: 1999 Facts and Figures,* Environmental Protection Agency, Washington, DC, 2000

FIGURE 3.9

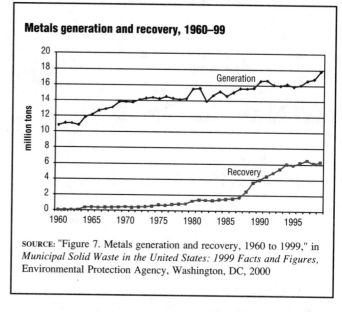

Metals generation and recovery, 1960–99

SOURCE: "Figure 7. Metals generation and recovery, 1960 to 1999," in *Municipal Solid Waste in the United States: 1999 Facts and Figures,* Environmental Protection Agency, Washington, DC, 2000

Figure 3.9 shows the increase in the generation and recovery of both ferrous and nonferrous metals from 1960 to 1999.

The EPA reported that 44.2 percent of all aluminum and 54.5 percent of aluminum cans were recovered for recycling in 1999. Making aluminum cans from bauxite (the ore from which new aluminum is made) requires huge amounts of electricity. Making aluminum cans from used aluminum cans uses 95 percent less energy. Aluminum is 100 percent recyclable. (See Figure 3.5.)

Plastics

Manufacturers are increasingly using plastic to package their products because plastic is so easy to use and to shape. As a result, plastics are the fastest-growing proportion of MSW in the United States. In 1960 plastics comprised less than 1 percent of MSW; by 1999, they comprised 10.5 percent. (See Figure 2.1 in Chapter 2.)

Overall recovery of plastics for recycling is relatively small—just 2 percent in 1999. (See Figure 3.3.) Recovery of some plastic products, though, is high. In 1999, 40 percent of plastic soft drink bottles were recovered, and 31.9 percent of plastic milk and water bottles were recovered. Figure 3.5 provides some facts on plastic container recycling. However, recovery of products such as plastic plates, cups, and trash bags is virtually zero. Figure 3.10 shows plastics generation and recovery rates from 1960 to 1999.

Although people often claim packaging, especially plastic packaging, is "the problem," plastic packaging has become 50 percent more efficient over the past 20 years. In 1970 an ounce of plastic could hold (deliver) 23 ounces of product, such as milk, aspirin, or soda. Today, an ounce of plastic delivers 34 ounces of product, due to improvements in strength. Furthermore, plastic accounts for 22 percent of all packaging, but delivers 65 percent of products.

THE HISTORY AND CURRENT STRENGTH OF RECYCLING

Recycling has become a major part of MSW management in the United States, and it will likely continue to grow, although at a slower pace than in the past. Recycling, however, did not enjoy immediate success. Recycling started out as a "do-good" activity. For a quarter-century after the first Earth Day (April 22, 1970), recycling advocates pleaded their case to skeptical decision-makers in the interest of environmental benefit. It evolved into a necessary burden for municipal governments.

In the early years of recycling, the economy was unable to use all the plastic, paper, and other materials that were recovered. Many private recycling companies were not able to make a profit. Instead of earning money from recycling, the programs cost them money. Some cities even started dumping their recycled materials into landfills because they could not sell them. Many city leaders felt that money spent on recycling should be used in other areas instead, such as education.

Critics of recycling pointed to the problems that recycling was experiencing as evidence that recycling programs could not work. Supporters of recycling thought that recycling problems stemmed from the success of collection programs, which recouped more than manufacturers were initially able to handle. Advocates of recycling programs had underestimated the wellspring of support for recycling that existed among the American people.

In fact, by the mid-1990s, that support translated into marketing success. Recycling had become a revenue-producer, and prices for nearly all recyclables skyrocketed. Cities that were once paying to get rid of waste could earn millions from selling the same material. Recycling

FIGURE 3.10

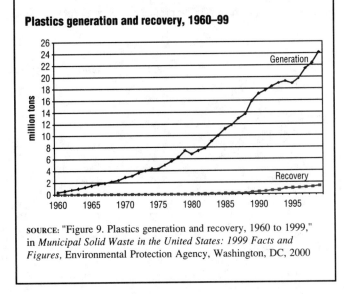

Plastics generation and recovery, 1960–99

SOURCE: "Figure 9. Plastics generation and recovery, 1960 to 1999," in *Municipal Solid Waste in the United States: 1999 Facts and Figures,* Environmental Protection Agency, Washington, DC, 2000

programs began to prosper. Theft of recyclables became commonplace. And private industry began to consider recycling as a way to cut expenses and even to add income, rather than as a nuisance that increased overhead costs. The new economics of recycling made it increasingly attractive to many city waste administrators.

As with any business, recycling is subject to the cyclical highs and lows of supply and demand. Recently, the recycling boom has leveled off, and prices have dropped. In the process, however, most Americans have come to understand that recovery is a viable industry as well as a necessary service.

There are several barriers, however, that continue to hinder the development of the recycling market:

- Consumers are often unaware of recycled products.
- Consumers often lack confidence in the quality of recycled products.
- The transportation costs of carrying recyclables to processing plants are high.
- Questions about supply and demand deter investors.
- It is difficult to recover or sort certain materials, such as oil, tires, and plastics.
- Recycled products are generally more expensive.

PACKAGING

The American way of life has changed greatly over the past few decades, as reflected in increases in the number of elderly and disabled living independently at home, women in the workforce, and latchkey children. (Latchkey children are those who are home alone after school until a parent returns from work.) Many products

TABLE 3.5

Recovery[1] of products in municipal solid waste, with detail on containers and packaging, 1960–99

Products	Percent of generation of each product							
	1960	1970	1980	1990	1995	1997	1998	1999
Durable goods	3.5%	6.4%	6.2%	11.6%	16.1%	17.0%	16.6%	16.6%
Nondurable goods	13.8%	14.9%	13.6%	16.9%	23.8%	23.7%	24.8%	26.8%
Containers and packaging								
Glass packaging								
Beer and soft drink bottles	6.4%	2.5%	10.8%	33.5%	32.6%	31.3%	31.4%	28.6%
Wine and liquor bottles	Neg.	Neg.	Neg.	10.3%	26.3%	24.2%	27.1%	24.0%
Food and other bottles & jars	Neg.	Neg.	Neg.	12.5%	21.6%	24.3%	26.3%	24.9%
Total glass packaging	1.6%	1.3%	5.4%	22.1%	27.2%	27.5%	28.9%	26.6%
Steel packaging								
Beer and soft drink cans	1.6%	1.3%	9.6%	26.7%	neg.	Neg.	Neg.	Neg.
Food and other cans	Neg.	1.7%	5.3%	23.2%	56.1%	60.5%	56.1%	56.1%
Other steel packaging	Neg.	Neg.	Neg.	30.0%	23.8%	66.7%	68.0%	70.8%
Total steel packaging	Neg.	1.5%	5.5%	23.9%	53.8%	61.0%	57.1%	57.3%
Aluminum packaging								
Beer and soft drink cans	Neg.	10.0%	36.5%	63.9%	56.6%	59.5%	53.9%	54.5%
Other cans	Neg.	Neg.	Neg.	Neg.	Neg.	Neg.	Neg.	Neg.
Foil and closures	Neg.	Neg.	Neg.	Neg.	Neg.	Neg.	Neg.	Neg.
Total aluminum pkg	Neg.	1.8%	25.2%	6.1%	8.6%	8.3%	8.1%	7.9%
Paper & paperboard pkg								
Corrugated boxes	34.4%	21.6%	37.4%	48.0%	64.2%	67.1%	66.5%	65.1%
Milk cartons[2]			Neg.	Neg.	Neg.	Neg.	Neg.	Neg.
Folding cartons[2]			Neg.	Neg.	20.3%	6.8%	4.1%	6.9%
Other paperboard packaging			Neg.	Neg.	Neg.	Neg.	Neg.	Neg.
Bags and sacks[2]			Neg.	Neg.	17.2%	15.5%	17.3%	13.6%
Wrapping papers[2]			Neg.	Neg.	Neg.	Neg.		
Other paper packaging	7.5%	9.2%	35.3%	neg.	Neg.	Neg.	Neg.	Neg.
Total paper & board pkg	19.4%	14.5%	27.4%	36.9%	52.3%	52.8%	51.9%	51.0%
Plastics packaging								
Soft drink bottles[2]			3.8%	32.6%	46.2%	35.5%	35.4%	40.0%
Milk bottles[2]			Neg.	3.8%	30.6%	31.3%	31.4%	31.9%
Other containers	Neg.	Neg.	Neg.	1.4%	12.7%	13.0%	10.7%	11.0%
Bags and sacks[2]			Neg.	3.2%	3.3%	2.6%	0.7%	0.6%
Wraps[2]			Neg.	2.0%	2.3%	2.3%	6.1%	5.1%
Other plastics packaging	Neg.	Neg.	Neg.	1.0%	0.9%	1.8%	2.7%	2.6%
Total plastics packaging	Neg.	Neg.	Neg.	3.8%	9.8%	8.7%	9.7%	9.7%
Wood packaging	Neg.	Neg.	Neg.	1.6%	7.3%	8.4%	9.8%	9.5%
Other misc. packaging	Neg.	Neg.	Neg.	Neg.	Neg.	Neg.	Neg.	Neg.
Total containers & pkg	10.5%	7.7%	16.1%	26.0%	39.1%	38.9%	38.3%	37.2%
Total product wastes[3]	10.3%	9.6%	13.3%	19.8%	28.9%	28.9%	29.0%	29.3%
Other wastes								
Food wastes	Neg.	Neg.	Neg.	Neg.	2.6%	2.4%	2.3%	2.2%
Yard trimmings	Neg.	Neg.	Neg.	12.0%	30.3%	41.4%	45.3%	45.3%
Miscellaneous inorganic wastes	Neg.	Neg.	Neg.	Neg.	Neg.	Neg.	Neg.	
Total other wastes	Neg.	Neg.	Neg.	7.2%	17.5%	21.7%	23.5%	23.3%
Total MSW recovered - percent	6.4%	6.6%	9.6%	16.2%	26.0%	27.1%	27.6%	27.8%

Note: Details may not add to totals due to rounding. Neg. = Less than 5,000 tons or 0.05 percent.
[1] Recovery of postconsumer wastes; does not include converting/fabrication scrap.
[2] Not estimated separately prior to 1980. Paper wraps not reported separately after 1996.
[3] Other than food products.

SOURCE: "Table 21: Recovery of Products in Municipal Solid Waste, 1960 to 1999 (With Detail on Containers and Packaging) (In percent of generation of each product)," in *Municipal Solid Waste in the United States: 1999 Facts and Figures*, Environmental Protection Agency, Washington, DC, 2000. Data from Franklin Associates.

and packages have been developed to meet the changing needs of these American consumers—single-serve meals, easy-to-open bottles and cans, and reclosable containers.

Packaging comprises a large proportion of MSW (one-third in 1999). (See Table 2.2.) Therefore, one of the major ways to reduce the amount of MSW is to reduce the amount of packaging used for products or to use materials that recycle or biodegrade easily. (See Figure 2.9, which diagrams the concepts of source reduction and waste reduction.)

As an example of source reduction in packaging, until recently CDs and cassettes were sold in packages far larger than needed. Many customers and recording artists complained to the manufacturers, who now put CDs and cassettes in smaller packages. Many other industries are also using less plastic and paper to package their products.

The EPA reported that 37.2 percent of packaging and containers were recovered in 1999, up from 10.5 percent in 1960, yet down from a high of 39.1 percent in 1995. The 1999 recovery figures for packaging and containers included 26.6 percent of glass, 57.3 percent of steel, 44.2 percent of aluminum, 51.0 percent of paper, 9.7 percent of plastics, and 9.5 percent of wood. (See Table 3.5.)

The National Consumers League (NCL), a private, non-profit consumer advocacy group, studied the amount of waste generated by a typical family consuming a year's worth of 10 common food items. They compared the packaging used to the same products with less packaging. The difference amounted to almost 286 pounds per year. (See Table 3.6; acronyms in the "less filling" column refer to types of plastic.)

"GREEN" PRODUCT DESIGN

Designing and manufacturing products with conservation and consideration for the environment in mind is called "green" product design. Figure 3.11 contrasts conventional and green design methods. Although costs of green design systems are generally greater initially, experts think that the long-term expense will be no greater and may be offset by recycling savings.

ENERGY SAVINGS

Disposing of MSW in landfills and by incineration wastes not only the materials but also the energy held within those products. The energy contained in materials is lost permanently when they are disposed of in landfills. Although significant amounts of energy can be recovered from waste through incineration, studies have found that recycling can recover three to five times more energy than incineration.

RECYCLING AROUND THE WORLD

The United States is not the only country facing waste disposal problems. Other industrial nations are confronting similar situations. Some landfills in Europe are reaching capacity, and most European countries are passing laws requiring more control over them. Unlike the United States, which still has much undeveloped territory, those nations do not. As a result, many European countries, like many American cities, are sending their waste to Africa and Latin America.

Several European countries, most notably Germany, require manufacturers to collect and recycle packaging they use for their products. A green dot is put on products sold in German supermarkets to show that the packaging is recyclable. Between one-half and two-thirds of products carry the green dot. France, Austria, and the United Kingdom have similar laws.

TABLE 3.6

Comparison of food packaging options

Based on Estimated Annual Household Consumption

	Less Filling: Market Basket 1	More Packaging: Market Basket 2	Annual Diff. (Pounds)
Beer	6 Aluminum cans, LDPE ring carrier	6 glass bottles, paperboard carton	166.30
Cereal, Toasted Oat	PE bag	Paperboard box, Plastic bag	8.58
Cheese, Cheddar	Plastic bag	Paperboard carton, servings wrapped in plastic	1.90
Eggs	PS foam carton	Paperboard carton	3.62
Juice	HDPE jug, 1 gal	Glass bottle, 1/2 gal	66.73
Lunch Meat, Ham	PE pouch	Paperboard outer carton, Inner plastic pouch	3.14
Pasta	Plastic bag, 32 oz.	Paperboard box, 16 oz.	2.82
Potato Chips	Laminated bag, 14 oz.	Paperboard tube, Foil bags	5.83
Soft Drinks	PET bottle, 2 liter	12 aluminum cans, Paperboard carton	19.03
Tuna	6 oz. steel can	3 small cans (8.25 oz.), Paperboard sleeve	7.98
SAVINGS			285.94

SOURCE: "NCL packaging study, selected statistics" [table] in "Great Taste, Less Landfilling," in *The ULS Report* vol. 6, no. 2, April-May-June 1999. Used with permission of the *The ULS Report*, Ann Arbor, MI.

The European Union Parliament reached agreement on a new End of Life Vehicle (ELV) Directive in January 2001. Member states will have 18 months from that time to introduce the final version of the Directive nationally. Under this law, manufacturers of cars face a 2007 deadline for recycling all scrap vehicles manufactured prior to January 1, 2001, and an immediate deadline for recycling all scrap vehicles manufactured after January 1, 2001. By 2015, 85 percent of the total weight of scrap vehicles will have to be recycled. The automobile manufacturers have the responsibility for arranging the takeback of cars. The ELV Directive also mandates that a number of metals, including lead, mercury, and cadmium, will be banned in the manufacture of vehicles beginning July 2003.

Sometimes cultural traditions can make it more difficult to control the amount of MSW a country produces. According to a July 22, 2001, report in the *Japan Economic Newswire*, Japan uses 2 billion tons of materials annually and buries 80 million tons of refuse in landfills. One of the major reasons for Japan's huge materials use and waste disposal is the amount of wrapping and packaging that manufacturers use. Often, the amount of wrapping on a gift shows the amount of respect or love the gift-giver has for the person receiving the gift; the more wrapping, the more respect or love. For example, it is not unusual to have a gift of cookies individually wrapped, laid in corrugated paper, put inside a plastic wrap, covered with fancy wrapping paper, and then delivered in a shopping bag. To change this will require a change in values for many Japanese.

FIGURE 3.11

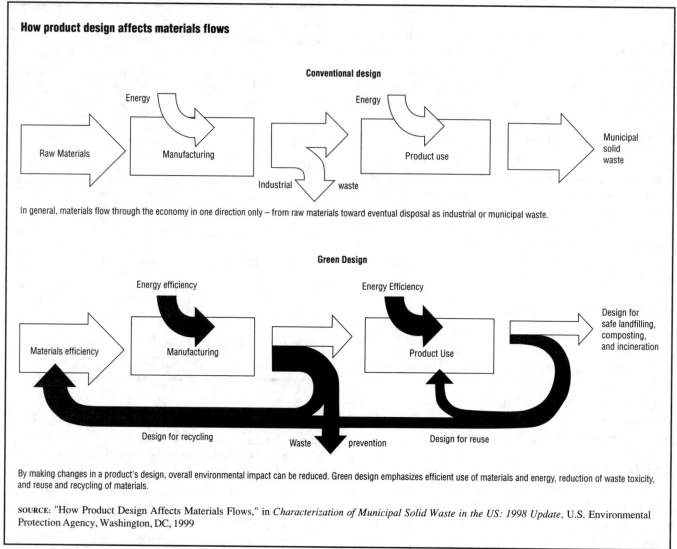

How product design affects materials flows

Conventional design

In general, materials flow through the economy in one direction only – from raw materials toward eventual disposal as industrial or municipal waste.

Green Design

By making changes in a product's design, overall environmental impact can be reduced. Green design emphasizes efficient use of materials and energy, reduction of waste toxicity, and reuse and recycling of materials.

SOURCE: "How Product Design Affects Materials Flows," in *Characterization of Municipal Solid Waste in the US: 1998 Update,* U.S. Environmental Protection Agency, Washington, DC, 1999

According to the EPA, as of 1995 (although later data exists for the United States, comparative data for the other countries was unavailable), the United States recycled a larger percentage of MSW than many industrialized countries. At a time when Americans recycled 23 percent of their MSW, Switzerland recovered 22 percent; Japan, 20 percent; Sweden, the Netherlands, and Germany, 16 percent each; Spain, 13 percent; and Canada, 10 percent. Italy, France, and the United Kingdom each recycled less than 3 percent of MSW.

PROJECTIONS FOR SOLID WASTE RECOVERY

Industry experts believe that recovery rates will increase to 30 to 35 percent between 2000 and 2005.

Figure 3.12 shows two projections: a more conservative projection (the line with squares) and a more optimistic projection (the line with triangles). Because the recycling infrastructure is already in place, growth could approach the upper range. However, recent lower prices for recovered waste do not bode well for expansion in the industry.

The EPA estimates that by 2005, 239.5 million tons of MSW will be generated and recovery could retrieve 76.7 million of these tons. This would mean that landfills and other disposal methods would handle a somewhat smaller percentage of waste (53.3 percent in 2000 and 52.1 percent in 2005) than in 1997 (55.1 percent). (See Table 3.7 and Figure 3.13.)

FIGURE 3.12

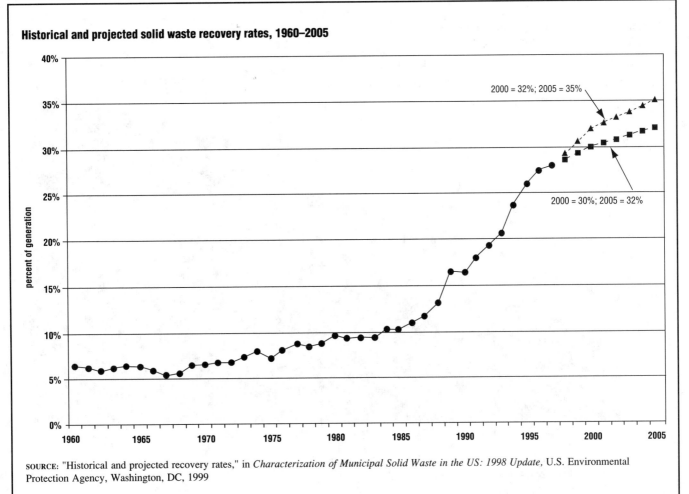

Historical and projected solid waste recovery rates, 1960–2005

2000 = 32%; 2005 = 35%

2000 = 30%; 2005 = 32%

SOURCE: "Historical and projected recovery rates," in *Characterization of Municipal Solid Waste in the US: 1998 Update,* U.S. Environmental Protection Agency, Washington, DC, 1999

TABLE 3.7

Generation, recovery, combustion, and disposal of municipal solid waste, 1997, 2000, and 2005

Recovery scenarios assumed: 30% in 2000, 32% in 2005
(In thousands of tons and percent of total generation)

	Thousands of tons			% of generation		
	1997	**2000**	**2005**	**1997**	**2000**	**2005**
Generation	216,970	223,230	239,540	100.0%	100.0%	100.0%
Recovery for recycling	48,630	53,850	61,840	22.4%	24.1%	25.8%
Recovery for composting*	12,070	13,100	14,900	5.6%	5.9%	6.2%
Total materials recovery	60,700	66,950	76,740	28.0%	30.0%	32.0%
Discards after recovery	156,270	156,280	162,800	72.0%	70.0%	68.0%
Combustion**	36,700	37,200	38,000	16.9%	16.7%	15.9%
Landfill, other disposal	119,570	119,080	124,800	55.1%	53.3%	52.1%

* Composting of yard trimmings and food wastes. Does not include backyard composting.

** Combustion of MSW in mass burn or refuse derived form, incineration without energy recovery, and combustion with energy recovery of source separated materials in MSW.
Details may not add to totals due to rounding.

SOURCE: "Generation, Recovery, Combustion, and Disposal of Municipal Solid Waste: 1997, 2000, and 2005," in *Characterization of Municipal Solid Waste in the US: 1998 Update,* U.S. Environmental Protection Agency, Washington, DC, 1999

FIGURE 3.13

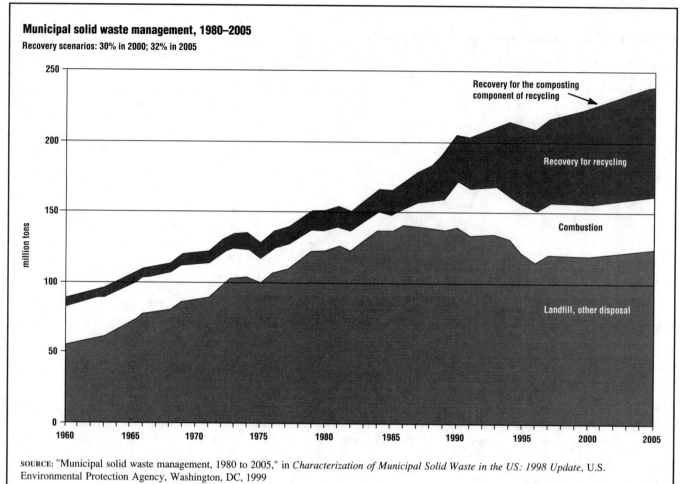

Municipal solid waste management, 1980–2005

Recovery scenarios: 30% in 2000; 32% in 2005

SOURCE: "Municipal solid waste management, 1980 to 2005," in *Characterization of Municipal Solid Waste in the US: 1998 Update*, U.S. Environmental Protection Agency, Washington, DC, 1999

CHAPTER 4

AIR POLLUTION

Air pollution is unwanted chemicals or other materials (pollutants) in the air we breathe. Many air pollutants occur as gases or vapors, but some are solid particles such as dust, smoke, and soot.

Air pollution can make people sick and can harm the environment. Trees, lakes, and animals can be harmed by air pollution. Air pollutants have made the ozone layer around Earth thinner, leading to increased skin cancer and cataracts (a disease of the eye that can cause blindness). Air pollution dirties and eats away the stone in buildings, monuments, and statues. Air pollution also causes haze that can make it harder to see.

Fossil fuels and chemicals have played a major role in society's pursuit of economic growth and higher standards of living. But the burning of fossil fuels and the use of chemicals alter the earth's chemistry and threaten the food, water, and air supplies on which humans depend.

SMOG

Smog, a word made from the combination of "smoke" and "fog," is probably the best-known form of air pollution. Ozone, a molecule containing three atoms of oxygen (O_3), is the most abundant photochemical pollutant in smog. Photochemical pollutants are formed when sunlight initiates chemical reactions among various pollutants directly emitted to the air from sources such as automobiles. Pollutants directly emitted to the air are termed primary pollutants. Those formed by reactions with other air pollutants are termed secondary pollutants.

Ozone can be good or bad, depending on where it is located. When ozone is high in the atmosphere, it shields ultraviolet light coming from the sun and protects human health and the environment. When ozone is at ground level, however, it becomes a harmful component of smog.

Wind often blows primary pollutants away from their sources of emission, and the chemical reactions that create the photochemical pollutants of smog can occur while primary pollutants are being blown through the air by the wind. For this reason, smog can be more serious miles away from the location where primary pollutants are emitted than at their source.

Weather and location determine where smog goes and how bad it will become. When thermal inversions occur (a layer of warm air over cool air), they trap air pollution near the ground. If winds are light as well, smog may stay in one place for days. As traffic and other pollution sources add more primary pollutants to the air, the smog gets worse. Some of the worst smog in the United States occurs in cities such as Los Angeles, Chicago, Houston, and New York. Mexico City, the capital city of neighboring Mexico, is generally considered to have the most polluted air in the world.

Breathing polluted air is not healthful. Sulfur dioxide gas is an air pollutant produced when fossil fuels such as gasoline or coal are burned, and is toxic to living things. Air, rain, or snow polluted with sulfur dioxide can harm buildings and statues, which indicates how potent it is.

Air pollution arises from both natural and human-made sources. The three principal human-made sources of air pollution are transportation, stationary fuel combustion, and industrial processes.

Criteria pollutants (see Table 4.1) are those for which the Environmental Protection Agency (EPA) has established air quality standards. In 1999 approximately 161 million Americans (about 43 percent of the population) lived in areas that failed to meet the air quality standard for at least one of the criteria pollutants. Such areas are called nonattainment areas. Table 4.2 shows the number of areas in 1999 that held nonattainment status compared to their original status after nonattainment designation resulting from the 1990 Clean Air Act Amendments.

Throughout the world, poor air quality contributes to hundreds of thousands of deaths and diseases each year,

TABLE 4.1

Common air pollutants (criteria air pollutants)

Ozone (ground-level ozone is the principal component of smog)
- **Source** - chemical reaction of pollutants; VOCs and NOx
- **Health Effects** - breathing problems, reduced lung function, asthma, irritates eyes, stuffy nose, reduced resistance to colds and other infections, may speed up aging of lung tissue
- **Environmental Effects** - ozone can damage plants and trees; smog can cause reduced visibility
- **Property Damage** - Damages rubber, fabrics, etc.

VOCs* (Volatile Organic Compounds); smog-formers
- **Source** - VOCs are released from burning fuel (gasoline, oil, wood coal, natural gas, etc.), solvents, paints glues and other products used at work or at home. Cars are an important source of VOCs. VOCs include chemicals such as benzene, toluene, methylene chloride and methyl chloroform
- **Health Effects** - In addition to ozone (smog) effects, many VOCs can cause serious health problems such as cancer and other effects
- **Environmental Effects** - In addition to ozone (smog) effects, some VOCs such as formaldehyde and ethylene may harm plants
  * All VOCs contain carbon (C), the basic chemical element found in living beings. Carbon-containing chemicals are called organic. Volatile chemicals escape into the air easily. Many VOCs, such as the chemicals listed in the table, are also hazardous air pollutants, which can cause very serious illnesses. EPA does not list VOCs as criteria air pollutants, but they are included in this list of pollutants because efforts to control smog target VOCs for reduction.

Nitrogen Dioxide (One of the NOx); smog-forming chemical
- **Source** - burning of gasoline, natural gas, coal, oil etc. Cars are an important source of NO^2.
- **Health Effects** - lung damage, illnesses of breathing passages and lungs (respiratory system)
- **Environmental Effects** - nitrogen dioxide is an ingredient of acid rain (acid aerosols), which can damage trees and lakes. Acid aerosols can reduce visibility.
- **Property Damage** - acid aerosols can eat away stone used on buildings, statues, monuments, etc.

Carbon Monoxide (CO)
- **Source** - burning of gasoline, natural gas, coal, oil etc.
- **Health Effects** - reduces ability of blood to bring oxygen to body cells and tissues; cells and tissues need oxygen to work. Carbon monoxide may be particularly hazardous to people who have heart or circulatory (blood vessel) problems and people who have damaged lungs or breathing passages

Particulate Matter (PM-10); (dust, smoke, soot)
- **Source** - burning of wood, diesel and other fuels; industrial plants; agriculture (plowing, burning off fields); unpaved roads
- **Health Effects** - nose and throat irritation, lung damage, bronchitis, early death
- **Environmental Effects** - particulates are the main source of haze that reduces visibility
- **Property Damage** - ashes, soots, smokes and dusts can dirty and discolor structures and other property, including clothes and furniture

Sulfur Dioxide
- **Source** - burning of coal and oil, especially high-sulfur coal from the Eastern United States; industrial processes (paper, metals)
- **Health Effects** - breathing problems, may cause permanent damage to lungs
- **Environmental Effects** - SO_2 is an ingredient in acid rain (acid aerosols), which can damage trees and lakes. Acid aerosols can also reduce visibilit y.
- **Property Damage** - acid aerosols can eat away stone used in buildings, statues, monuments, etc.

Lead
- **Source** - leaded gasoline (being phased out), paint (houses, cars), smelters (metal refineries); manufacture of lead storage batteries
- **Health Effects** - brain and other nervous system damage; children are at special risk. Some lead-containing chemicals cause cancer in animals. Lead causes digestive and other health problems.
- **Environmental Effects** - Lead can harm wildlife.

SOURCE: "Common Air Pollutants (Criteria Air Pollutants)," in *The Plain English Guide to the Clean Air Act,* Environmental Protection Agency, Washington, DC, 1993. Updated on 5/7/2001 at [Online] http://www.epa.gov/oar/oaqps/peg_caa/pegcaa11.html [Accessed 8/30/01]

---

to dying forests and lakes, and to corroding buildings and monuments. Air pollution, particularly acid precipitation, devastates forests, crops, and waterways and works its way into the water cycle and food chains. Table 4.3 shows the pollutants most harmful to plant life.

THE HEALTH EFFECTS OF AIR POLLUTION

The quality of the air plays a role in public health. While focusing on air quality is an obvious and often successful approach to improving public health, such a focus is complex. Among the factors that must be considered are the levels of pollutants in the air, levels of individual exposure to these pollutants, individual susceptibility to toxic substances, and exposure times to substances. In addition, attributing health problems to specific pollutants is complicated by the effect of non-environmental factors, such as smoking, heredity, and diet, on health.

Air pollution is related to a number of respiratory diseases, including bronchitis, pulmonary emphysema, lung cancer, bronchial asthma, and premature lung tissue aging. In addition, air pollution may cause eye irritation and weaken the immune system. Lead contamination in the air can cause neurological and kidney disease and can be responsible for impaired fetal development and impaired cognitive development in children. The American Lung Association estimates the annual health costs of exposure to the most serious air pollutants to be $40 to $50 billion.

The EPA estimates that emissions of toxic materials (hazardous air pollutants such as dioxins) into the air cause at least 2,000 cancer deaths a year. The EPA and the Harvard School of Public Health suggest that as many as 50,000 to 60,000 deaths a year are caused by particulate matter (soot) in the air. Scientists report that some types of particles can be fatal in concentrations even lower than those set as safe by the EPA.

TABLE 4.2

Areas redesignated to attainment between September 1999 and September 2000

Pollutant	Original # areas	1999 # areas	1999 Population (in 1000s)
CO	43	20	33,230
Pb	12	8	1,116
NO_2	1	0	0
O_3	101	32	92,505
PM_{10}	85	77	29,880
SO_2	51	31	4,371

SO_2	Coshocton Co., OH; Gallia Co., OH; and Lorain Co., OH
PM_{10}	Canon City, CO
CO	Colorado Springs, CO; Longmont, CO; and Minneapolis-St. Paul, MN
Pb	Collin Co., TX and Marios Co. (Indianapolis), IN
O_3	Cincinnati-Hamilton, OH-KY

SOURCE: Adapted from "Table 4-3. Nonattainment Status," in *National Air Quality and Emissions Trends Report, 1998,* Environmental Protection Agency, Office of Air Quality Planning and Standards, Emissions Monitoring and Analysis Division, Air Quality Trends Analysis Group, Research Triangle Park, NC, March, 2000 and "Table 4-1. Areas Redesignated Between September 1999 and September 2000," in *National Air Quality and Emissions Trends Report, 1999,* Environmental Protection Agency, Washington, DC, Office of Air Quality Planning and Standards, Emissions Monitoring and Analysis Division, Air Quality Trends Analysis Group, Research Triangle Park, NC, March, 2001

WHAT ARE THE AIR POLLUTANTS?

The Clean Air Act of 1970 and the Clean Air Act Amendments of 1990 address the six pollutants associated with the National Ambient Air Quality Standards (NAAQS). These pollutants in the ambient, or surrounding, air are ozone, nitrogen dioxide (sometimes referred to more generally as the family of nitrogen oxides, Nox), carbon monoxide, particulate matter, sulfur dioxide, and lead. They are called criteria pollutants and are identified as serious threats to human health. Table 4.1 shows the criteria air pollutants, their sources, and their effects on health, the environment, and property. This table also includes VOCs, which are not criteria pollutants but are hazardous air pollutants targeted for reduction.

The EPA has documented air pollution trends in the United States annually since 1973. Its *National Air Quality and Emissions Trends Report, 1999* (2001) reports two kinds of trends for criteria pollutants. Emissions are calculated estimates of the total tonnage of these pollutants released into the air annually. Air quality concentrations measure pollutant concentrations in the air at monitoring stations. Nationally, air quality has improved since 1980 and 1990 for all six pollutants, although particulates were not measured in 1980. All criteria pollutant emissions except NO_x decreased as well. (See Table 4.4.)

Ozone

Ozone (O_3) is the principal component of photochemical smog. It is a gas that is formed when energy from

TABLE 4.3

Air pollutants, in order of harm to plants

Pollutant	Primary or secondary pollutant	Form	Major source(s)
Ozone (O_3)	Secondary	Gas	Product of chemical reactions in the atmosphere
Acidic deposition (sulfates and nitrates)	Secondary	Particulate	Product of chemical reactions in the atmosphere
Sulfur dioxide (SO_2)	Primary	Gas	Power generation, smelter operation
Nitrogen dioxides (NO_x)	Primary and secondary	Gas	From direct release and atmospheric transformation
Hydrogen fluoride (HF)	Primary	Gas/ Particulate	Superphosphate production, and aluminum smelters
Ethylene	Primary	Gas	Combustion, natural causes

SOURCE: "Air pollutants, in order of harm to plants," in *Agriculture and the Environment,* U.S. Department of Agriculture, Washington, DC, 1992

TABLE 4.4

Percent change in air quality and emissions, 1980–1999

Percent Change in Air Quality

	1980–1999	1990–1999
CO	-57	-36
Pb	-94	-60
NO_2	-25	-10
O_3 1-hr	-20	-4
8-hr	-12	no change
PM_{10}	—	-18
SO_2	-50	-36

Percent Change in Emissions

	1980–1999	1990–1999
CO	-22	-7
Pb	-95	-23
NO_x	+1	+2
VOC	-33	-15
PM_{10}	-55	-16
SO_2	-28	-21

SOURCE: *Latest Findings on National Air Quality: 1999 Status and Trends,* U.S. Environmental Protection Agency, Washington, DC, August 2000

sunlight causes nitrogen oxides from power plants and automobiles to react with VOCs, a wide variety of hydrocarbons from industrial processes and automobile emissions. Hydrocarbons are compounds containing the elements hydrogen and carbon.

Ozone has become a persistent problem in many parts of the world. Even the smallest amounts of ozone can cause breathing difficulty. Moderate or heavy exertion in ozone-laden air can result in chest pain and cough. Ozone can also result in lung inflammation, aggravation of preexisting respiratory diseases such as asthma, and increased

FIGURE 4.1

Classified ozone nonattainment areas

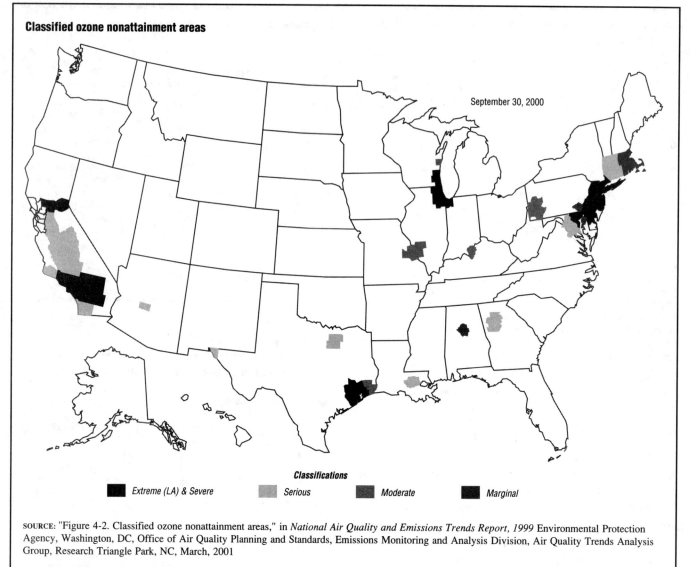

SOURCE: "Figure 4-2. Classified ozone nonattainment areas," in *National Air Quality and Emissions Trends Report, 1999* Environmental Protection Agency, Washington, DC, Office of Air Quality Planning and Standards, Emissions Monitoring and Analysis Division, Air Quality Trends Analysis Group, Research Triangle Park, NC, March, 2001

susceptibility to respiratory infection. Ozone causes environmental damage as well, particularly to vegetation.

Ground-level ozone is the most complex, pervasive, and difficult to control of the six criteria pollutants. Figure 4.1 shows the areas that failed to attain standards set for ozone in 2000. (Do not confuse ground-level ozone in pollution with the useful ozone layer high above the earth, which shields the planet from much ultraviolet, or UV, radiation from the sun.)

Volatile Organic Compounds

Volatile organic compounds (VOCs), such as benzene, toluene, and formaldehyde, are released from burning fuels such as coal, natural gas, gasoline, and wood. The health and environmental effects of VOCs are similar to those of ozone.

Figure 4.2 shows the sources of VOC emissions and their relative proportions in 1999. Vehicle emissions and

industrial processes are the major sources of VOC emissions. Solvent use comprises 60 percent of the industrial processes emissions category.

From 1940 through 1970, VOC emissions increased about 77 percent, mainly because of the increase in car and truck traffic, and in industrial production. Since 1970 national VOC emissions have decreased as a result of emission controls on cars and trucks, and less open burning of solid waste. From 1980 to 1999, VOC emissions decreased 31 percent. From 1990 to 1999, VOC emissions from highway vehicles dropped 18 percent. During that time, industrial VOC emissions decreased 21 percent, in part due to the implementation of controls that affect specific chemical and solvent industries.

Nitrogen Dioxide

Nitrogen dioxide (NO_2) comes from burning fuels such as gasoline, natural gas, coal, and oil. Vehicle

FIGURE 4.2

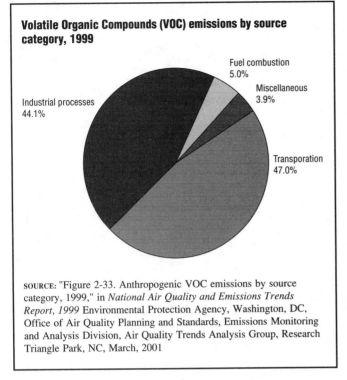

Volatile Organic Compounds (VOC) emissions by source category, 1999

Industrial processes
44.1%

Fuel combustion
5.0%

Miscellaneous
3.9%

Transporation
47.0%

SOURCE: "Figure 2-33. Anthropogenic VOC emissions by source category, 1999," in *National Air Quality and Emissions Trends Report, 1999* Environmental Protection Agency, Washington, DC, Office of Air Quality Planning and Standards, Emissions Monitoring and Analysis Division, Air Quality Trends Analysis Group, Research Triangle Park, NC, March, 2001

FIGURE 4.3

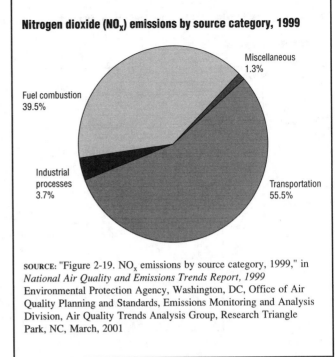

Nitrogen dioxide (NO$_x$) emissions by source category, 1999

Miscellaneous
1.3%

Fuel combustion
39.5%

Industrial processes
3.7%

Transportation
55.5%

SOURCE: "Figure 2-19. NO$_x$ emissions by source category, 1999," in *National Air Quality and Emissions Trends Report, 1999* Environmental Protection Agency, Washington, DC, Office of Air Quality Planning and Standards, Emissions Monitoring and Analysis Division, Air Quality Trends Analysis Group, Research Triangle Park, NC, March, 2001

emissions and stationary source fuel combustion, such as coal-fired power plants, are the primary sources of nitrogen dioxide in the atmosphere. (See Figure 4.3.) (Although most of the nitrogen compounds from combustion sources are emitted as nitrogen oxide [NO], it is readily converted into nitrogen dioxide in the atmosphere, so this book will often discuss nitrogen oxides as nitrogen dioxide. Collectively, nitrogen oxides are typically shown as NO$_x$.)

Nitrogen dioxide is a major part of smog. Those with preexisting respiratory illness and children aged 5 to 12 are most affected by short-term exposure to this pollutant. Long-term exposure may result in increased susceptibility to respiratory infection. Nitrogen dioxide also contributes to global warming and acid precipitation.

From 1940 to 1970, nitrogen dioxide emissions increased because of a rise in the burning of natural gas and the increase in the number of vehicles on the nation's roads. From 1980 to 1999, these emissions increased as well, but only by 4 percent. However, the air quality concentration of nitrogen dioxide decreased 25 percent from 1980 to 1999.

How can emissions of nitrogen dioxide increase while the amount in the air decreases? The EPA, in its *National Air Quality and Emissions Trends Report, 1999* (Washington, DC, 2001), suggests that this situation may be the result of nitrogen chemistry in the atmosphere, which may form intermediate compounds not measured by EPA monitoring devices.

Figure 4.4 shows the trends in annual mean NO$_2$ concentrations from 1980 to 1989 and 1990 to 1999 in rural, suburban, and urban locations. The highest annual mean NO$_2$ concentrations are typically found in urban areas, with significantly lower annual mean concentrations recorded at rural sites. The 1999 composite mean at 137 urban sites was 24 percent lower than the 1980 level, compared to a 27 percent reduction at 180 suburban sites. At 66 rural sites, the composite mean NO$_2$ concentration was about the same in 1999 as it was in 1980.

Carbon Monoxide

A colorless, odorless gas, carbon monoxide (CO) reduces the ability of blood to carry oxygen. Those most at risk from carbon monoxide, therefore, are people with cardiovascular disease, who may already have problems with circulation and the delivery of oxygen to critical organs such as the heart and brain. High levels of CO can be deadly to anyone.

Carbon monoxide is formed when the carbon in fuels, such as gasoline, natural gas, wood, coal, and oil, is not burned completely. As Figure 4.5 shows, more than three-fourths of atmospheric carbon monoxide emissions in 1999 were formed by the incomplete combustion of fuel in vehicles.

In 1940 cars and trucks created only about 28 percent of carbon monoxide emissions, while homes burning coal and oil made up about 50 percent. From 1940 through 1970, emissions from cars and trucks nearly tripled. By

FIGURE 4.4

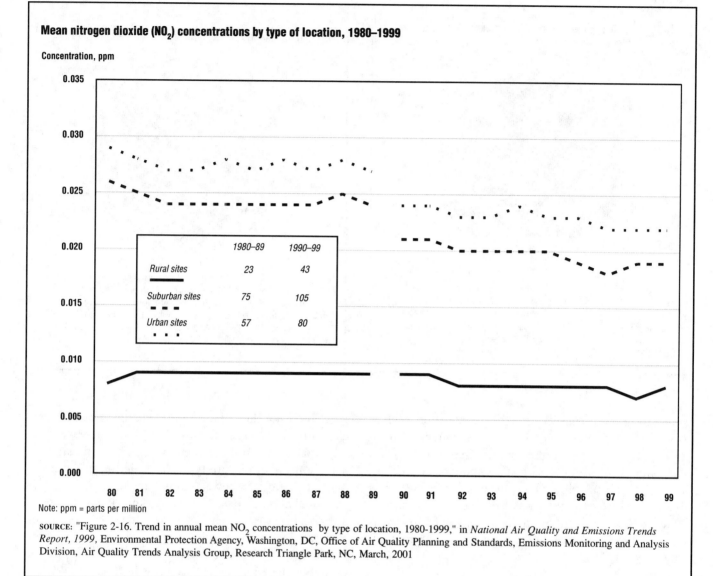

Mean nitrogen dioxide (NO₂) concentrations by type of location, 1980–1999

Concentration, ppm

	1980–89	1990–99
Rural sites	23	43
Suburban sites	75	105
Urban sites	57	80

Note: ppm = parts per million

SOURCE: "Figure 2-16. Trend in annual mean NO₂ concentrations by type of location, 1980-1999," in *National Air Quality and Emissions Trends Report, 1999,* Environmental Protection Agency, Washington, DC, Office of Air Quality Planning and Standards, Emissions Monitoring and Analysis Division, Air Quality Trends Analysis Group, Research Triangle Park, NC, March, 2001

1970 cars and trucks accounted for 71 percent of all carbon monoxide, and a dozen years later, in 1982, they produced 80 percent of the total carbon monoxide emissions. By 1999 that figure had dropped by only 2.9 percent.

The total amount of carbon monoxide emissions from on-road vehicles has dropped 56 percent since 1980, due to automobile emissions control programs. This drop occurred even though there was a 57 percent increase in vehicle miles traveled. Carbon monoxide emissions from all transportation sources have decreased only 23 percent over the same period, primarily due to a 42 percent increase in off-road emission. (See Figure 4.6.)

From 1980 to 1999 the amount of CO in the air decreased by 57 percent. In one year alone, from 1998 to 1999, the concentration of carbon monoxide decreased by 3 percent.

Particulate Matter

Particulate matter (PM-10) is the general term for coarse solid particles and/or liquid droplets—dust, smoke, and soot—that come from paved and unpaved roads (fugitive dust), agriculture and forestry, residential wood stoves and fireplaces (other combustion), and fuel combustion in vehicles, power plants, and industry (traditionally inventoried sources). Figure 4.7 shows total PM-10 emissions by source category.

When particulate matter hangs in the air, it creates a haze that can irritate the nose, throat, and lungs. It can also aggravate respiratory conditions such as asthma. People most susceptible to the effects of particulate matter in the air are the elderly and children, and those with preexisting respiratory or cardiovascular diseases or conditions.

From 1940 to 1971, the amount of particulate matter in the air increased. During the 1970s, however, pollution

FIGURE 4.5

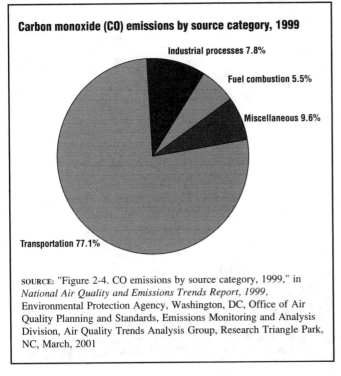

Carbon monoxide (CO) emissions by source category, 1999

SOURCE: "Figure 2-4. CO emissions by source category, 1999," in *National Air Quality and Emissions Trends Report, 1999*, Environmental Protection Agency, Washington, DC, Office of Air Quality Planning and Standards, Emissions Monitoring and Analysis Division, Air Quality Trends Analysis Group, Research Triangle Park, NC, March, 2001

FIGURE 4.6

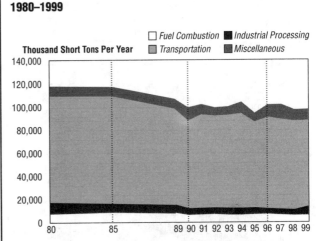

Trend in national total carbon monoxide (CO) emissions, 1980–1999

Notes: Emissions data not available for consecutive years 1980–1989. Emission estimation methods continue to evolve and improve over time. Methods have changed for many significant categories beginning with the years 1985, 1990, and 1996 and consequently are not consistent across all years in this trend period.

SOURCE: "Figure 2-6. Trend in national total CO emissions, 1980-1999," in *Air Quality and Emissions Trends Report, 1999* Environmental Protection Agency, Washington, DC, Office of Air Quality Planning and Standards, Emissions Monitoring and Analysis Division, Air Quality Trends Analysis Group, Research Triangle Park, NC, March, 2001

control laws led to a drop in particulate matter concentrations in the air. Between 1990 and 1999, there was an 18 percent decrease in the air quality concentrations of PM-10.

Between 1990 and 1999, particulate emissions dropped 15 percent. Figure 4.8 shows the trend of emissions of PM-10 from fuel combustion, industrial processing, and transportation (traditionally inventoried sources) from 1980 through 1999. The first five years of the 1980s showed a dramatic decline in particulate matter from these sources, followed by a somewhat steady decline since that time.

Sulfur Dioxide

Sulfur dioxide (SO_2) is formed when fuel is burned that contains sulfur (mainly coal and oil). It is also formed during metal smelting and some other industrial processes.

Inhaling sulfur dioxide in polluted air can impair breathing in those with asthma or even in healthy adults who are active outdoors. As with other air pollutants, children, the elderly, and those with preexisting respiratory and cardiovascular diseases and conditions are most susceptible to adverse effects from breathing this gas. The environment is susceptible to sulfur dioxide as well. Together, sulfur dioxide and nitrogen dioxide are the major components of acid precipitation, which can damage vegetation, bodies of water, statues, monuments, and buildings.

From 1940 to 1970, sulfur dioxide emissions increased as a result of the growing use of fossil fuels, especially coal, by industry and electrical utility plants. Since 1970 total sulfur dioxide emissions have dropped

FIGURE 4.7

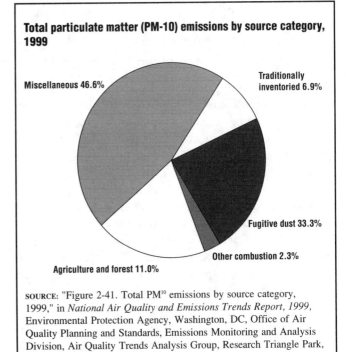

Total particulate matter (PM-10) emissions by source category, 1999

SOURCE: "Figure 2-41. Total PM¹⁰ emissions by source category, 1999," in *National Air Quality and Emissions Trends Report, 1999*, Environmental Protection Agency, Washington, DC, Office of Air Quality Planning and Standards, Emissions Monitoring and Analysis Division, Air Quality Trends Analysis Group, Research Triangle Park, NC, March, 2001

because of cleaner fuels with lower sulfur content and the greater use of anti-pollution devices, such as scrubbers, that clean the factory emissions.

FIGURE 4.8

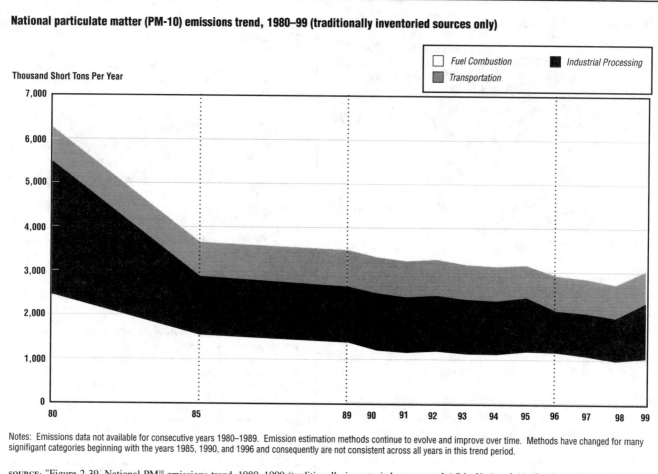

National particulate matter (PM-10) emissions trend, 1980–99 (traditionally inventoried sources only)

Notes: Emissions data not available for consecutive years 1980–1989. Emission estimation methods continue to evolve and improve over time. Methods have changed for many signifigant categories beginning with the years 1985, 1990, and 1996 and consequently are not consistent across all years in this trend period.

SOURCE: "Figure 2-39. National PM[10] emissions trend, 1980–1999 (traditionally inventoried sources only)," in *National Air Quality and Emissions Trends Report, 1999,* Environmental Protection Agency, Washington, DC, Office of Air Quality Planning and Standards, Emissions Monitoring and Analysis Division, Air Quality Trends Analysis Group, Research Triangle Park, NC, March, 2001

As shown in Figure 4.9, most sulfur emissions today still come from fuel combustion, and the electric utility industry accounts for most of the emissions in that category. However, from 1990 to 1999, sulfur dioxide emissions decreased 20 percent, with a sharp decline between 1994 and 1995. (See Figure 4.10.) This decline was due to the implementation of the EPA's Acid Rain Program. The overall goal of the Acid Rain Program is to reduce emissions of sulfur dioxide and nitrogen dioxide, the primary causes of acid rain (precipitation). Phase II of the Acid Rain Program was implemented in 2000 and is expected to result in new reductions in sulfur dioxide emissions.

Not only did emissions of sulfur dioxide decrease, but also the concentration of SO_2 in the air decreased as well. From 1980 to 1999, the air quality concentration of sulfur dioxide decreased 50 percent. From 1990 to 1999, it decreased by 36 percent.

Lead

Lead poisoning is the most common and most devastating environmental disease affecting young children,

FIGURE 4.9

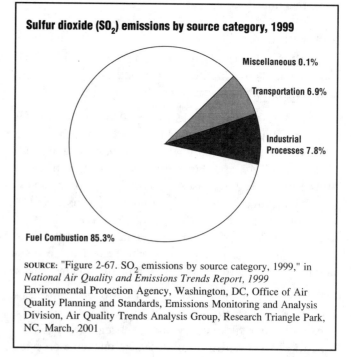

Sulfur dioxide (SO_2) emissions by source category, 1999

SOURCE: "Figure 2-67. SO_2 emissions by source category, 1999," in *National Air Quality and Emissions Trends Report, 1999* Environmental Protection Agency, Washington, DC, Office of Air Quality Planning and Standards, Emissions Monitoring and Analysis Division, Air Quality Trends Analysis Group, Research Triangle Park, NC, March, 2001

FIGURE 4.10

National sulfur dioxide (SO₂) emissions trend, 1980–99

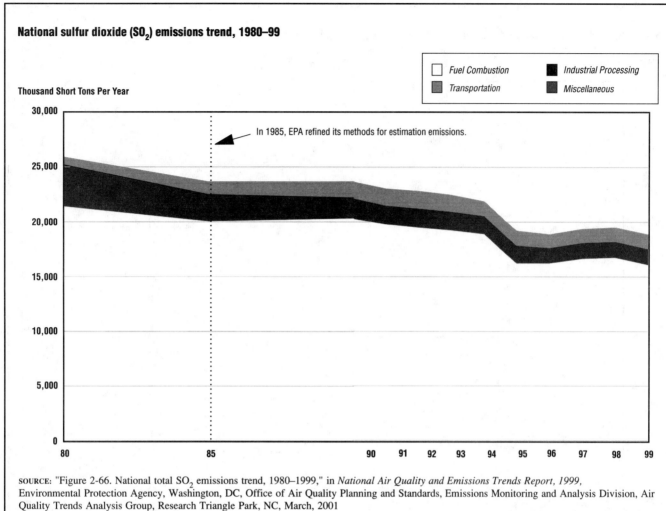

Thousand Short Tons Per Year

In 1985, EPA refined its methods for estimation emissions.

Legend: Fuel Combustion | Industrial Processing | Transportation | Miscellaneous

SOURCE: "Figure 2-66. National total SO₂ emissions trend, 1980–1999," in *National Air Quality and Emissions Trends Report, 1999*, Environmental Protection Agency, Washington, DC, Office of Air Quality Planning and Standards, Emissions Monitoring and Analysis Division, Air Quality Trends Analysis Group, Research Triangle Park, NC, March, 2001

according to the Centers for Disease Control and Prevention (CDC). The chemical element lead (Pb) can damage the brain and nervous system. Until recently, the main source of lead pollution was leaded gasoline for cars. Today, smelters and battery plants, followed by transportation, are the leading sources of lead emissions. (See Figure 4.11.) Most of the transportation sector's lead emissions come from aircraft, which still use leaded fuel.

From 1980 to 1999, lead emissions decreased 94 percent, primarily because of the EPA's efforts to phase out automotive leaded gasoline. Air quality concentrations of lead fell 94 percent over that time as well. Figure 4.12 shows the overall downward trend in lead concentrations for rural, suburban, and urban sites. (In Figure 4.12, the concentration of lead is noted as µg/m³, which means micrograms per cubic meter. A microgram is one-millionth of a gram.)

The primary cause of the most severe cases of lead poisoning in children is exposure to lead in paint. Lead-based paint was once widely used in housing in the United States.

FIGURE 4.11

Lead (Pb) emissions by source category, 1999

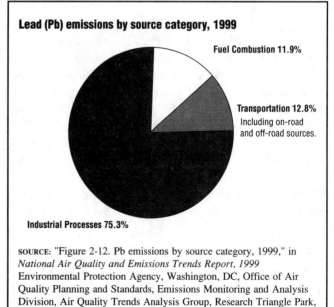

Fuel Combustion 11.9%

Transportation 12.8%
Including on-road and off-road sources.

Industrial Processes 75.3%

SOURCE: "Figure 2-12. Pb emissions by source category, 1999," in *National Air Quality and Emissions Trends Report, 1999* Environmental Protection Agency, Washington, DC, Office of Air Quality Planning and Standards, Emissions Monitoring and Analysis Division, Air Quality Trends Analysis Group, Research Triangle Park, NC, March, 2001

FIGURE 4.12

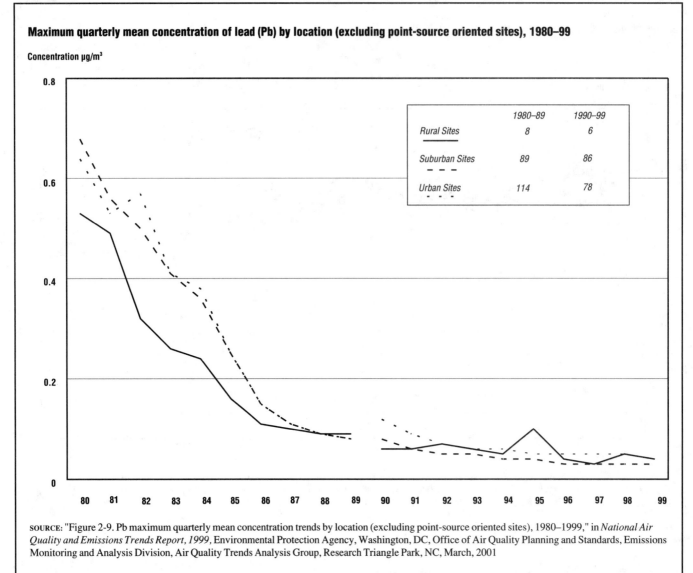

Maximum quarterly mean concentration of lead (Pb) by location (excluding point-source oriented sites), 1980–99

Concentration µg/m³

	1980–89	1990–99
Rural Sites	8	6
Suburban Sites	89	86
Urban Sites	114	78

SOURCE: "Figure 2-9. Pb maximum quarterly mean concentration trends by location (excluding point-source oriented sites), 1980–1999," in *National Air Quality and Emissions Trends Report, 1999,* Environmental Protection Agency, Washington, DC, Office of Air Quality Planning and Standards, Emissions Monitoring and Analysis Division, Air Quality Trends Analysis Group, Research Triangle Park, NC, March, 2001

The Office of Housing and Urban Development (HUD) estimates that 57 million, or about three-fourths, of the 77 million privately owned and occupied homes built before 1980 contain lead-based paint. Families with children under seven years of age, who are the most vulnerable to lead poisoning, occupy almost 10 million of these homes. In 1997 the EPA and the Department of Housing and Urban Development (HUD) issued a regulation requiring the disclosure of known lead-based paint hazards when homes are sold or rented. In addition, many states have passed laws requiring the disclosure of lead content. (See Figure 4.13.)

AIR TOXICS

Hazardous air pollutants (HAPs), also referred to as air toxics, are pollutants that may cause severe health effects or ecosystem damage. Examples of air toxics are volatile chemicals, such as benzene; combustion byproducts, such as dioxins; heavy metals, such as mercury; and solvents, such as carbon tetrachloride. The Clean Air Act (CAA) lists 188 substances as hazardous air pollutants and directs the EPA to regulate sources emitting major amounts of these pollutants. Air toxics are emitted from many sources, including industrial facilities, dry cleaners, vehicles, building materials, and wildfires.

Certain manufacturing facilities are required to report to the EPA their estimated releases of 650 listed chemicals each year. These reports are compiled into an annual database called the Toxics Release Inventory (TRI), which was established under the Emergency Planning and Community Right-to-Know Act of 1986. Data were first collected in 1987 and compiled in 1988.

Although the TRI has the limitations that data are self-reported and certain facilities are not required to participate, the TRI estimates help show trends in toxic air emissions. Table 4.5 shows the toxic chemical releases by state in 1999. The states are ranked according to

FIGURE 4.13

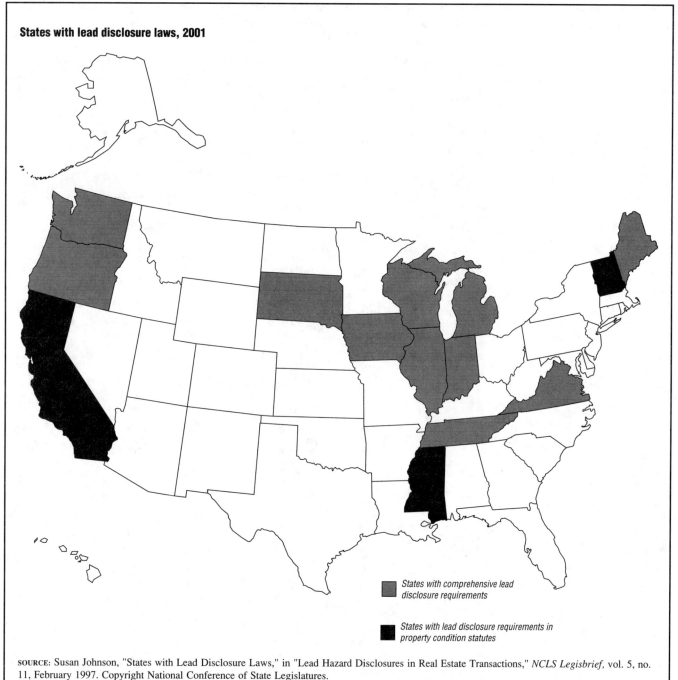

States with lead disclosure laws, 2001

States with comprehensive lead
disclosure requirements

States with lead disclosure requirements in
property condition statutes

SOURCE: Susan Johnson, "States with Lead Disclosure Laws," in "Lead Hazard Disclosures in Real Estate Transactions," *NCLS Legisbrief,* vol. 5, no. 11, February 1997. Copyright National Conference of State Legislatures.

pounds of total on-site and off-site releases. Nevada had the highest releases in 1999, followed by Utah, Arizona, Alaska, Texas, Ohio, New Mexico, Pennsylvania, Indiana, and Illinois. (On this table, original industries are manufacturers that have been reporting since 1987 and federal facilities that have been reporting since 1994. New industries are manufacturers that have been reporting since 1998.)

Figure 4.14 shows the percent of emissions by source type of each of the 33 urban HAPs that have available emis-

sions information. It also contains information on diesel particulate matter. To read this bar graph, note that the center vertical line is "zero." Bars extend to the right and left from this zero point for the two categories noted at the top.

The right-hand column of bars on Figure 4.14 shows which HAPs come primarily from mobile sources (such as cars or airplanes); few do. Many EPA motor vehicle and fuel emission control programs of the past have reduced air toxics from mobile sources. However, the EPA is still reassessing the need for further vehicle and

TABLE 4.5

TRI (Toxic Release Inventory) total releases by state, original and new industries, 1999

State	Original Industries		New Industries		All TRI Industries	
	Pounds	Rank	Pounds	Rank	Pounds	Rank
Alabama	75,132,585	10	62,995,934	17	138,128,519	16
Alaska	1,671,982	48	431,345,804	4	433,017,786	4
American Samoa	0	—	5,628	54	5,628	55
Arizona	50,782,129	18	912,547,939	3	963,330,068	3
Arkansas	37,592,186	23	3,933,290	43	41,525,476	33
California	42,747,339	21	26,298,645	25	69,045,984	27
Colorado	6,675,202	40	19,409,489	29	26,084,691	39
Connecticut	6,359,752	41	1,475,523	48	7,835,275	47
Delaware	7,708,180	39	3,672,174	44	11,380,354	45
District of Columbia	18,096	53	79,871	52	97,967	54
Florida	76,714,040	9	72,692,580	13	149,406,620	13
Georgia	60,950,277	14	65,974,004	16	126,924,281	19
Guam	0	—	501,108	49	501,108	53
Hawaii	401,133	52	2,173,658	47	2,574,791	49
Idaho	26,517,444	27	59,458,895	19	85,976,339	22
Illinois	95,873,821	6	69,181,076	15	165,054,897	10
Indiana	125,781,848	5	73,088,864	11	198,870,712	9
Iowa	34,665,540	25	14,126,889	32	48,792,429	30
Kansas	33,069,818	26	9,504,240	38	42,574,058	32
Kentucky	45,813,925	20	60,391,397	18	106,205,322	20
Louisiana	134,825,056	4	15,327,549	31	150,152,605	12
Maine	7,728,607	38	120,061	50	7,848,668	46
Maryland	13,626,221	36	30,354,865	24	43,981,086	31
Massachusetts	5,602,815	43	6,273,390	42	11,876,205	44
Michigan	72,468,757	11	69,817,757	14	142,286,514	15
Minnesota	20,080,339	34	11,142,248	36	31,222,587	36
Mississippi	62,452,276	13	13,343,582	34	75,795,858	25
Missouri	56,780,432	17	72,960,345	12	129,740,777	17
Montana	48,659,575	19	78,959,073	9	127,618,648	18
Nebraska	19,012,631	35	8,254,822	41	27,267,453	38
Nevada	4,368,476	44	1,164,039,385	1	1,168,407,861	1
New Hampshire	3,114,421	46	2,757,533	46	5,871,954	48
New Jersey	21,818,000	30	9,465,385	39	31,283,385	35
New Mexico	20,463,178	33	241,812,999	5	262,276,177	7
New York	35,840,928	24	35,973,300	23	71,814,228	26
North Carolina	67,121,835	12	91,228,696	8	158,350,531	11
North Dakota	2,595,162	47	21,060,751	28	23,655,913	40
Northern Marianas	0	—	3,412	55	3,412	56
Ohio	140,208,448	*2	163,019,708	6	303,228,156	6
Oklahoma	22,961,015	29	14,108,242	33	37,069,257	34
Oregon	21,811,249	31	45,884,507	22	67,695,756	28
Pennsylvania	160,461,734	*3	92,314,818	7	252,776,552	8
Puerto Rico	6,324,486	42	11,848,219	35	18,172,705	42
Rhode Island	1,296,069	49	95,029	51	1,391,098	50
South Carolina	59,730,443	15	24,330,454	26	84,060,897	23
South Dakota	3,564,241	45	8,564,736	40	12,128,977	43
Tennessee	88,470,887	7	55,840,140	21	144,311,027	14
Texas	257,858,098	1	56,008,033	20	313,866,131	5
Utah	82,785,620	8	1,079,001,349	2	1,161,786,969	2
Vermont	646,780	51	0	—	646,780	52
Virgin Islands	699,418	50	69,495	53	768,913	51
Virginia	57,411,080	16	23,158,525	27	80,569,605	24
Washington	24,804,178	28	3,670,737	45	28,474,915	37
West Virginia	21,762,246	32	78,729,865	10	100,492,111	21
Wisconsin	40,990,645	22	17,391,132	30	58,381,777	29
Wyoming	9,689,355	37	9,740,423	37	19,429,778	41
Total	**2,326,509,998**		**5,445,527,573**		**7,772,037,571**	

Note: Off-site Releases include metals and metal compounds transferred off-site for solidification/stabilization and for wastewater treatment, including to POTWs. Off-site Releases do not include transfers to disposal sent to other TRI Facilities that reported the amount as an on-site release. Facilities/forms are included in the original industry category if they did not report a new industry SIC code. Facilities/forms are included in the new industry category if the facility/form has a new industry SIC code and no SIC code in 20–39. If the facility reported in any year prior to 1998 and the facility/form has a combination of original and new industry SIC codes, then the facility/form is included in the original industry category. If the facility reported for the first time in 1998 or later and the facility/form has a combination of original and new industry SIC codes, then the facility/form is included in the new industry category. One facility, Phelps Dodge Miami Inc. in Claypool, AZ, that reported under SIC code 33 and SIC code 10 in 1999 and previous years has been included in the new industry category SIC code 10 for the purpose of this analysis.

*Due to an EPA data entry error, three chemical reporting revisions for 1999 by one facility, the US Army Letterkenny Depot in Chambersburg, PA, reporting in the original industry sector were not included in tables in this report (except in federal facility tables). The effect of the revisions is to change the facility's total releases for zinc compounds from 17,147,839 pounds to zero and lead compounds from 60,123 pounds to zero. The facility anticipated revising total releases for manganese compounds from 5,584,900 pounds to below 500 pounds. The effect of the revisions is to change the rank for the original industries in Pennsylvania to 3 and in Ohio to 2, as noted in this table.

SOURCE: "Table E-2. TRI Total Releases by State, Original and New Industries, 1999," in "Toxics Release Inventory 1999 Executive Summary," in *1999 Toxics Release Inventory*, U.S. Environmental Protection Agency, Washington, DC, April 2001

FIGURE 4.14

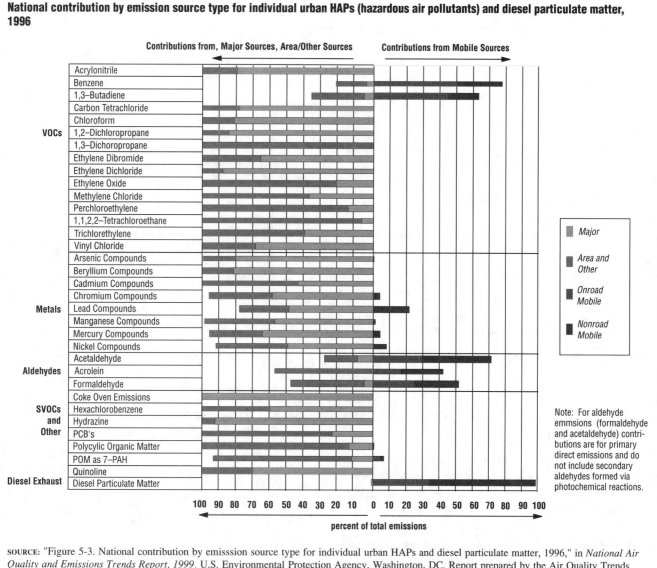

National contribution by emission source type for individual urban HAPs (hazardous air pollutants) and diesel particulate matter, 1996

SOURCE: "Figure 5-3. National contribution by emisssion source type for individual urban HAPs and diesel particulate matter, 1996," in *National Air Quality and Emissions Trends Report, 1999*, U.S. Environmental Protection Agency, Washington, DC. Report prepared by the Air Quality Trends Analysis Group, Research Triangle Park, NC, March 2001

fuel controls for mobile sources of toxics, and will finalize its decisions by 2004.

Figure 4.14 shows that major stationary sources, such as industrial facilities, are the primary sources of HAPs. Since the implementation of the 1990 Clean Air Act Amendments, the EPA has made considerable progress in reducing emissions of air toxics in stationary sources primarily via technology-based emissions standards. The EPA is currently assessing the need for additional stationary source standards.

The Clinton Administration expanded "right to know" initiatives, which are environmental programs designed to inhibit pollution, not with legislation and regulation, but by exposing polluters to pressure from a well-informed public. One of these initiatives is the Sector Facility Indexing Pro-

ject (SFIP), which was initiated by the EPA in early 1995. SFIP expands on the Toxics Release Inventory by providing data on the Internet in one location (http://www.epa.gov/oeca/sfi/) about 621 facilities in five industries: automobile, steel, metals, oil refining, and papermaking. In June 2001, data for 253 major federal facilities in the United States were added to SFIP. The environmental profiles of facilities include inspections, noncompliance, enforcement, pollution releases, and pollution spills. SFIP also includes information on the location of each facility and the population of the surrounding area.

AUTOMOBILES AND AIR POLLUTION

In the early 1950s, a California researcher studying the smog over Los Angeles made the first link between air

FIGURE 4.15

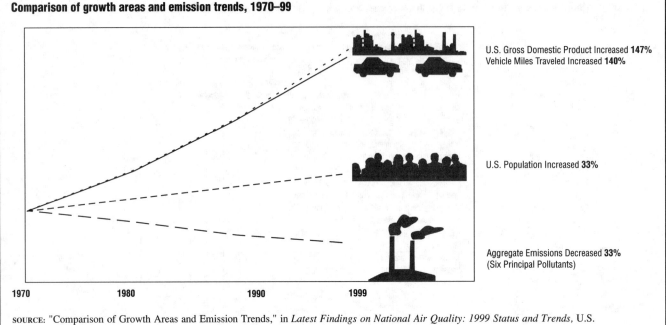

Comparison of growth areas and emission trends, 1970–99

U.S. Gross Domestic Product Increased **147%**
Vehicle Miles Traveled Increased **140%**

U.S. Population Increased **33%**

Aggregate Emissions Decreased **33%**
(Six Principal Pollutants)

1970   1980   1990   1999

SOURCE: "Comparison of Growth Areas and Emission Trends," in *Latest Findings on National Air Quality: 1999 Status and Trends*, U.S. Environmental Protection Agency, Washington, DC, August 2000

pollution and automobiles. Since that initial discovery, the federal government has set standards to bring down levels of automobile emissions.

In 1970 Congress enacted the Clean Air Act, which gave the EPA broad responsibility for regulating motor vehicle pollution. The law called for a 90 percent reduction in auto emissions. In response to these standards, the auto industry developed new emission control technologies. For example, by 1971, auto manufacturers developed charcoal canisters to trap gasoline vapors. Exhaust gas recirculation valves, which reduced nitrogen dioxide emissions, appeared in cars by 1972. And by 1975, the first generation of catalytic converters were in use. Catalytic converters cut down on emissions of VOCs (hydrocarbons) and carbon monoxide. Unleaded gasoline was introduced that same year, which reduced lead emissions.

In 1985 the EPA adopted stringent emission standards for diesel-powered trucks and buses. These standards took effect in 1991 and 1994. In 1990 the Clean Air Act Amendments required further reduction in VOC, carbon monoxide, nitrogen dioxide, and particulate emissions. The Clean Air Act Amendments also developed programs aimed at reducing pollution from cars by such approaches as more stringent emission testing procedures, new vehicle technologies, and clean fuels programs.

The Clean Air Act and the resultant response from the auto industry have had a tremendous effect on reducing automobile emissions. Figure 4.15 shows that between 1970 and 1999, total emissions of the six criteria air pollu-

tants fell about 30 percent while vehicle miles traveled increased 140 percent. However, millions of vehicles still pollute the air. Some experts believe that additional efforts are needed to eliminate emissions further, by promoting alternative fuels for cars and alternative transportation, such as mass transit systems, carpools, and bicycles.

**Reducing Emissions and Energy Use—
The CAFE Standards**

In addition to reducing emissions, a governmental goal is to conserve energy and reduce America's dependence on foreign oil. In 1973 the Organization of Petroleum Exporting Countries (OPEC) imposed an oil embargo that reminded America how dependent it had become on foreign sources of fuel. In 1972, the year before the embargo, the United States had consumed 31 percent of the world's oil, and depended on foreign sources—particularly the Middle East—for 28 percent of that oil. As a result of the embargo, and in an effort to make the United States less dependent on foreign oil, Congress passed the 1975 Automobile Fuel Efficiency Act, which set the initial Corporate Average Fuel Efficiency (CAFE) standards.

The CAFE standards required each domestic automaker to increase the average fuel economy of its new cars each year, until achieving 27.5 miles per gallon (mpg) by 1985. In the aftermath of the Persian Gulf War in the early 1990s, another strong reminder of U.S. dependence on foreign oil, some members of Congress wanted to raise the CAFE standards by as much as 40 percent, to 45 mpg for cars and 35 mpg for light trucks. Those in favor of raising the standards claimed that it would save about 2.8 million barrels of oil a day. They also noted that if cars became even more fuel-efficient, emissions of carbon dioxide would be significantly reduced. Carbon dioxide has been identified as the main "greenhouse" gas that contributes to global warming. This gas (and other greenhouse gases) trap some of the outgoing energy, retaining heat like the glass panels of a greenhouse.

Opponents to raising CAFE standards believe that the congressional fuel economy campaign would saddle American motorists with car features they would not like and would not buy. They also pointed out that the only way to additionally raise fuel efficiency levels is to manufacture much smaller cars and trucks and to limit the number of larger vehicles. They claim smaller cars would raise the numbers of highway deaths and injuries, limit consumer choice of larger and family-sized vehicles, and place thousands of auto-related jobs at risk. Thus far, legislators have not passed further legislation to increase CAFE standards. The required efficiency standards are still being met, but average fuel efficiency has not increased much beyond the standards. In contrast, the European Commission (the executive board of the European Union, a league of European countries) has proposed an ambitious target of 47 mpg for gasoline-driven European cars (compared to the current average of 29 mpg) and 52 mpg for diesel-powered European cars by 2005.

In recent years, passenger cars have been losing market share to sport utility vehicles (SUVs). Because SUVs are classified as light trucks, they are subject to a less stringent fuel economy standard of 20.7 mpg. Additionally, SUVs and light trucks fall under less stringent emissions standards and are allowed to emit three times more nitrogen dioxide than cars. However, in December 1999, the EPA announced tougher pollution regulations on new cars, including sport utility vehicles, minivans, and light trucks, which together currently account for half the new vehicles sold. The regulations are aimed at slashing tailpipe releases by 90 percent by 2009 and reducing sulfur in gasoline by 90 percent. The regulations will take effect with 2004 model cars.

Reducing Emissions and Energy Use—Alternative Fuels

The use of alternative non-petroleum-based fuels is becoming an increasingly popular way to reduce vehicle emissions and overall energy use. The U.S. Department of Energy (DOE) defines alternative fuels as those that are substantially non-petroleum, yield energy security (lower our dependence on foreign oil), and yield environmental benefits. The DOE currently recognizes the following as alternative fuels: methanol and denatured ethanol (which are both mixed with gasoline to yield a fuel containing no less than 70 percent alcohol), natural gas (compressed or

TABLE 4.6

Characteristics of alternative transportation fuels

	Compressed Natural Gas (CNG)	Ethanol (E85)	Liquefied Natural Gas (LNG)	Liquefied Petroleum Gas (LPG)
Chemical Structure	CH_4	CH_3CH_2OH	CH_4	C_3H_8
Primary Components	Methane	Denatured ethanol and gasoline	Methane that is cooled cryogenically	Propane
Main Fuel Source	Underground reserves	Corn, grains or agricultural waste	Underground reserves	A by-product of petroleum refining or natural gas processing
Energy Content per Gallon	29,000 Btu	80,460 Btu	73,500 Btu	84,000 Btu
Energy Ratio Compared to Gasoline	3.94 to 1 or 25% at 3000 psi	1.42 to 1 or 70%	1.55 to 1 or 66%	1.36 to 1 or 74%
Liquid or Gas	Gas	Liquid	Liquid	Liquid

SOURCE:"What are the current characteristics of the alternative fuels?," in *Alternative Fuels Data Center: Frequently Asked Questions,* U.S. Department of Energy, Office of Transportation Technology, Alternative Fuels Data Center, Washington, DC [Online] http://www.afdc.nrel.gov/questions.html [accessed October, 2001]

liquefied), liquefied petroleum gas, hydrogen, coal-derived liquid fuels, fuels derived from biological materials, and electricity (including solar energy). The characteristics of alternative fuels are shown in Table 4.6.

All the alternative fuels recognized by the DOE reduce ozone-forming tailpipe emissions. Additionally, compressed natural gas vehicles show an estimated 80 percent reduction in combined carbon monoxide and nitrogen dioxide emissions from reformulated gasoline-powered vehicles; liquefied natural gas vehicles show an estimated 60 percent reduction; methanol vehicles show an estimated 40 percent reduction; and ethanol vehicles show an estimated 25 percent reduction. (Reformulated gasoline is gas that has been blended to reduce emissions and smog formation from emissions.)

According to Department of Energy projections, there were expected to be about 456,000 alternative-fuel vehicles on American roads in 2001. Since 1992 the number of alternative-fueled vehicles has nearly doubled. Table 4.7 shows the estimated number of alternative-fueled vehicles in use in the United States, by fuel, from 1992 to 2001.

ETHANOL. To help reduce the nation's dependence on imported oil, Congress enacted the National Defense Authorization Act in 1991. The law includes a provision directing federal agencies to purchase gasohol when it is available at prices equal to or lower than those of gasoline.

TABLE 4.7

Estimated number of alternative-fueled vehicles in use, by fuel, 1992–2001

Fuel	1992	1993	1994	1995	1996	1997	1998	1999	2000	2001
Liquefied Petroleum Gases (LPG)[a]	221,000	269,000	264,000	259,000	263,000	263,000	266,000	267,000	268,000	*269,000*
Compressed Natural Gas (CNG)	23,191	32,714	41,227	50,218	60,144	68,571	78,782	89,556	100,530	*109,730*
Liquefied Natural Gas (LNG)	90	299	484	603	663	813	1,172	1,681	1,900	*2,039*
Methanol, 85 Percent (M85)[b]	4,850	10,263	15,484	18,319	20,265	21,040	19,648	18,964	18,365	*16,918*
Methanol, Neat (M100)	404	414	415	386	172	172	200	198	195	*184*
Ethanol, 85 Percent (E85)[b c]	172	441	605	1,527	4,536	9,130	12,788	22,464	34,680	*48,022*
Ethanol, 95 Percent (E95)[b]	38	27	33	136	361	347	14	14	13	*13*
Electricity	1,607	1,690	2,224	2,860	3,280	4,453	5,243	6,964	8,661	*10,400*
Non-LPG Subtotal	**30,352**	**45,848**	**60,472**	**74,049**	**89,421**	**104,526**	**117,847**	**139,841**	**164,344**	***187,306***
Total	**251,352**	**314,848**	**324,472**	**333,049**	**352,421**	**367,526**	**383,847**	**406,841**	**432,344**	***456,306***

[a] Values are rounded to thousands. Accordingly, these estimates are not equal to the sum of Federal fleet data (for which exact counts are available) and non-Federal fleet estimates (rounded to thousands).
[b] The remaining portion of 85-percent methanol and both ethanol fuels is gasoline.
[c] In 1997, some vehicle manufacturers began including E85-fueling capability in certain model lines of vehicles. For 1999, the EIA estimated that the number of E-85 vehicles that are capable of operating on E85, gasoline, or both, is 725,464. Many of these AFVs are sold and used as traditional gasoline-powered vehicles. In this table, alternative fuel vehicles (AFV's) in use include only those E85 vehicles believed to be intended for use as alternative-fuel vehicles (AFV's). These are primarily fleet-operated vehicles.

Note: Estimates for 1999 are revised. Estimates for 2000 are preliminary and estimates for 2001, in italics, are based on plans or projections.

SOURCE: "Table 1. Estimated Number of Alternative-Fueled Vehicles in Use in the United States, by Fuel, 1992–2001," in *Alternatives to Traditional Transportation Fuels 1999*, U.S. Department of Energy, Energy Information Administration, Washington, DC, 1999

Gasohol is made from a mixture of gasoline (90 percent) and ethanol (10 percent), often obtained by fermenting agricultural crops or crop wastes, or gasoline (97 percent) and methanol (3 percent), made commonly from natural gas or coal. Gasohol burns more slowly, coolly, and completely than gasoline, resulting in reduced emissions of some pollutants. However, gasohol has negative aspects. It vaporizes more readily than gasoline, potentially aggravating ozone pollution in warm weather. Ethanol-based gasohol can damage rubber seals, diaphragms, and certain finishes. Methanol-based gasohol is toxic and corrosive, and its emissions produce cancer-causing formaldehyde.

Nevertheless, federal agencies have taken a number of steps to encourage the use of gasohol. In 1991 Executive Order 12759 required federal agencies that operate more than 300 vehicles to reduce their gas consumption by 10 percent—an incentive to use gasohol. Despite these measures, however, use of gasohol has increased only slightly, mainly because gasohol costs more than gasoline and is sometimes unavailable due to the high cost of transporting and storing it. Most support for gasohol seems to come from farm states, where the main ingredients for ethanol are grown.

Fueling stations for gasohol and ethanol are hard to find. The National Ethanol Vehicle Coalition in Jefferson City, Missouri, now promotes the use of E85—which consists of 85 percent ethanol and 15 percent gasoline—but stations that sell ethanol are few and far between, and are concentrated in the Midwest. Nonetheless, the major American automobile manufacturers all produce flexible-fuel vehicles than can run on ethanol, gasoline, or a mixture of the two. These flex-fuel systems are available on several regular-production models.

NATURAL GAS AND PROPANE. Drivers who choose to use propane and natural gas as fuel for their vehicles face the same dilemma as ethanol users: where to find a pump? Experts believe that any fueling system needs a large customer base and that no one will buy cars that run on alternative fuel until a fueling system has been set up. Natural gas requires less refinery work than gas and is already distributed around the continental United States; it also burns cleaner than gasoline. However, the public has been slow to embrace it.

Compressed natural gas (CNG) fueling stations have been built across the country, but they are not yet commonplace. In 1999 there were only about 1,300 natural gas refueling stations in the country, compared with more than 200,000 gasoline stations. In some cases, local natural gas companies build the CNG stations; large companies that have their own fleet of natural gas vehicles build others. Still, it is difficult to sell CNG technology with few fueling stations, and even more difficult to establish a network of fueling stations without a mass market for the fuel. In spite of fueling station scarcity, the number of

CNG vehicles in the United States has grown from slightly over 23,000 in 1992 to a projected number of nearly 110,000 in 2001. (See Table 4.7.)

Propane, also called liquefied petroleum gas (LPG), has worked the best of any alternative fuel to date, but its growth has not been as dramatic as that of natural gas. Only 90 LPG vehicles were in use in the United States in 1992; that figure was expected to grow only to about 2,000 in 2001. (See Table 4.7.)

HYDROGEN. For decades, advocates of hydrogen have promoted it as the fuel of the future—abundant, clean, and cheap. Hydrogen researchers from universities, laboratories, and private companies claim their industry has already produced vehicles that could be ready to market if problems of fuel supply and distribution could be solved. Other experts contend that economics and safety concerns may limit hydrogen's wider use for decades.

ELECTRIC VEHICLES. In the early days of the automobile, electric cars outnumbered internal-combustion vehicles. With the introduction of technology for producing low-cost gasoline, however, electric vehicles fell out of favor. But as cities became choked with air pollution, the idea of an efficient electric car once again emerged. In order to make it acceptable to the public, however, several considerations had to be addressed: How many miles could an electric car be driven before needing to be recharged? How light would the vehicle need to be? And could the car keep up with the speed and driving conditions of busy freeways and highways?

In 1993 tax breaks became available for people who buy cars that run on alternative energy sources; these breaks are especially generous for purchasers of electric cars. The breaks are intended to compensate for the price difference between electric cars and the average gas-powered car, and to jump-start production of these vehicles. By 2003, 10 percent of all new cars offered for sale in California must be zero-emission vehicles. New York, Massachusetts, Maine, and Vermont each have similar laws, all set to take effect in 2003.

Electric vehicles (EVs) come in three types: battery-powered; fuel cell; and hybrids, which are powered by both an electric motor and a small conventional engine. EV1, a two-seater by General Motors (GM), was the first commercially available electric car. In 1999 GM introduced its second-generation EV1, the Gen II. It uses a lead-acid battery pack and has a driving range of approximately 95 miles. The Gen II is also offered with an optional nickel-metal hydride battery pack, which increases its range to 130 miles. Ford is currently producing a Ford Ranger in an EV model. EV drivers have a charger installed at their home, allowing them to recharge the car overnight. There are also some public places where rechargers are available.

Fuel cell electric vehicles use an electrochemical process that converts a fuel's energy into usable electricity. Some experts think that, in the future, vehicles driven by fuel cells could replace vehicles with combustion engines. Fuel cells produce very little sulfur and nitrogen dioxide, and generate less than half the carbon dioxide of internal-combustion engines. Rather than needing to be recharged, they are simply refueled. Hydrogen, natural gas, methanol, and gasoline can all be used with a fuel cell.

DaimlerChrysler's Mercedes-Benz division has produced the first prototype fuel-cell car. The NECAR4 produces zero emissions and runs on liquid hydrogen. The hydrogen must be kept cold at all times, which makes the design impractical for widespread use. However, they will soon have another model, which runs on methanol and should be more practical. The NECAR4 travels 280 miles on a full 11-gallon tank. The prototype was introduced in 1999, and consumers may be able to purchase a production version by 2004.

Ecostar, an alliance between Ford, DaimlerChrysler, and Ballard Power Systems, is working on developing new fuel cells to power vehicles. Other automakers have experimented with fuel-cell prototype cars as well, but these vehicles are not yet commercially available. They are expected to be on the roads by 2004.

Hybrid cars have both an electric motor and a small internal-combustion engine. A sophisticated computer system automatically shifts from using the electric motor to the gas engine, as needed, for optimum driving. The electric motor is recharged while the car is driving and braking. Because the gasoline engine does only part of the work, the car gets very good fuel economy. The engine is also designed for ultra-low emissions.

As of 2001 there are two hybrids on the market in the United States: the Toyota Prius, a comfortable sedan with front and back seating; and the two-passenger Honda Insight. Both cars were sold in Japan for several years before being introduced to the U.S. market. Ford has created a hybrid SUV, the Ford Escape, which will be available in 2003.

Mandating the Use of Alternative Fuel Vehicles (AFVs)

The Energy Policy Act of 1992, which passed in the wake of the 1991 Persian Gulf War, required that federal and state governments and fleet owners increase the percentages of vehicles powered by alternative fuels. The fleet requirements affect those who own or control at least 50 vehicles in the United States and fleets of at least 20 vehicles that are centrally fueled or capable of being centrally fueled within a metropolitan area of 250,000 or more. (Table 4.8 shows the percentages of new vehicle purchases that must be AFVs.) In doing so, many municipal governments and the U.S. Postal Service have put into

TABLE 4.8

Percentage of new fleet light duty vehicle acquisitions that must be AFVs (Alternative Fuel Vehicles), 1997–2006

Year	Federal	State	Alternative Fuel Provider	Municipal and Private*
1997	33%	10%	30%	
1998	50%	15%	50%	
1999	75%	25%	70%	
2000	75%	50%	90%	
2001	75%	75%	90%	
2002	75%	75%	90%	20%
2003	75%	75%	90%	40%
2004	75%	75%	90%	60%
2005	75%	75%	90%	70%
2006	75%	75%	90%	70%

*Percentages listed for municipal and private fleets are tentative; there are currently no mandates under EPAct.

SOURCE: *EPAct/Clean Fuel Fleet Program Fact Sheet,* U.S. Department of Energy, Office of Transportation Technologies, September 1998

operation fleets of natural gas and electric vehicles, such as garbage trucks, transit buses, and postal vans.

AIRPLANES AND AIR POLLUTION

As air travel in affluent nations rose, it caused a number of environmental problems. The average American flew 1,739 miles a year by 2000. Europeans, though they flew fewer miles, had the world's most crowded skies, while the world's most rapid growth in flying took place in Asia.

Flying carries an environmental price; it is the most energy-intensive form of transport. In much of the industrialized world, air travel is replacing more energy-efficient rail or bus travel. Despite a rise in fuel efficiency of jet engines, jet fuel consumption has risen 65 percent since 1970.

Another problem with air travel is its impact on global warming due to aircraft emissions of nitrogen oxide. Results from a study of ten regional areas by the EPA's Office of Mobile Sources show that in 1990, for nitrogen oxide, the aircraft component of the regional mobile source emissions ranged from 0.6 percent to 3.6 percent. The projected nitrogen oxide emissions for 2010 range from 1.9 percent to 10.4 percent of the regional mobile source emissions (*Evaluation of Air Pollutant Emissions from Subsonic Commercial Jet Aircraft,* 1999). The Intergovernmental Panel on Climate Change (IPCC) notes that greenhouse gas emissions deposited in the upper atmosphere do greater harm than those released at the earth's surface.

In 1998 Pratt and Whitney announced plans to introduce a radical new engine design that would be cleaner, more efficient, and more reliable than conventional designs. The new engine, expected to enter service in 2002, would reduce emissions by 40 percent and would be much quieter than airplane engines now in service. The engine is designed for use on single-aisle planes carrying 120 to 180 passengers, such as the Boeing 737 or the Airbus A320.

There is also a movement toward action on other engines in the airline industry—those in trucks, cars, and carts that service airplane fleets. The Electric Power Research Institute launched a research study in 1993 to show that the use of electric vehicles can significantly reduce total airport emissions. In mid-1998, at the completion of the study, researchers concluded that the use of electric vehicles and equipment at airports was an economically and environmentally viable method for reducing current airport emissions or for offsetting future emissions. Many large airports, such as Los Angeles International, San Francisco International, and Dallas/Fort Worth have already replaced or currently are replacing high-pollution ground vehicles with zero-emission (electric) vehicles.

BOATS AND AIR POLLUTION

Boat engines have not changed much since the 1930s. Running an outboard motor for an hour is estimated to pollute as much as driving 800 miles. In 1996 the Environmental Protection Agency (EPA) adopted standards to slash emissions from boats and other water vehicles, such as jet skis, which on some days in some places, according to the EPA, can account for up to 15 percent of total smog. The new standards set a goal of a 75 percent emissions reduction by 2006. Under the new regulations, engine prices have risen approximately 14 percent, but these new engines will make up some of this extra funding by using less gas.

In 1998 air-quality regulators in California proposed state rules tougher than federal standards to limit emissions from personal watercraft and motorboats. California is the nation's second largest boating state after Michigan.

THE CLEAN AIR ACT—A HUGE SUCCESS

In 1970 the U.S. Congress passed the landmark Clean Air Act (CAA), proclaiming that it would restore urban air quality. It was no coincidence that the law was passed during a 14-day Washington, D.C., smog alert. Although the CAA has had mixed results and many goals still have not been met, most experts credit it with making great strides toward cleaning up the air (United States General Accounting Office, *Air Pollution: Status of Implementation and Issues of the Clean Air Act Amendments of 1990,* 2000). Since its adoption, airborne lead has declined 90 percent, primarily due to the reduced sale of leaded gasoline, and most other measured emissions have also decreased. Los Angeles, for example, while still far from attaining air quality standards, has cleaner air than at any time since measurements were first taken in the 1940s.

Nationwide, more than half the areas not meeting standards for ozone in 1990 did so by the year 2000, as did two-thirds of the areas not attaining carbon monoxide standards in 1990.

The Clean Air Act Amendments of 1990

The overall goal of the Clean Air Act Amendments of 1990 was to reduce the pollutants in the air by 56 billion pounds a year—224 pounds for every man, woman, and child in America—when the law is fully phased in by the year 2005. Other aims were to cut acid precipitation in half by the year 2000, reduce smog and other pollutants, and protect the ozone layer by phasing out chlorofluorocarbons (CFCs) and related chemicals.

The Economic Value of the Clean Air Act and Its Amendments

In *The Benefits and Costs of the Clean Air Act, 1970 to 1990* (1997), the first report mandated by the CAA on the monetary costs and benefits of controlling pollution, the EPA concluded that the economic value of clean air programs was 42 times greater than the total costs of air pollution control over the 20-year period. The study found numerous positive economic consequences in the U.S. economy because of CAA programs and regulations. The CAA affected industrial production, investment, productivity, consumption, employment, and economic growth. In fact, the study estimated total agricultural benefits from the CAA at almost 10 billion dollars. The EPA compared benefits to direct costs or expenditures. The total costs of the CAA were $523 billion for the 20-year period; total benefits equaled $22.2 trillion—a net benefit of approximately $21.7 trillion.

The National Conference of State Legislatures, in its *Two Decades of Clean Air: EPA Assesses Costs and Benefits* (1998), used data from the EPA analysis and found that the Act produced major reductions in pollution that caused illness and disease, smog, acid rain, haze, and damage to the environment.

The second mandated review of the CAA, *The Benefits and Costs of the Clean Air Act Amendments of 1990* (2000), the most comprehensive and thorough review of the CAA's amendments ever conducted, found similar results. Using a sophisticated array of computer models and the latest cost data, the EPA found that by 2010 the Act will have prevented 23,000 Americans from dying prematurely and averted more than 1.7 million asthma attacks. The CAA will prevent 67,000 episodes of acute bronchitis, 91,000 occurrences of shortness of breath, 4.1 million lost work days, and 31 million days in which Americans would have had to restrict activity because of illness. Another 22,000 respiratory-related hospital admissions will be averted, as well as 42,000 admissions for heart disease and 4,800 emergency room visits.

The EPA estimated that the benefits of CAA amendment programs totaled about $110 billion in reduction of illness and premature death. The study found that the costs of achieving these benefits were only about $27 billion, a fraction of the value of the benefits. In addition, the study reported that there were other benefits that scientists and economists cannot quantify and express in dollar terms, such as controlling cancer-causing air toxics and benefiting crops and ecosystems by reducing pollutants.

The Continuing Problem of Ozone and Particulates

The CAA requires the EPA to review public health standards at least every five years to ensure that they reflect the best current science. In 1997, in response to what many consider compelling scientific evidence of the harm caused by ozone and fine particles to human health, the EPA issued new, stricter air quality standards for ozone and particulate matter.

This was the first revision in ozone standards in 20 years and the first-ever standard for fine particulates. The provisions tightened the standard for ground-level ozone from the level of 0.12 parts per million (ppm) at the highest daily measurement to 0.08 ppm average over an eight-hour period. The new particulate matter standard included particles larger than 2.5 microns in diameter instead of the original standard of those larger than 10 microns.

In May 1999 a three-judge federal appeals panel overturned the new standards. The EPA appealed, but in October 1999 the full U.S. Court of Appeals for the District of Columbia refused to overturn the decision. Finally, in February 2001, the Supreme Court returned a unanimous decision reaffirming the federal government's authority to set clean air standards. The court ordered the EPA to adopt a more reasonable interpretation for enforcing ozone standards in some areas, but they agreed that the agency has the right to enforce the stringent regulations set in 1997.

Despite improvements in ozone levels, few large urban areas in the United States comply with ozone standards. (See Figure 4.1 and Table 4.2.) Under the proposed standard, many smaller population centers would also become noncompliant, and states will be forced to take further pollution control measures to comply.

THE COST OF CUTTING EMISSIONS FURTHER

In the United States, an increasing problem in the effort to reduce air pollution further is that most of the "cheap fixes" have already been made. Many economists argue that the expensive ones may not be worth the price. The very premise that air pollution can be reduced to levels at which it no longer poses any health risk is now being questioned by some academics as well as by industry analysts.

Virtually all gains in the war on ozone have been achieved by reducing auto emissions. The costs for future air quality improvements may exceed, from some points of view, the value of any improvement, and the disparity may only get worse over time. For example, by 1994 the tailpipe pollution standard had reduced the exhaust of volatile organic compounds (VOCs) by 98 percent. Reducing the figure by a total of 99.5 percent will at least double the cost.

Some "cheap fixes" are still available, however. The steps by the EPA in 1999 to toughen pollution regulations on new cars, including sport utility vehicles, minivans, and light trucks, will help improve air quality when the regulations take effect with 2004 model cars. Other possible improvements could come from changes in "grandfather" clauses, loopholes that exempt companies from compliance with laws because the companies existed prior to the law. Power plants rank first in grandfathered emissions. Other top industries affected by grandfather clauses include aluminum smelters and oil refineries.

REDUCING MANY POLLUTANTS BUT MISSING SOME

Progress in cutting air pollution in the United States has been uneven. Although reductions in emissions of all six criteria pollutants have occurred, carbon dioxide (CO_2) emissions continue to rise. Carbon dioxide is not a criteria pollutant, but it is a major greenhouse gas that contributes to global warming.

The equilibrium of CO_2 in the atmosphere has been altered since the Industrial Revolution, which began in the United States in the early 1800s. Since that time, atmospheric concentrations of carbon dioxide have risen about 28 percent, principally because of fossil fuel combustion (the burning of fuels such as gasoline and coal).

Carbon dioxide emissions from fossil fuel combustion have gone up even within the last decade. From 1990 to 1999, emissions of CO_2 from fossil fuel combustion increased at an average annual rate of 1.4 percent. Of the total carbon dioxide emissions in 1999, fossil fuel combustion accounted for 98 percent (EPA, Office of Atmospheric Programs, *Inventory of U.S. Greenhouse Gas Emissions and Sinks: 1990–1999*, 2001).

Fossil fuels produce energy when burned; they are used predominantly in the United States to fuel industrial processes and automobiles, to provide heat in homes, and to generate electricity. In fact, 84 percent of the energy needs of Americans in 1999 was supplied by the burning of fossil fuels. Of the fossil fuels, petroleum supplied the largest share of U.S. energy demands, accounting for an average of 39 percent of total energy consumption from 1990 through 1999. Natural gas and coal followed, accounting for averages of 24 and 23 percent of total ener-gy consumption, respectively. Most petroleum was consumed in transportation, while the vast majority of coal was used by electric utilities, and natural gas was consumed largely in industries and residences (EPA, Office of Atmospheric Programs, *Inventory of U.S. Greenhouse Gas Emissions and Sinks: 1990–1999*, 2001).

When fossil fuels are burned to supply energy, pollutants beyond carbon dioxide are created. Some of these have been missed by governmental controls. Electrostatic precipitators (electrical cleaning systems) and filters, which have been designed to control emissions from power plants, do nothing about gaseous emissions. Additionally, sulfur dioxide scrubbers, which use a spray of water or reactant to trap pollutants and remove 95 percent of the sulfur dioxide emissions from smoke stacks, create scrubber ash, a hazardous waste. (Scrubbers also do nothing to control carbon dioxide emissions.)

Although a car built today produces only one-tenth the pollution per mile traveled as one built two decades ago, fuel efficiency standards have not been tightened in years, Americans are buying less-efficient vehicles, and total miles traveled increase each year. This is just the opposite of what was promised at the 1992 United Nations Conference on the Environment in Rio de Janeiro (also known as the Rio Earth Summit). The U.S. goal of reducing carbon dioxide emissions to 1990 levels by 2000, as agreed at the Conference, was not reached. Other industrialized nations also fell short of this voluntary treaty goal.

The 1997 Kyoto Global Warming Treaty

In December 1997 the United Nations convened a 160-nation conference on global warming in Kyoto, Japan, in hopes of producing a new treaty on climate change that would place binding caps on industrial emissions. Participants hoped to ratify the treaty and have it enacted in 2002, the 10th anniversary of the Rio Earth Summit. At the time of this writing, ratification of the treaty was tenuous.

The treaty, called the Kyoto Protocol to the United Nations Framework Convention on Climate Change (or simply the Kyoto Protocol), binds industrialized nations to reducing their emissions of six greenhouse gases below 1990 levels by 2012, with each country having a different target. The six greenhouse gases are: carbon dioxide, methane, nitrogen oxide, hydrofluorocarbons, sulfur dioxides, and perfluorocarbons. Under the terms of initial drafts of the treaty, the United States must cut emissions by 7 percent, most European nations by 8 percent, and Japan by 6 percent. Reductions must begin by 2008 and be achieved by 2012. Developing nations are not required to make such pledges.

The United States had proposed a program of voluntary pledges by developing nations, but that section was deleted, as was a tough system of enforcement. Instead, each country decides for itself how to achieve its goal. The treaty provides market-driven tools, such as buying and selling credits, for reducing emissions. It also sets up a Clean Development Fund to help provide poorer nations with technology to reduce their emissions.

Although it is the first time nations have made such sweeping pledges, many sources expect difficulty in getting ratification. In the United States, President Bill Clinton signed the Protocol but the Senate did not ratify it. Business leaders believe the treaty goes too far, while environmentalists believe standards do not go far enough. Some experts doubt that any action emerging from Kyoto will be sufficient to prevent the doubling of greenhouse gases. Representatives of the oil industry and business community contend the treaty will spell economic hardship for the United States. The fossil-fuel industry and conservative politicians portray the Protocol as unworkable and too costly to the American economy.

By 2001 the Kyoto Protocol was near collapse. However, diplomats from 178 nations met in Bonn, Germany in July 2001 and drafted a compromise to preserve the global-warming treaty. U.S. President George W. Bush stood firm on rejecting the Kyoto Protocol and characterized it as "fatally flawed," stating that implementing it would harm the economy and unfairly require only the industrial nations to cut emissions.

To take effect, the treaty must be ratified by 55 of the nations responsible for 55 percent of industrialized nations' carbon dioxide emissions in 1990. In October 2001, 2,000 delegates from 160 countries began 12 days of talks in Marrakesh, Morocco, aimed at completing a final draft of the Kyoto Protocol. However, without the United States' ratification of the treaty, the only way it could be ratified is if Japan agrees. Public opinion in Japan is strongly in favor of the Protocol, but Japan feels that it would be at an economic disadvantage if it ratifies the treaty and incurs costs not shared by American industries (if the United States does not ratify the treaty as well).

Although President Bush has rejected the Kyoto Protocol, he has promised to address the issues of greenhouse gas emissions and global warming. Thus far, he has proposed studying the problem and funding new technologies to reduce carbon dioxide emissions.

Fossil Fuel Use in the Developing World

Environmental pollution is worldwide and environmental problems are expected to become increasingly regional and global in the future. Evidence mounts that human activities—especially the production of gases from the combustion of coal, oil, and natural gas—may be causing atmospheric warming worldwide. Developing countries stand on the brink of economic growth, but that explosion of growth will undoubtedly be fueled by fossil fuels, as was the case in America and Europe decades earlier. The filthiest smoke and water generally arise in the early stages of industrialization.

China, especially, faces a dilemma—coal harms the environment but it just as surely fuels economic growth. China's heavy reliance on coal, along with its inefficient and wasteful patterns of energy use, will make it the largest single producer of carbon dioxide by 2020, surpassing even the United States. Between 1970 and 1990, energy consumption in China rose 208 percent, compared with an average rise of 28 percent in developed countries during the same period. More than 5 million Chinese participate in coal extraction, feeding China's enormous and growing appetite for energy.

Five of China's largest cities are among the world's ten most polluted cities. Polluted air reportedly kills 178,000 Chinese people prematurely each year, primarily from emphysema and bronchitis. Children with sooty faces dodge traffic; rain brings rivers of black flowing down city streets.

China's situation is repeated, on a lesser scale, in India, Brazil, and the rest of the developing world, where meeting environmental goals is considered a rich country's luxury. Chinese officials believe, as do officials in many other developing nations, that developed countries cause 80 percent of the world's pollution. Chinese leadership believes the developed nations should be held responsible for the problems and, as a result, should help pay for cleaner coal-burning technologies in the third world, as well as financing hydroelectric plants, nuclear power stations, and alternative energy sources.

In India, the country's residents have adjusted to living in a haze of dust and fumes. In December 2000 the World Health Organization reported that the level of microscopic particles in the air was nearly seven times the amount the organization deems healthy. On the streets, pedestrians use handkerchiefs or saris (wrapped garments worn by some Indian women) to cover their faces in protection from airborne pollutants. In 1994 the Indian Supreme Court ruled that cars sold in the largest cities must run on unleaded fuel and have catalytic converters. But unleaded fuel is expensive and hard to find—less than 1 percent of the fuel sold in New Delhi, India's capital, is unleaded. Inefficient two-wheeled scooters spew out much pollution and, with 400 new scooters added every day in New Delhi alone, the air quality continues to deteriorate.

INDOOR AIR QUALITY

Although most people think of the outdoor air when they think of air pollution, recent studies have shown that indoor environments are not necessarily safe havens from air pollution. In fact, certain pollutants are often found in greater concentrations indoors than out. This fact is especially important

FIGURE 4.16

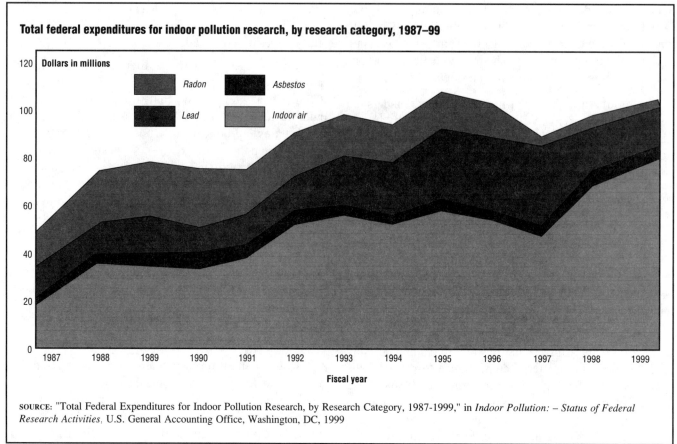

Total federal expenditures for indoor pollution research, by research category, 1987–99

Dollars in millions

Legend: Radon, Asbestos, Lead, Indoor air

Fiscal year

SOURCE: "Total Federal Expenditures for Indoor Pollution Research, by Research Category, 1987-1999," in *Indoor Pollution: – Status of Federal Research Activities*, U.S. General Accounting Office, Washington, DC, 1999

since 90 percent of people's time is spent in indoor environments, including residences, workplaces, public transportation, and public and commercial establishments. Particularly vulnerable groups, such as infants, the elderly, and the ill, may be inside virtually all the time.

Modern indoor environments contain a variety of sources for pollution, including synthetic building materials, consumer products, and dust mites (microscopic insects that live on house dust and human skin residue). People, pets, and indoor plants also contribute to airborne pollution. Efforts to lower energy costs by tightly sealing and insulating buildings have increased the likelihood that pollutants will accumulate.

Reports of illness and allergy among building occupants have become commonplace. Scientific evidence suggests that respiratory diseases, allergies, mucous membrane irritation, nervous system defects, cardiovascular symptoms, reproductive problems, and lung cancer may be linked to exposure to indoor air pollution. Scientists consistently rank indoor air pollution among the top environmental health risks, although public opinion polls report that most Americans do not perceive the risks of indoor pollution to be great.

Providing healthful air quality is not only a complex scientific and technical issue, but also a complicated issue of public policy, in determining the proper role of the government in safeguarding people's health. For example, the EPA estimates that exposure of nonsmokers to cigarette smoke may cause as many as 3,000 lung-cancer deaths annually in the United States. It also contributes to a wide range of diseases, including asthma, pneumonia, and bronchitis, and incurs enormous expense in work-time loss and medical and insurance expenses.

The first legislation to deal specifically with indoor air quality was Title IV of the Superfund Amendments and Reauthorization Act of 1986, which called for the EPA to establish an advisory committee to conduct research and disseminate information. In October 1991 the General Accounting Office (GAO) reported on the progress of the legislation in *Indoor Air Pollution: Federal Efforts Are Not Effectively Addressing a Growing Problem*. The GAO concluded that not only was the EPA's emphasis on indoor pollution not commensurate with the health risks posed by the problem, but also that research had been, and would likely continue to be, constrained by lack of funding. Accordingly, the proposed Indoor Air Quality Act of 1991 was not enacted by Congress.

Federal agencies reported that they spent almost $1.1 billion on indoor-related research from 1987 through 1999. Most of that amount went toward indoor air

FIGURE 4.17

Total federal expenditures for indoor pollution research, by agency, 1987–1999

Dollars in millions

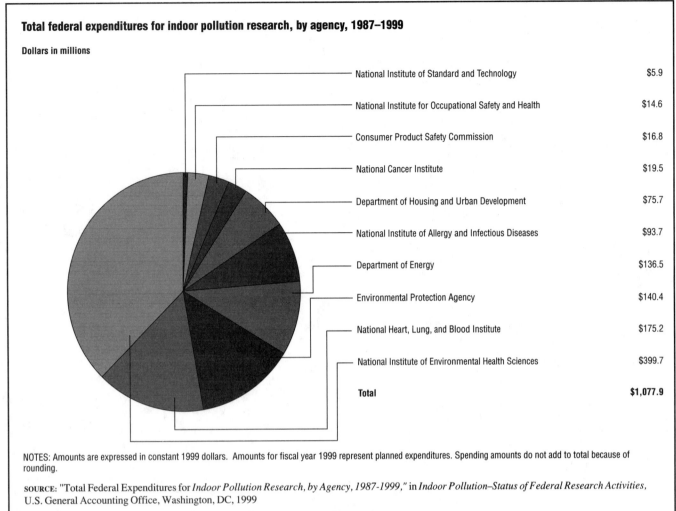

National Institute of Standard and Technology	$5.9
National Institute for Occupational Safety and Health	$14.6
Consumer Product Safety Commission	$16.8
National Cancer Institute	$19.5
Department of Housing and Urban Development	$75.7
National Institute of Allergy and Infectious Diseases	$93.7
Department of Energy	$136.5
Environmental Protection Agency	$140.4
National Heart, Lung, and Blood Institute	$175.2
National Institute of Environmental Health Sciences	$399.7
Total	**$1,077.9**

NOTES: Amounts are expressed in constant 1999 dollars. Amounts for fiscal year 1999 represent planned expenditures. Spending amounts do not add to total because of rounding.

SOURCE: "Total Federal Expenditures for *Indoor Pollution Research, by Agency, 1987-1999,"* in *Indoor Pollution–Status of Federal Research Activities,* U.S. General Accounting Office, Washington, DC, 1999

research, followed by studies of lead, radon, and asbestos in the indoor environment. (See Figure 4.16.) Figure 4.17 shows the federal agencies that participated in such research and their expenditures.

In 1999 the GAO once again reviewed the status of indoor air quality activities in its *Indoor Pollution: Status of Federal Research Activities,* its latest publication on this topic. It found that significant strides have been made in understanding the risks posed by chemicals and other contaminants commonly found in homes, offices, and schools. Nonetheless, it concluded that "many gaps and uncertainties remain in the assessment of exposures to known indoor pollutants." These gaps include specific sources of exposures; the magnitude of exposures; the relative role of specific exposures such as inhalation, ingestion, and skin contact; the nature, duration, and frequency of human activities that contribute to exposures; and the geographic distribution of exposures to certain pollutants for the U.S. population as a whole.

CHAPTER 5

POLLUTION OF SURFACE WATERS— OCEANS, ESTUARIES, LAKES, AND RIVERS

Water is as important to living things as the air they breathe. Water is also crucial to activities in industry, farming, fishing, and transportation, and provides opportunities for recreation. Since water plays critical roles in the lives of all Americans, it is extremely serious when our nation's waterways become polluted.

Polluted water is that which is unusable for its intended purposes. The U.S. Public Health Service classifies water pollutants into eight categories: (1) oxygen-demanding wastes, such as plant and animal material; (2) infectious agents, such as bacteria and viruses; (3) plant nutrients, such as fertilizers; (4) organic chemicals, such as pesticides; (5) inorganic chemicals, such as acids from coal mine drainage; (6) sediment from land erosion, such as clay silt on a stream bed; (7) radioactive substances, such as wastes from processing radioactive material; and (8) heat from industry, such as cooling water used in steam generation of electricity.

GROWTH AND POLLUTION

As America grew and cities increased in size, pollution became increasingly worse. In the 1800s and early 1900s, factories poured their wastes directly into rivers. Big cities, with huge amounts of waste, dumped their refuse onto the street, and later into big holes in the ground. (See Figure 1.1.) Pollution from that waste seeped into the ground water. Many cities poured their sewage directly into rivers. Other cities loaded their waste onto big barges that sailed out into the ocean and dumped the garbage and trash there.

Farmers, wanting to raise more food for the growing nation, used increased amounts of pesticides and fertilizers. When they watered their fields or when it rained, some of the pesticides and fertilizers ran off with the excess water into the lakes and rivers.

In cities, streets became coated with oil and other chemicals from cars and trucks. Homeowners used fertil-

TABLE 5.1

Pollution sources

Category	Examples
Industrial	Pulp and paper mills, chemical manufacturers, steel plants, metal process and product manufacturers, textile manufacturers, food processing plants
Municipal	Publicly owned sewage treatment plants that may receive indirect discharges from industrial facilities or businesses
Combined Sewer Overflows	Single facilities that treat both storm water and sanitary sewage, which may become overloaded during storm events and discharge untreated wastes into surface waters
Storm Sewers/Urban Runoff	Runoff from impervious surfaces including streets, parking lots, buildings, and other paved areas
Agricultural	Crop production, pastures, rangeland, feedlots, animal operations
Silvicultural	Forest management, tree harvesting, logging road construction
Construction	Land development, road construction
Resource Extraction	Mining, petroleum drilling, runoff from mine tailing sites
Land Disposal	Leachate or discharge from septic tanks, landfills, and hazardous waste sites
Hydrologic Modification	Channelization, dredging, dam construction, flow regulation
Habitat Modification	Removal of riparian vegetation, streambank modification, drainage/filling of wetlands

SOURCE: "Table 1-1. Pollution Source Categories Used in This Report," in *National Water Quality Inventory: 1998 Report to Congress,* Environmental Protection Agency, Washington, DC, 2000

izers to make their lawns grow. When it rained, some of the oil and fertilizer ran off with the rain into storm sewers. Melting snow also carried pollutants, including the salts used to melt ice on streets and roads, into storm sewers. Eventually, storm sewers emptied into rivers or lakes.

Water pollution is characterized by its composition (the eight types listed in the previous section), its source, and its fate. Table 5.1 lists sources of water pollution and

FIGURE 5.1

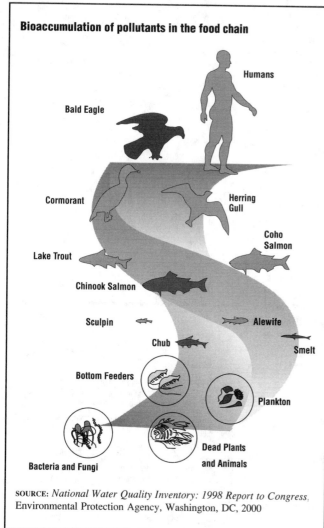

Bioaccumulation of pollutants in the food chain

Humans

Bald Eagle

Cormorant

Herring Gull

Coho Salmon

Lake Trout

Chinook Salmon

Sculpin

Alewife

Chub

Smelt

Bottom Feeders

Plankton

Bacteria and Fungi

Dead Plants and Animals

SOURCE: *National Water Quality Inventory: 1998 Report to Congress,* Environmental Protection Agency, Washington, DC, 2000

Water Pollution and Illness

CONTAMINATION OF FISH AND SHELLFISH BY METALS. Fish and shellfish (such as oysters, clams, shrimp, and lobsters) that live in polluted waters can become very dangerous to eat because of a concept called biomagnification. Biomagnification works like this: Many pollutants stick to aquatic vegetation and are readily stored in the fatty tissues of animals. As a result, as small fish and shellfish eat aquatic plants, and larger fish eat smaller fish and shellfish, and birds eat large fish, and humans eat birds and large fish, these pollutants accumulate in organisms in increasing concentrations as they move up the food chain. Figure 5.1 shows the movement of pollutants through the food chain.

Perhaps the most widely publicized case of a waterborne health hazard to humans resulting from biomagnification occurred in Minamata, Japan, in 1956. More than 600 people died and many others suffered severe neurological damage from eating shellfish contaminated with methyl mercury.

CONTAMINATION OF FISH AND SHELLFISH BY PATHOGENS. Over the past several years, dozens of people have contracted cholera after eating shellfish (such as oysters, clams, and mussels) from the coastal marshlands of southwestern Louisiana. In fact, it is not unusual to have three or four cases of cholera in Louisiana during the summer months. Table 5.2 lists pathogens (disease-causing organisms) and the swimming-associated illnesses they cause. Such illnesses cause dehydration, vomiting and, in extreme cases, collapse.

Although some pathogens are present naturally in marine waters, human activity has greatly increased their types and quantities. Human pathogens come mainly from discharges of raw sewage and from sewage sludge and wastewater outflow from sewage treatment plants, although they can enter marine waters directly through surface runoff. Viruses, bacteria, and protozoa can exist in marine environments for months or years. Concentrations of some intestinal viruses may be 10 to 10,000 times greater in coastal sediments than in other waters.

When states find dangerous pollutants in their fish or shellfish, they issue warnings for people to limit their consumption of or to stop eating fish or shellfish from certain lakes, rivers, and estuaries or from certain ocean waters. Figure 5.2 shows the number of advisories against eating fish and wildlife in each of the states in 1998. In 1998, 47 states, the District of Columbia, and American Samoa issued 2,506 advisories against eating fish from their waters, up from 2,196 in 1996. Mercury, PCBs, chlordane, dioxin, and DDT caused virtually all the advisories. (See Figure 5.3.) (Chlordane and DDT are pesticides; PCBs, or polychlorinated biphenyls, are toxic compounds used in hundreds of industrial and commercial applications.) Air

provides examples of each. The rest of this chapter will discuss the fate of water pollution: in which bodies of water pollutants are found.

THE NEED FOR POLLUTION CONTROL

People have always settled on the shores of oceans, lakes, and rivers. They establish homes, then towns, cities, and industries, benefiting from the many advantages of nearby sources of water. In the past, one of these advantages has been that lakes or rivers were convenient places to dispose of wastes. As industrialized societies developed, the amount of waste became enormous and contained synthetic and toxic materials that could not be assimilated by the waters' ecosystems. Millions of tons of sewage, pesticides, chemicals, and garbage were dumped into waterways until there were few in the United States and in other industrialized countries that were not polluted. Some were (and some remain) contaminated to the point of ecological "death"; that is, they were or are unable to sustain life. Additionally, some polluted waterways are a source of illness.

pollution is believed to be the most significant source of mercury contamination in these waters. The mercury is deposited in the water in rain, snow, fog, or dust particles. In 1996 only 12 of the 27 coastal states, plus one interstate commission, reported the extent of their waters affected by shellfish harvesting restrictions—more than 2,325 square miles. (See Table 5.3.)

PATHOGENS IN BEACH WATERS. Thousands of times each year, American beaches are closed to protect the public from disease-carrying organisms. But there are many coastal states that do not regularly monitor surf pollution, and millions of tourists may be unaware of whether it is safe to swim, boat, or fish at any given time or place. Even heavily visited beaches such as those in Key West and Miami Beach in Florida; Myrtle Beach, South Carolina; the Outer Banks of North Carolina; and Santa Barbara, California are inadequately protected. Currently, the federal government does not monitor beach water or require the states to do so.

Every summer since 1991, the Natural Resources Defense Council (NRDC), a not-for-profit environmental organization based in New York, has performed a nationwide survey of beach closings and beach water monitoring programs in coastal states. Its latest report, *Testing the Waters—A Guide to Water Quality at Vacation Beaches* (2001), found that during 2000 there were at least 11,270 days of closing and advisories at U.S. ocean, bay, Great Lakes, and some freshwater beaches, up from 6,160 in 1999. There were 48 extended closings and advisories (6–12 weeks), up from 23 in 1999, and 50 permanent closings and advisories (more than 12 weeks), up from 28 in 1999. Since 1988 there have been more than 47,426 closings and advisories and 185 extended closings and advisories. (See Table 5.4.)

The major causes of beach closings and advisories in 2000 were as follows:

- 85 percent were due to excessive bacteria levels.

- 8 percent were in response to a known pollution event, such as breaks in sewage pipes.

- 6 percent were precautionary, due to rain known to carry pollution into swimming waters.

- 2 percent were due to other causes, such as chemical spills, fish kills, strong waves, and red tides. (Red tides are caused by population explosions of fire algae in coastal waters. These organisms produce powerful toxins, or poisons.)

(The figures do not add up to 100 percent due to rounding.)

The major pollution sources responsible for the closings and advisories in 2000 included polluted runoff and storm water, sewage spills and overflows, and rain. Almost every coastal and Great Lakes state reported having at least one beach where storm water drains onto or near bathing beaches. California, Connecticut, Massachusetts, New Jersey, Florida, and Michigan had the most beaches with storm water pollution sources.

Despite the threat of pollution, many states with popular beach areas still do not have regular beach-monitoring programs. The NRDC found that only nine states—Connecticut, Delaware, Illinois, Indiana, New Hampshire, New Jersey, New York, North Carolina, and Ohio—monitor most or all of their beach waters weekly and notify the public. Other states monitor infrequently or monitor only a portion of their recreational beaches. Legislation passed by Congress in 2000 requires that states adopt EPA standards or the equivalent by 2004 for beach closings and advisories.

Coastal water pollution has a significant economic impact on coastal states. Failing to invest in clean waters costs states economic growth—jobs, job productivity, tourism, and property tax dollars. Beaches are popular vacation destinations in the United States, generating over $100 billion in revenues in 12 coastal states alone. Polluted waters cause economic losses both from swimming-related illnesses and the loss of beachgoers' use of beaches.

TABLE 5.2

Pathogens and swimming-related illnesses

Pathogenic Agent	Disease
Bacteria	
E. coli	Gastroenteritis
Salmonella typhi	Typhoid fever
Other salmonella species	Various enteric fevers (often called paratyphoid), gastroenteritis, septicemia (generalized infections in which organisms multiply in the bloodstream)
Shigella dysenteriae	Bacterial dysentery and other species
Vibrio cholera	Cholera
Viruses	
Rotavirus	Gastroenteritis
Norwalkvirus	Gastroenteritis
Poliovirus	Poliomyelitis
Coxsackievirus (some strains)	Various, including severe respiratory diseases, fevers, rashes, paralysis, aseptic meningitis, myocarditis
Echovirus	Various, similar to coxsackievirus (evidence is not definitive except in experimental animals)
Adenovirus	Respiratory and gastrointestinal infections
Hepatitis	Infectious hepatitis (liver malfunction), also may affect kidneys and spleen
Protozoa	
Cryptosporidium	Gastroenteritis
Giardia lambia	Diarrhea (intestinal parasite)
Entamoeba histolytica	Amoebic dysentery, infections of other organs
Isospora belli and Isospora hominus	Intestinal parasites, gastrointestinal infection
Balantidium coli	Dysentery, intestinal ulcers

SOURCE: Mark Dorfman, "Table 4: Pathogens and Swimming-Related Illnesses," in *Testing the Waters XI: A Guide to Beach Water Quality at Vacation Beaches,* Natural Resources Defense Council, New York, NY, August 2001

FIGURE 5.2

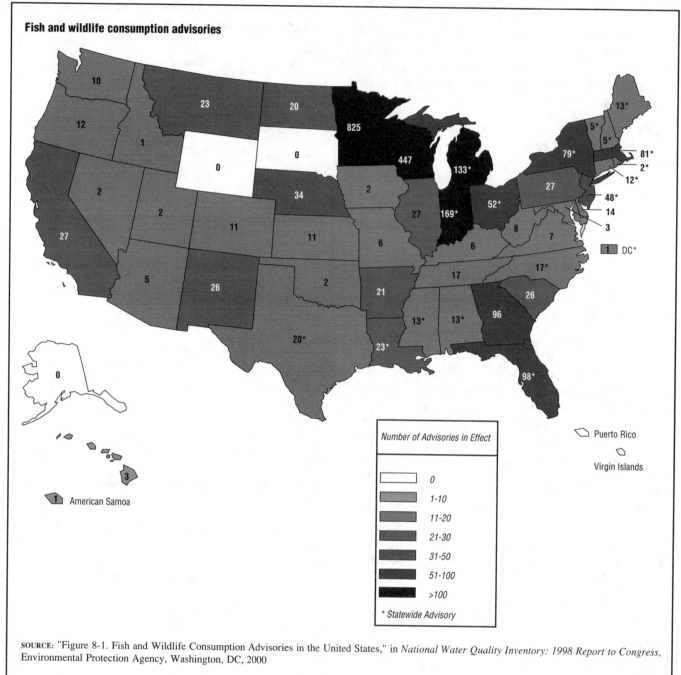

Fish and wildlife consumption advisories

Number of Advisories in Effect

☐	0
	1-10
	11-20
	21-30
	31-50
	51-100
	>100

* Statewide Advisory

SOURCE: "Figure 8-1. Fish and Wildlife Consumption Advisories in the United States," in *National Water Quality Inventory: 1998 Report to Congress*, Environmental Protection Agency, Washington, DC, 2000

Acid and U.S. Waters

Acid pollutes many waterways in the United States. This acid comes from two sources—acid precipitation and wastes from mines.

ACID PRECIPITATION. Acid precipitation (rain, snow, or fog) is produced when smoke or emissions from factories and coal-burning electric power plants, which contain sulfur dioxide, nitrogen oxides, and hydrocarbons, mix with the water in the air to form a mild acid. (Figure 5.4 shows how acid precipitation develops.) This precipitation may fall close to the factories or power plants, or it may be carried many hundreds of miles away by winds high in the atmosphere. If there is no water in the air, the acid may fall to the earth as dust, which mixes with rainwater.

Acid precipitation falls everywhere—on cities, on forests, and into bodies of water. When it falls in cities, it can damage stone statues and buildings as well as vegetation. When it is in smog, it can harm people's lungs. When it falls in forests, it can kill trees and other vegetation. When it falls into bodies of water, it acidifies the water. That, in turn, harms aquatic plants and animals. Small increases in the acid level in a body of water can affect physiological processes, making it more difficult for fish to reproduce, and large increases can kill aquatic life.

FIGURE 5.3

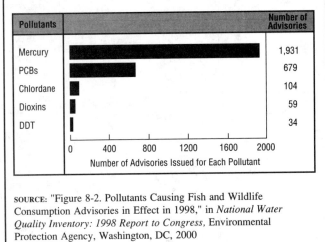

Pollutants causing fish and wildlife consumption advisories in effect in 1998

Pollutants	Number of Advisories
Mercury	1,931
PCBs	679
Chlordane	104
Dioxins	59
DDT	34

SOURCE: "Figure 8-2. Pollutants Causing Fish and Wildlife Consumption Advisories in Effect in 1998," in *National Water Quality Inventory: 1998 Report to Congress*, Environmental Protection Agency, Washington, DC, 2000

TABLE 5.3

Shellfish harvesting restrictions

State	Number of Water-bodies with Restrictions	Size (square miles)
Alabama	—	—
Alaska	—	—
California	—	—
Connecticut	—	—
Delaware	—	—
Delaware River Basin	—	97.0
District of Columbia[a]	—	—
Florida	—	—
Georgia	—	395.0
Hawaii	0	0
Louisiana	26	—
Maine	—	—
Maryland	37	171.2
Massachusetts	12	541.7
Mississippi	—	—
New Hampshire	11	16.8
New Jersey	—	254.0
New York	—	312.5
North Carolina	—	—
Oregon	7	58.0
Puerto Rico	—	—
Rhode Island	39	66.5
South Carolina	122	266.5
Texas	—	—
Virginia	—	146.0
Virgin Islands	—	—
Washington	—	—
Totals	**254**	**2,325.1**

[a]The District of Columbia prohibits commercial harvest of shellfish in all of its waters.
— Not reported in a numerical format.

SOURCE: "Table 8-1. Shellfish Harvesting Restrictions Reported by the States," in *National Water Quality Inventory: 1998 Report to Congress*, Environmental Protection Agency, Washington, DC, 2000

Most aquatic organisms cannot live outside the pH range of 5 to 9. (See Figure 5.5.) Even within that range, fish health may be affected. (See Table 5.5.)

Many states are very concerned about the effects of acid precipitation on their waterways. Many add limestone or other alkaline materials to neutralize the acidic affect in these bodies of water, although this often works for only a short time.

In April 1999 the National Acid Precipitation Assessment Program (NAPAP), an agency created by Congress in 1980 to assess the damage caused by acid precipitation, released findings from its latest study, *National Acid Precipitation Assessment Program Biennial Report to Congress: An Integrated Assessment*. The agency warned that, despite important strides in reducing air pollution, acid precipitation remains a serious problem in sensitive areas and provided more evidence that acid deposition is more "complex and intractable than was believed 10 years ago." Among the findings were:

• New York's Adirondack Mountain waterways suffer from serious levels of acid. Even though sulfur levels are declining, nitrogen levels are still climbing. The agency predicted that by 2040, about half the region's 2,800 lakes and ponds would be too acidic to sustain life.

• The Chesapeake Bay is suffering from excess nitrogen, which is causing algal blooms (sharp increases in the growth of algae) that can suffocate other life forms.

• High elevation forests in Colorado, West Virginia, Tennessee, and Southern California are nearly saturated with nitrogen, a key ingredient in acid precipitation. (Nitrogen saturation is a condition in which the nitrogen levels in the soil exceed the plant needs with the result

that excess nitrogen is flushed into streams where it can cause undesirable plant growth. As the nitrogen moves through the soil it strips away chemicals essential for forest fertility, increasing lake and stream acidity.)

• High elevation lakes and streams in the Sierra Nevada, the Cascades, and the Rocky Mountains may be on the verge of "chronically high acidity."

The agency concluded in its report that further reductions in sulfur and nitrogen would be needed. The agency also found, however, that the 1990 Clean Air Act Amendments have reduced sulfur emissions and acid deposition in much of the United States. In 1998 the EPA ordered 22 states in the East and Midwest to reduce nitrogen oxides, which, when accomplished, should lower acid levels further.

ACID FROM MINES. Mining companies must separate the stone and dirt that they take from mines from the mineral ore that they want. To do this, they use chemicals, many of which are acidic. Sometimes the wastes from this method of extracting ore end up in waterways. When this happens, it can make water too acidic, resulting in the

TABLE 5.4

Ocean, bay, and Great Lakes beach closings and advisories, 1988–2000

	Monitoring for swimmer safety	1988	1989	1990	1991	1992	1993	1994	1995	1996	1997	1998	1999	2000
AL	Limited	**	**	**	**	**	**	**	**	**	**	**	0	6
CA	Comprehensive	**	At least 64	At least 338	745 + 5(p)	609 + 1(e) + 1(p)	1397[1] + 2(e)+ 2(p)	At least 910 + 2(e)+ 6(p)	At least 1305 + 3(e) + 11(p)	At least 1054 + 7(e)+ 9(p)	At least 1141 + 1(e) + 37(p)	At least 3273 + 30(e)+ 12(p)[2]	At least 3547 + 11(e)+ 3(p)	At least 5,780 + 17(e) + 23(p)
CT	Comprehensive	**	At least 103	218	293 + 1(e)	223	At least 174	At least 162 + 1(e)	251 + 1(e)	196 + 2(e)	At least 214 + 1(e)	At least 272	At least 81 + 1(e)	At least 397
DE	Comprehensive	1	62	11	11	5	0	0	0	16	3(p)	14	5	5
FL	Limited	**	**	303	299	772[3] + 1(e)	At least 101 + 1(e)[4]	At least 215 + 1(e)	At least 830	At least 174 + 2(e) + 1(p)	At least 706 + 5(e) + 4(p)	1868 + 3(e) + 5(p)	At least 671 + 6(e) 18(p)	527 + 9(e) + 8(p)
GA	Limited (began 1999)												1(p)	0
Guam	Comprehensive	**	**	**	**	**	0	0	2 + 1(e)	**	688 + 7(e) + 2(p)	**	**	1,691 + 15(e) + 5(p)
HI	Comprehensive	At least 9	At least 23	At least 22	106	29	6	22	13[1]	70	1	0	2	15
IL	Comprehensive	**	**	**	**	**	73	36	55	66	At least 90	38	196	103
IN	Comprehensive	**	**	**	**	**	At least 30	36	14	34	30	154 + 1(p)	269	341 + 1(p)
LA	No regular monitoring	**	**	**	1(p)	1(p)	1(p)	1(p)	1(p)	1(p)	1(p)	4(p)	4(p)	4(p)
ME	Limited	**	1	30 + 1(e)	47 + 3(p)	At least 3(p)	35 + 3(p)	At least 15 + 3(p)	At least 10 + 3(p)	At least 20 + 3(p)	20+ 3(p)	25 + 1(p)	At least 1	At least 13
MD	Limited	0	0	0	24 + 3(p) + 2(e)	At least 6 + 3 (p) + 2(e)	At least 106 + 1(e) +3(p)	82 + 3(p)	At least 200	307 + 24 + 3(p)	4(p) + 1(e)	At least 10	25	111 + 1(e)
MA	Limited	At least 75	At least 60	At least 59	At least 59	At least 60	At least 61	At least 58	132 + 1(p)	At least 152 + 2(p)	78 + 1(e)	231 + 1(e) + 2(p)	At least 95 + 1(e) + 1(p)	At least 390 + 2(p)
MI	Limited	**	**	**	**	**	**	26 + 3(e) + 2(p)	96 + 1(e)	At least 18 + 1(e) + 1(p)	236	227 + 1(p)	At least 100 +1(e)	At least 276
MN	Limited	**	**	**	**	**	0	0	0	0	0	0	0	1(p)
MS	Limited (began 1997)	**	**	**	**	**	**	**	**	**	**	**	9	15 1(e)

TABLE 5.4

Ocean, bay, and Great Lakes beach closings and advisories, 1988–2000 [CONTINUED]

	Monitoring for swimmer safety	1988	1989	1990	1991	1992	1993	1994	1995	1996	1997	1998	1999	2000
NH	Comprehensive (coastal only)	**	**	**	1(e)	0	0	0	0	0	0	0	52	21+1(e)
NJ	Comprehensive	126	266	228	108	112	88	238	86	87	42	31	34	33
NY	Limited (Great Lakes)	273+1(p)	473+5(p)	383+3(p)	314+2(e)+3(p)	799[5]	At least 212[6]+1(e)	227+1(e)+24 days restricted use	283+3(e)	219+4(e)	273+1(e)	178+3(e)	At least 104+1(e)	At least 388+1(p)
NC	Comprehensive (began 1997)					28					44+1(p)	279+4(e)+7(p)	154+2(e)+1(p)	128+1(p)
OH	Comprehensive	**	**	**	**	**	0	96	67	119	100	288	257	501
OR	No regular monitoring											**	**	**
PA	Comprehensive	**	**	**	**	**	19	14	10	6	0	18	3	41
PR	Limited	**	**	**	**	**		1(e)			**	**	**	At least 3
RI	Limited	0	0	0	0	0	0	0	0	0	0	191	54	62+3(p)
SC	Limited	**	**	**	**	2						0	89	118
TX	Limited	**	**	**	0	1 medical advisory	42	0	0	0	0	0	0	4(e)
USVI	Limited	**	**	**	**	**	0	0	0	4	43	**	At least 307	At least 34
VA	Limited	**	**	**	2	0	0	0		0	3	0	At least 9	0
WA	Limited	**	**	**	**	**	At least 94	At least 148	At least 114+1(e)	At least 120	At least 137	139+3(p)	At least 96	At least 34+1(p)
WI	Limited													At least 237
Total		At least 484+3(p)	At least 1,052+5(p)	At least 1,592+4(p)+1(e)	At least 2,008+14(p)+7(e)	At least 2,619+8(p)+6(e)	At least 2,438+9(p)+5(e)	At least 2,279+15(p)+12(e)	At least 3,522+16(p)+9(e)	At least 2,596+20(p)+16(e)	At least 4,153+55(p)+17(e)	At least 7,236+36(p)+41(e)	At least 6,160+28(p)+23(e)	At least 11,270+48(e)+50(p)

Note: Every day of an advisory/closure is counted as one beach closing. Because of inconsistencies in monitoring and closing practices among states and over time, it is difficult to make comparisons between states or to assess trends over time based on the closing data.

** NRDC received no data.

(e) Extended beach closure (6 to 12 weeks)

(p) Permanent beach closure (12 or more weeks)

[1] This increase appears to be the result of 700 San Diego County closings/advisories due to heavy winter storms.

[2] This increase appears to be due to 2,937 closings and advisories in southern California as a result of heavy El Niño rains.

[3] This increase appears to be due to 506 warnings in Dade County against swimming after heavy rains caused sewage spills.

[4] The decrease in the number of Florida closings/advisories appears to be due to significantly less rainfall in 1993 compared with 1992, particularly in Pasco and Dade Counties.

[5] Included in this total are 706 rainfall advisories issued in New York City.

[6] The decrease in New York closings/advisories appears to be due to less rainfall in 1993 compared with 1992 and a change in New York City's standing rainfall advisory, which covered fewer beaches for a shorter time.

SOURCE: Mark Dorfman, "Table 2: U.S. Ocean, Bay, and Great Lakes Beach Closings and Advisories, 1988<en>2000," in Testing the Waters XI: A Guide to Beach Water Quality at Vacation Beaches, Natural Resources Defense Council, New York, NY, August 2001

FIGURE 5.4

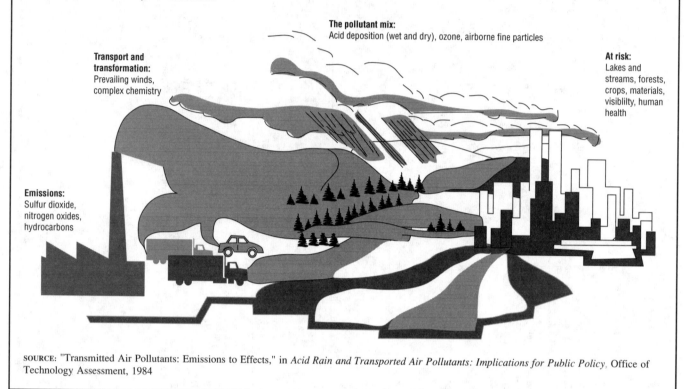

Transmitted air pollutants: emissions to effects

The transported pollutants considered result from emissions of three pollutants: sulfur dioxide, nitrogen oxides, and hydrocarbons. As these pollutants are carried away from their sources, they form a complex "pollutant mix" leading to acid deposition, ozone, and airborne fine particles. These transported air pollutants pose risks to surface waters, forests, crops, materials, visibility, and human health.

The pollutant mix:
Acid deposition (wet and dry), ozone, airborne fine particles

Transport and transformation:
Prevailing winds, complex chemistry

At risk:
Lakes and streams, forests, crops, materials, visiblilty, human health

Emissions:
Sulfur dioxide, nitrogen oxides, hydrocarbons

SOURCE: "Transmitted Air Pollutants: Emissions to Effects," in *Acid Rain and Transported Air Pollutants: Implications for Public Policy*, Office of Technology Assessment, 1984

death of aquatic plants and fish. Table 5.6 lists the metals that threaten marine environments. It includes information about these metals as well, such as their properties and health effects.

THE CLEAN WATER ACT

On June 22, 1969, the Cuyahoga River in Cleveland burst into flames, the result of oil and debris that had accumulated on the river's surface. Five-story-high flames destroyed two bridges and thrust the problem of environmental pollution into the public consciousness. Many people became aware—and wary—of the nation's polluted waters, and in 1972 Congress passed the Federal Water Pollution Control Act, commonly known as the Clean Water Act (CWA).

The objective of the CWA was to "restore and maintain the chemical, physical, and biological integrity of the Nation's waters." It called for an end to the discharge of all pollutants into the navigable waters of the United States and for achieving "wherever possible, water quality which provides for the protection and propagation of fish, shellfish, and wildlife and provides for recreation in and on the water." The second provision was that waters were to be restored to "fishable/swimmable" condition.

The CWA required that each state prepare and submit to the Environmental Protection Agency (EPA) a report on

- the water quality of all navigable waters in the state,

- the extent to which the waters provided for the protection and propagation of marine animals and allowed recreation in and on the water,

- the extent to which pollution had been eliminated or was under control, and

- the sources and causes of pollutants.

Congress stated in the CWA that these reports, known as *National Water Quality Inventories*, would be submitted every two years to the EPA.

The Clean Water Act, in a single generation, reversed the decline in the health of the nation's water that had been occurring since the mid-1800s. Since 1995, however, certain groups have proposed legislation to change the CWA, giving more authority to the states and more weight to economic considerations. The proponents of change argue that enough has been accomplished and that now is the time to make the law more flexible. They claim the huge cost of maintaining clean water risks making the United States uncompetitive in the international marketplace and

FIGURE 5.5

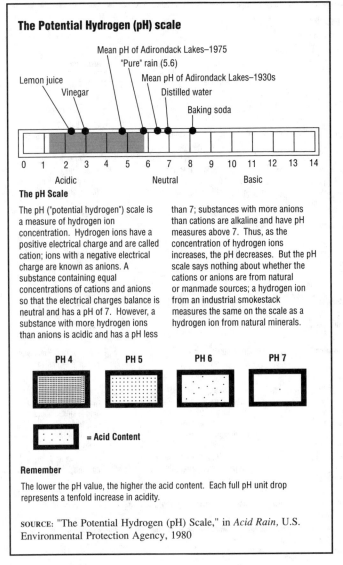

The Potential Hydrogen (pH) scale

Mean pH of Adirondack Lakes–1975

"Pure" rain (5.6)

Mean pH of Adirondack Lakes–1930s

Lemon juice

Vinegar

Distilled water

Baking soda

| 0 | 1 | 2 | 3 | 4 | 5 | 6 | 7 | 8 | 9 | 10 | 11 | 12 | 13 | 14 |

Acidic   Neutral   Basic

The pH Scale

The pH ("potential hydrogen") scale is a measure of hydrogen ion concentration. Hydrogen ions have a positive electrical charge and are called cation; ions with a negative electrical charge are known as anions. A substance containing equal concentrations of cations and anions so that the electrical charges balance is neutral and has a pH of 7. However, a substance with more hydrogen ions than anions is acidic and has a pH less than 7; substances with more anions than cations are alkaline and have pH measures above 7. Thus, as the concentration of hydrogen ions increases, the pH decreases. But the pH scale says nothing about whether the cations or anions are from natural or manmade sources; a hydrogen ion from an industrial smokestack measures the same on the scale as a hydrogen ion from natural minerals.

PH 4   PH 5   PH 6   PH 7

```
: : : :  = Acid Content
```

Remember

The lower the pH value, the higher the acid content. Each full pH unit drop represents a tenfold increase in acidity.

SOURCE: "The Potential Hydrogen (pH) Scale," in *Acid Rain*, U.S. Environmental Protection Agency, 1980

TABLE 5.5

Effects of pH on aquatic life

pH Range	General Biological Effects
6.5 to 6.0	Some adverse effects for highly acid-sensitive species
6.0 to 5.5	Loss of sensitive minnows and forage fish; decreased reproductive success for trout and walleye
5.5 to 5.0	Loss of many common sports fish and additional nongame species
5.0 to 4.5	Loss of most sports fish; very few fishes able to survive and reproduce where pH levels commonly below 4.5

SOURCE: "Effects of pH on aquatic life," in *National Water Quality Inventory: 1996 Report to Congress,* U.S. Environmental Protection Agency, Washington, DC, 1998

Because of the sparse reporting by the states and differences in support criteria and measurement techniques between states, a complete assessment of the quality of the nation's surface waters is not possible. However, the reports are valuable to estimate overall water quality and identify the major sources and causes of water pollution.

Designated Uses

Defining water quality is a little like trying to determine "how good is good?" or "how clean is clean?" Generally, the key measure of the quality of any body of surface water—river, lake, or estuary—is the degree to which the water is able to support the uses for which it has been officially designated. These uses may include high-quality cold-water fishing, swimming, or propagation of aquatic life; or the ability to supply water for drinking, crop irrigation, or hydroelectric power production. For example, if the designated use for a particular body of water is irrigation, it is not considered to be polluted if it can be safely used for that purpose, even if it is unfit for other purposes such as drinking.

Under federal mandate, each state must designate uses for the rivers, streams, lakes, and estuaries within its boundaries. Following EPA guidelines, the states then determine whether the bodies of water meet the standards set for their use. It is not uncommon for a body of water to have more than one designated use. However, most bodies of water are designated primarily for recreation, drinking, and the support of fish populations. Figure 5.6 lists and defines the "use support levels" reported by the states. They range from "fully supporting all uses" to "not attainable."

that government regulations demand more than is necessary to maintain drinkable water.

THE EPA'S 1998 *NATIONAL WATER QUALITY INVENTORY*

Due to funding limitations, most states assess only a portion of their total water resources during each two-year reporting cycle required under the Clean Water Act, with the goal of assessing all their waters over a five- to ten-year period. The most recent EPA water quality inventory is the *National Water Quality Inventory: 1998 Report to Congress* (Washington, DC, 2000). To check their water for this report, the states used chemical and biological monitoring and other types of data, such as surveys of fisheries, water quality models, and information from citizens. The purpose of these evaluations is to determine what percent of each type of body of water is supporting its intended uses (such as drinking water supply, recreation, and warm and cold water fisheries) as part of the EPA-approved water quality standards.

Point and Nonpoint Sources of Pollution

Pollution is the main reason that a body of water cannot support its designated uses. There are a vast number of pollutants that can make water use threatened, impaired, or not attainable, but to control pollution it is

TABLE 5.6

Properties and effects of metals of primary concern in marine environments

	Arsenic	Cadmium	Lead	Mercury
Bioaccumulation	Low except in some fish species	Moderate	Low or none	Significant (methylated form)
Biomagnification	Low or none	Low or none	Low or none	Significant (methylated form)
Properties	Metallic form: insoluble Readily methylated by sediment bacteria to become highly soluble, but low in toxicity	Metalic form: relatively soluble Not subject to biomethylation Less bioavailable in marine than in fresh water Long biological residence time Synergistic effects with lead	Generally insoluble Adsorption rate age-dependent, 4 to 5 times higher in children than adults Synergistic effects with cadmium	Metallic form: relatively insoluble Readily methylated by sediment bacteria to become more soluble, bioavailable, persistent, and highly toxic
Major environmental sink	Sediments	Sediments	Sediments	Sediments
Major routes of human exposure:				
Marine environments	Seafood: very minor route, except for some fish species	Seafood contributes approximately 10% of total for general population	Seafood comparable to other food sources	Seafood is primary source of human exposure
Other environments	Inhalation: the major route	Food, primarily grains	Diet and drinking water	Terrestrial pathways are minor sources in comparison
Health effects	Acute: gastrointestinal hemorrhage; loss of blood pressure; coma and death in extreme cases Chronic: liver and peripheral nerve damage; possibly skin and lung cancer	Emphysema and other lung damage; anemia; kidney, pancreatic, and liver impairment; bone damage; animal (and suspected human) carcinogen and mutagen	Acute: gastrointestinal disorders Chronic: anemia; neurological and blood disorders; kidney dysfunction; joint impairments; male/female reproductive effects; teratogenic	Kidney dysfunction; neurological disease; skin lesions; respiratory impairment; eye damage; animal teratogen and carcinogen

SOURCE: Adapted from "Table 8. Properties and effects of metals of primary concern in marine environments," in *Wastes in Marine Environments,* U.S. Congress, Office of Technology Assessment, Washington, DC, 1987

necessary to find out what the pollutant is, as well as its source. Although there are many ways in which pollutants can enter waterways, sources of pollution are generally categorized as point sources and nonpoint sources.

Point sources are localized sources of water pollution that disperse pollutants from a single point, such as a sewage drain or an industrial discharge pipe. Pollutants that are commonly discharged from point sources include bacteria from a sewer pipe, and toxic chemicals and heavy metals from industrial plants.

Nonpoint sources are nonlocalized sources of water pollution that are spread out over a large area and have no specific outlet or discharge point, such as the pollution of ground water (water beneath the earth's surface) from water seeping through land containing pollutants in farm fields and urban areas. Nonpoint source pollutants can include pesticides, fertilizers, toxic chemicals, and asbestos and salts from road construction. The EPA estimates that as much as 65 percent of surface water pollutants comes from nonpoint sources.

THE QUALITY OF U.S. OCEAN WATERS

Marine Debris

The Ocean Conservancy (formerly the Center for Marine Conservation), located in Washington, D.C., defines marine debris as human-made items, such as those made of glass, plastic, metal, or paper, that have been lost or disposed of in the marine (ocean) environment. The items may have been intentionally discarded, accidentally dropped, or indirectly deposited from the land. The debris may sink to the bottom of the water, float on top of the water, or drift beneath the surface.

The International Coastal Cleanup is a program coordinated by the Ocean Conservancy. The mission of the Coastal Cleanup program is to remove debris from U.S. shorelines, collect information on the amount and types of debris, educate people about marine debris, and use the information collected to effect positive change.

In 2000 data from the International Coastal Cleanup revealed the top 12 debris items found along the U.S. coastline. Table 5.7 lists these items, the total number reported,

FIGURE 5.6

Summary of use support

For water bodies with more than one designated use, the states, tribes and other jurisdictions consolidate the individual use support information into a summary use support determination:

Good/Fully Supporting All Uses – Based on an assessment of available data, water quality supports all designated uses. Water quality meets narrative and/or numeric criteria adopted to protect and support a designated use.

Good/Threatened for One or More Uses – Although all the assessed uses are currently met, data show a declining trend in water quality. Projections based on this trend indicate water quality will be impaired in the future, unless action is taken to prevent further degradation.

Impaired for One or More Uses – Based on an assessment of available data, water quality does not support one or more designated uses.

Use Not Attainable – The state, tribe, or other jurisdiction performed a use-attainability analysis and demonstrated that one or more designated uses are not attainable due to one of six conditions specified in the *Code of Federal Regulations* (40CFR 131.10).

SOURCE: "Summary of Use Support," in *National Water Quality Inventory: 1998 Report to Congress,* Environmental Protection Agency, Washington, DC, 2000

TABLE 5.7

Most prevalent coastal debris items, 2000

Debris Items	Total number reported	Percentage of total collected
1. cigarette butts	1,027,303	20.25%
2. plastic pieces	337,384	6.65%
3. food bags/wrappers (plastic)	284,287	5.60%
4. foamed plastic pieces	268,945	5.30%
5. caps, lids (plastic)	255,253	5.03%
6. paper pieces	219,256	4.32%
7. glass pieces	209,531	4.13%
8. beverage cans	184,294	3.63%
9. beverage bottles (glass)	177,039	3.49%
10. straws	161,639	3.19%
11. beverage bottles (plastic)	150,129	2.96%
12. bottle caps (metal)	130,401	2.57%
Dirty Dozen Totals	**3,405,461**	**67.12%**

SOURCE: "2000 international coastal cleanup—United States dirty dozen," in *The International Coastal Cleanup,* Center for Marine Conservation, Ocean Conservancy, Washington, DC [Online] http://www.cmc-ocean.org/cleanupbro/00calc.php3 [accessed October, 2001]

and the percentage each comprised of the total debris collected. Cigarette butts make up slightly more than 20 percent of shoreline debris. Taken together, various types of plastic items make up approximately another 25 percent.

The Ocean Conservancy uses data from the Coastal Cleanup Program to identify sources of marine debris. The Conservancy has identified ocean-based sources as sea-going vessels (from small recreational vehicles to large ships), and offshore rigs and drilling platforms. Land-based sources include beach visitors and overflowing sewer systems. Creeks, rivers, and storm water drains carry debris from these sources downstream to the ocean.

MARINE DEBRIS IS A THREAT TO AQUATIC LIFE. The debris found in the ocean can be a great danger to ocean wildlife. An animal, such as a seal, might get trapped in a net, rope, or line, and drown. In fact, some scientists think this might be the reason why the seal population has declined over the past two decades. Whales and dolphins also get caught in old fishing nets. The New England Aquarium reported that 56 percent of endangered whales photographed by Aquarium personnel had scars from plastic gill nets or lobster gear entanglement.

Ocean debris can be a serious threat to seabirds and shorebirds. They become caught in fishing nets, fishing lines, or plastic beer and soda container rings and drown or choke to death. Sometimes pelicans get fishing line or plastic beer container rings caught around their beaks so they cannot catch food. As a result, they starve to death. Pelicans and egrets may get fishing line caught around their wings and legs so they cannot fly. They, too, starve to death.

Plastic items are a particular hazard to marine organisms. Some birds and sea turtles eat little pieces of plastic, thinking it is food. Dead whales and dolphins have been found with their stomachs full of plastic bags. Adult birds eat small plastic pellets resembling fish eggs and feed them to their young. An estimated 2 million sea birds and 100,000 marine animals die each year as a result of ingesting or becoming entangled in plastic.

In 1988, 31 nations ratified an agreement making it illegal for their ships to dump plastic debris, including fishing nets, into the ocean. As part of that agreement, the United States enacted the Marine Plastics Pollution Research and Control Act, which, among other things, imposed a $25,000 fine for each violation.

FIGURE 5.7

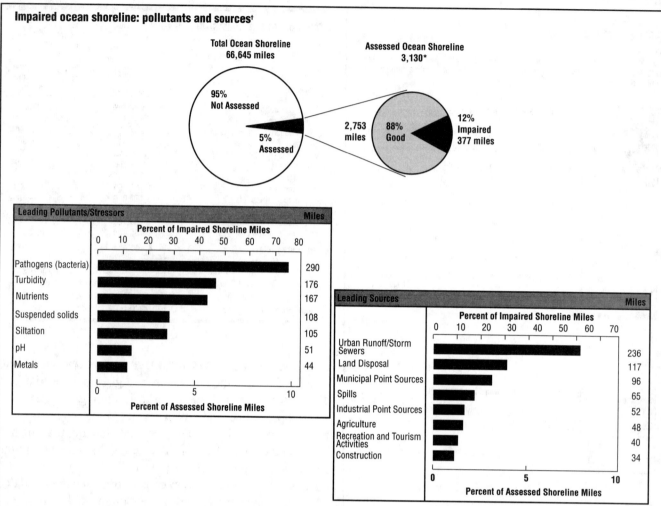

Impaired ocean shoreline: pollutants and sources†

States assessed 5% of the total miles of ocean shoreline for the 1998 report. The larger pie chart on the left illustrates this proportion. The smaller pie chart on the right shows that, for the subset of assessed water, 88% are rated as good and 12% as impaired. When states identify waters that are impaired, they describe the pollutants or processes causing or contributing to the impairment and the sources of pollutants associated with the impairment. The upper bar chart presents the leading causes and the number of ocean shoreline miles impacted, and the lower bar chart presents the leading sources and the number of ocean shoreline miles they impact. The percent scales on the upper and lower x-axis of the bar charts provide different perspectives on the magnitude of the impact of these pollutants and sources. The lower axis compares the miles impacted by the pollutant or source to the total assessed miles. The upper axis compares the miles impacted by the pollutant or source to the total impaired miles.

†Excluding natural sources

*Includes miles assessed as not attainable.

Note: Percentages do not add up to 100% because more than one pollutant or source may impair a segment of ocean shoreline.

SOURCE: Adapted from "Figure 5-12. Leading POLLUTANTS In Impaired Ocean Shoreline Waters*," and "Figure 5-13. Leading SOURCES of Ocean Shoreline Impairment," both in *National Water Quality Inventory: 1998 Report to Congress,* Environmental Protection Agency, Washington, DC, 2000

MARINE DEBRIS AFFECTS HUMANS. Diving and boating safety can be jeopardized by marine debris. Skin divers and scuba divers can be caught in old nets and fishing lines. Fishing nets can wrap around boat propellers, making it impossible for boats to operate. The junk washed up on shores fouls beaches and makes them less attractive to visitors. Fewer people will want to visit the beach if it is littered, which hurts the economy of beach areas.

Causes and Sources of Marine Pollution

In its 1998 *National Water Quality Inventory* (2000) of U.S. ocean coastal waters, the Environmental Protection Agency (EPA) reported that 15 of the 27 coastal states provided information on their coastal waters. Fourteen rated general water quality conditions in some of their coastal waters, and ten identified pollutants and sources of pollutants. The states assessed 14 percent of the national coastline waters excluding Alaska, or 5 percent including Alaska. Of the coastline waters assessed, 80 percent fully supported their designated uses, 8 percent were threatened for one or more uses but currently supported their designated uses, and 12 percent were impaired for one or more designated uses. Figure 5.7 shows that 88 percent of assessed

FIGURE 5.8

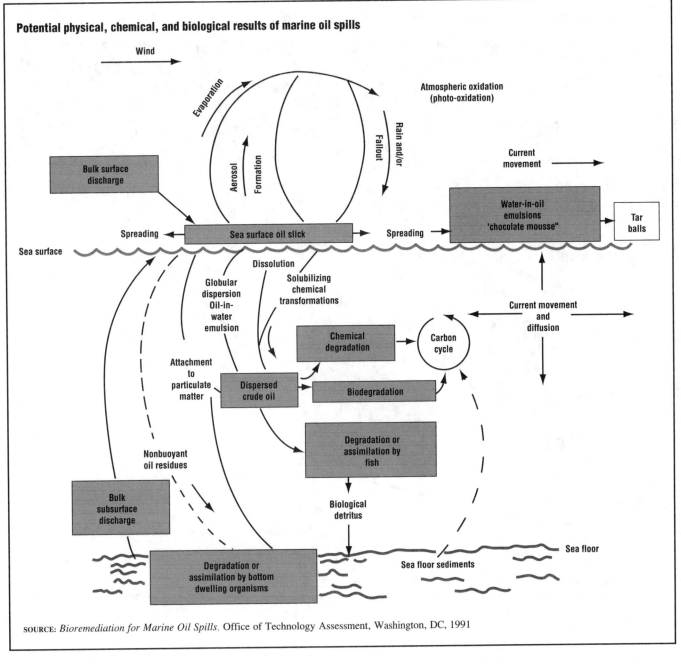

Potential physical, chemical, and biological results of marine oil spills

SOURCE: *Bioremediation for Marine Oil Spills*, Office of Technology Assessment, Washington, DC, 1991

ocean shoreline was rated "good," and the remaining 12 percent was rated "impaired."

Figure 5.7 also shows the major pollutants affecting U.S. coastal waters. Pathogens (disease-causing bacteria) were the leading contaminant, followed by turbidity (muddy or unclear water) and nutrients (such as fertilizers). The primary sources of these pollutants were urban runoff and storm sewers, land disposal of wastes, municipal sewage treatment plants, accidental spills, industrial discharges, agriculture, recreation and tourism activities, and construction. However, the leading pollutant may not originate from the leading source because major pollutants may be released from many minor sources.

Other Potential Threats to the Marine Environment

MEDICAL WASTE. During the summers of 1987 and 1988, medical wastes from hospitals, including containers of blood and syringes used to give injections, floated onto the shore along the East Coast, mainly in New York and New Jersey. Some of this waste was infected with the human immunodeficiency virus (HIV, the virus that causes AIDS) and a virus that causes a type of hepatitis (a serious liver disease). As a result, the government closed the beaches in these areas for several weeks. In 1988 medical waste also washed up onshore along the Great Lakes, and those beaches had to be shut down.

The sensational nature of medical waste appearing on beaches prompted quick legislation. Congress passed

FIGURE 5.9

Oil spill boundary defining the area affected by the Exxon Valdez oil spill and federal lands located within the boundary

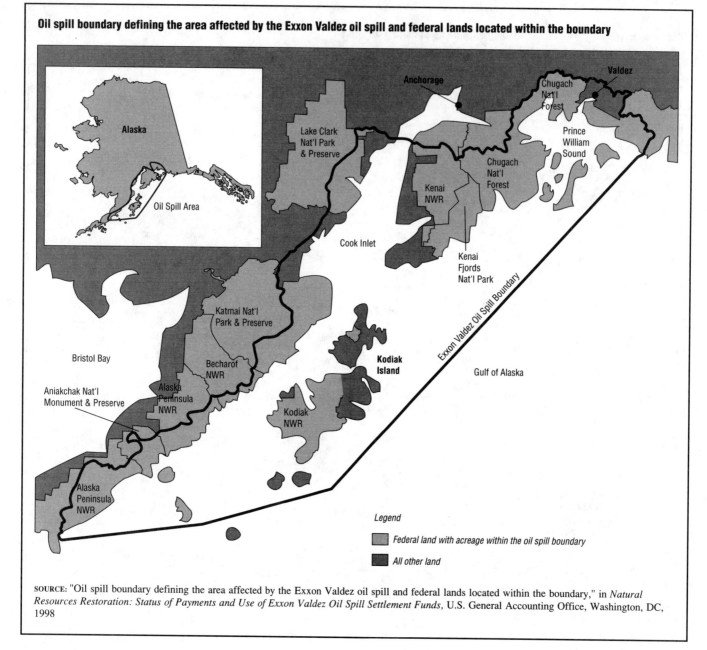

SOURCE: "Oil spill boundary defining the area affected by the Exxon Valdez oil spill and federal lands located within the boundary," in *Natural Resources Restoration: Status of Payments and Use of Exxon Valdez Oil Spill Settlement Funds,* U.S. General Accounting Office, Washington, DC, 1998

the 1988 Medical Waste Tracking Act, requiring producers of medical waste to be held accountable for safe disposal of the waste or face up to $1 million in fines and five years in prison.

In 1990 the Agency for Toxic Substances and Disease Registry (ATSDR), a division of the U.S. Department of Health and Human Services, concluded that medical waste presents little danger to the general public. Results of an ATSDR investigation revealed that the general public does not normally come in contact with medical waste unless it originates from homes in which health care is provided and the waste is carelessly discarded. The public may also be at risk when encountering needles and syringes disposed of by intravenous drug users. Furthermore, despite the furor raised by the public over medical waste, studies show that it accounts for only 0.01 percent of all waste collected and analyzed on the nation's beaches.

DREDGING. Every year, millions of tons of materials are dredged from the bottoms of harbors and coastal areas to clear or enlarge navigational channels or for development purposes. This material ends up in U.S. marine waters, most of it in the Gulf of Mexico. Dredged materials may contain high concentrations of pesticides, metals, and toxic chemicals. During dredging or when the dredged material is dumped, pollutants that have settled into the sediment are stirred up and released into open water, giving them a greater potential to harm marine life.

COASTAL DEVELOPMENT AND RECREATION. Almost three-fourths of the U.S. population lives within 50 miles of a coastline, and more people move to coastal regions each year. Millions visit seaside areas, drawn by the mild climates, scenic beauty, and recreational activities. To accommodate an increasing number of residents and tourists, developers are building more houses, resorts, marinas, and boatyards. Commercial establishments built to accommodate the influx of new residents add to the population density.

Development often comes at the expense of ocean life. Destruction of marine habitats is common in populated areas. Many aquatic organisms and animals have little tolerance for disturbances such as light and temperature changes. When one species is eliminated from an ecosystem, the food chain is broken, and other species will often be destroyed or leave the area in search of a more suitable habitat. Other marine animals are sometimes harmed by collisions with recreational and fishing boats, causing extensive injuries or death.

OIL SPILLS. Oil spills are a dramatic form of water pollution. They are highly visible, and their impact is sometimes immediate and severe. While it is true that oil can have a devastating effect on marine life, the size of the spill itself is often not the determining factor in the amount of damage it causes. Other factors include the amount and type of marine life in the area and weather conditions that might disperse the oil. Figure 5.8 shows the physical, chemical, and biological results of marine oil spills.

When the *Exxon Valdez* ran into a reef in Prince William Sound, Alaska, in 1989, 11 million gallons of oil spilled into one of the richest and most ecologically sensitive areas in North America. (Figure 5.9 shows the area affected.) A slick the size of Rhode Island threatened fish and wildlife. Otters, which cannot tolerate even a small amount of oil on their fur, died by the thousands, despite efforts by trained environmentalists and local volunteers to save them. Oil-soaked birds lined the shores, only to be eaten by larger predator birds, which then died from the ingested oil.

In response to the *Exxon Valdez* disaster, Congress passed the Oil Pollution Act of 1990, which called for prompt reaction and a $1 billion cleanup-damage fund, early planning for response to spills, stricter crew standards, and double hulls on new tankers. (When equipped with two hulls, if the tanker's exterior hull is punctured, the interior hull holding the oil will still likely remain intact.) The law requires older tankers to be fitted with double hulls by the year 2010. The *Exxon Valdez* was not double-hulled. An Alaskan state commission estimated that if the *Valdez* had been equipped with a double-hull design, 20 to 60 percent of the spill might have been prevented.

Until a decade or so ago, the only way to battle oil spills was intensive, manual cleanup. In 1990 an explo-

TABLE 5.8

Potential advantages and disadvantages of bioremediation

Advantages:
- Usually involves only minimal physical disruption of a site
- No significant adverse effects when used correctly
- May be helpful in removing some of the toxic components of oil
- Offers a simpler and more thorough solution than mechanical technologies
- Possibly less costly than other approaches

Disadvantages:
- Of undetermined effectiveness for many types of spills
- May not be appropriate at sea
- Takes time to work
- Approach must be specifically tailored for each polluted site
- Optimization requires substantial information about spill site and oil characteristics

SOURCE: *Bioremediation for Marine Oil Spills*, Office of Technology Assessment, Washington, DC, 1991

sion occurred on the Norwegian tanker *Mega Borg* 57 miles off the Texas coast, spilling 4 million gallons of crude oil into the ocean. At the request of several Texas agencies, a new method of cleaning the spill was tried: bioremediation.

Bioremediation is the process of adding materials to the oil spill area, such as fertilizers or microorganisms, that will increase the rate at which natural biodegradation of the oil occurs. It is often used after mechanical methods have been used. Mechanical methods include using booms to block the spread of oil on the water's surface and using skimmers to remove it from the surface.

For the *Mega Borg* spill, 110 pounds of microbes were sprayed over the 40 acres of oil. (There are over a trillion microbes in each gram.) The process worked like this: Once the bacteria began "eating," they multiplied until their food source, the oil, was depleted. The microbes then died and were eaten by other microbes. The resulting waste was a fatty acid that harmlessly re-entered the food chain. Table 5.8 shows the advantages and disadvantages of using bioremediation.

The U.S. National Research Council estimates that approximately 8.4 billion gallons of oil enter marine waters each year, not from major oil spills, but from street runoff, industrial liquid wastes, and intentional discharge from ships flushing their oil tanks. The agency indicated concern for areas that are habitually exposed to oil pollution, since as little as one part of oil per million parts of water can be detrimental to the reproduction and growth of fish, crustaceans, and plankton.

THE QUALITY OF U.S. ESTUARIES

An estuary is an inlet, bay, or area where a river meets the ocean. Estuaries and the nearby coastal areas are among the biologically richest and most useful areas in the world. Fish and shellfish lay their eggs in estuaries,

FIGURE 5.10

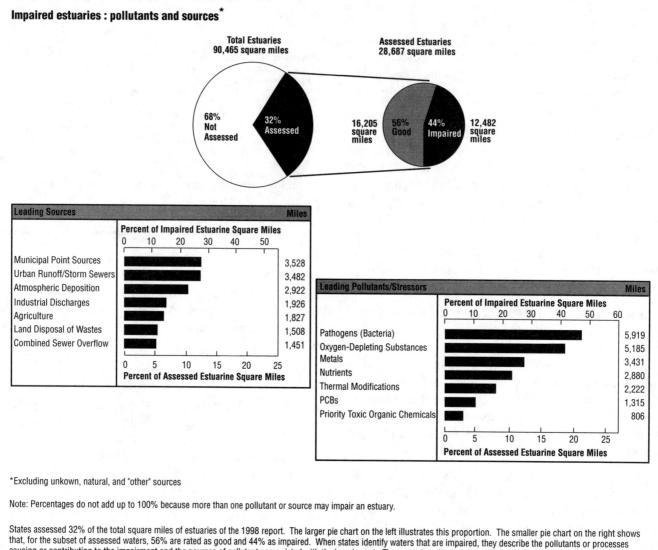

Impaired estuaries : pollutants and sources*

*Excluding unkown, natural, and "other" sources

Note: Percentages do not add up to 100% because more than one pollutant or source may impair an estuary.

States assessed 32% of the total square miles of estuaries of the 1998 report. The larger pie chart on the left illustrates this proportion. The smaller pie chart on the right shows that, for the subset of assessed waters, 56% are rated as good and 44% as impaired. When states identify waters that are impaired, they describe the pollutants or processes causing or contributing to the impairment and the sources of pollutants associated with the impairment. The upper bar chart presents the leading causes and the number of estuarine square miles impacted, and the lower bar chart presents the leading sources and the number of estuarine square miles they impact. The percent scales on the upper and lower x-axis of the bar charts provide different perspectives on the magnitude of the impact of these pollutants and sources. The lower axis compares the square miles impacted by the pollutant or source to the total assessed square miles. The upper axis compares the square miles impacted by the pollutant or source to the total impaired square miles.

SOURCE: Adapted from "Figure 5-3. Leading POLLUTANTS in Impaired Estuaries," and "Figure 5-4. Leading SOURCES of Estuary Impairment*," both in *National Water Quality Inventory: 1998 Report to Congress,* Environmental Protection Agency, Washington, DC, 2000

where the progeny hatch and develop into adult fish. About two-thirds of all fish caught are hatched in estuaries. Birds and many animals live in the wetlands that border estuaries.

Causes and Sources of Estuary Pollution

In its 1998 *National Water Quality Inventory* (2000) of U.S. estuaries, the EPA reported that 22 of the 27 coastal states, the District of Columbia, the Virgin Islands, and the Delaware River Basin Commission assessed 32 percent of the nation's estuarine waters. Of the 28,687 square miles assessed, 47 percent fully supported their uses, 9 percent were threatened for one or more uses but at the time supported their designated uses, and 44 percent

were impaired. Figure 5.10 shows that 56 percent of assessed estuaries was rated "good," and the remaining 44 percent were "impaired."

Figure 5.10 also shows the major pollutants in U.S. estuaries. Pathogens were the most common pollutant, followed by oxygen-depleting substances and metals. Most estuarine pollution came from municipal point sources, urban runoff/storm sewers, and atmospheric deposition.

The National Estuary Program

As part of the Water Quality Act of 1987, the United States government is working to improve the condition of the nation's beaches and coastal waters through the National Estuary Program. From data collected, program

FIGURE 5.11

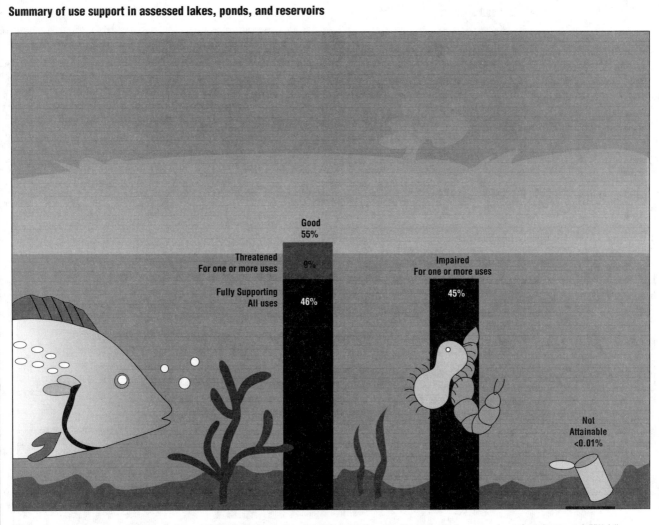

Summary of use support in assessed lakes, ponds, and reservoirs

Good
55%

Threatened
For one or more uses   9%

Impaired
For one or more uses

45%

Fully Supporting
All uses   46%

Not
Attainable
<0.01%

This figure presents the status of the assessed acres of lakes, reservoirs, and ponds. Of the more than 17 million acres of lakes, reservoirs, and ponds assessed, 55% fully support their designated uses and 45% are impaired for one ore more uses. Nine percent of the assessed waters are fully supporting uses but threatened.

SOURCE: "Figure 4-2. Summary of Use Support in Assessed Lakes, Ponds, and Reservoirs," in *National Water Quality Inventory: 1998 Report to Congress,* Environmental Protection Agency, Washington, DC, 2000

officials concluded that the biggest problem faced by estuaries is development—the building of houses, roads, malls, factories and schools near estuaries. With more people, more businesses, and more industry comes added pollution. The second most important finding from an analysis of the data was that states and local governments, not the federal government, should be the primary decision-makers to promote estuarine health. Wise zoning decisions—what types of businesses, factories, and housing can be built and where they can be built—are very important for controlling pollution.

THE QUALITY OF U.S. LAKES, RESERVOIRS, AND PONDS

There are approximately 41.6 million acres of lakes, reservoirs, and ponds in the United States. These lakes,

reservoirs, and ponds (which will be subsequently referred to simply as lakes) provide water for drinking, swimming, fishing, and generating electric power. In its 1998 *National Water Quality Inventory* (2000) of U.S. estuaries, the EPA reported that 45 states, Puerto Rico, the District of Columbia, and two Native American tribes evaluated 42 percent of the nation's lakes. Forty-six percent fully supported their designated uses, 9 percent were threatened for one or more uses but at the time supported their designated uses, and 45 percent were impaired. (See Figure 5.11.)

Causes and Sources of Lake Pollution

Lakes are products of their watersheds (the area that drains into a lake); therefore, a lake's water quality reflects the condition and management of the lake's watershed. The states that reported pollution of their lakes

FIGURE 5.12

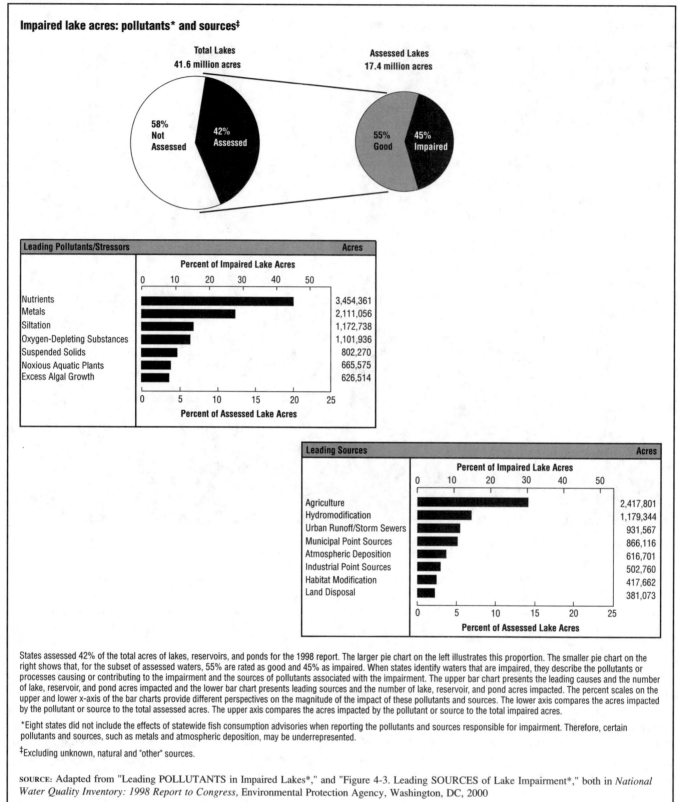

Impaired lake acres: pollutants* and sources‡

States assessed 42% of the total acres of lakes, reservoirs, and ponds for the 1998 report. The larger pie chart on the left illustrates this proportion. The smaller pie chart on the right shows that, for the subset of assessed waters, 55% are rated as good and 45% as impaired. When states identify waters that are impaired, they describe the pollutants or processes causing or contributing to the impairment and the sources of pollutants associated with the impairment. The upper bar chart presents the leading causes and the number of lake, reservoir, and pond acres impacted and the lower bar chart presents leading sources and the number of lake, reservoir, and pond acres impacted. The percent scales on the upper and lower x-axis of the bar charts provide different perspectives on the magnitude of the impact of these pollutants and sources. The lower axis compares the acres impacted by the pollutant or source to the total assessed acres. The upper axis compares the acres impacted by the pollutant or source to the total impaired acres.

*Eight states did not include the effects of statewide fish consumption advisories when reporting the pollutants and sources responsible for impairment. Therefore, certain pollutants and sources, such as metals and atmospheric deposition, may be underrepresented.

‡Excluding unknown, natural and "other" sources.

SOURCE: Adapted from "Leading POLLUTANTS in Impaired Lakes*," and "Figure 4-3. Leading SOURCES of Lake Impairment*," both in *National Water Quality Inventory: 1998 Report to Congress,* Environmental Protection Agency, Washington, DC, 2000

in 1998 often cited multiple pollutants in any given lake acre. Because a single acre of a lake can be affected by several sources of pollution, the states were asked to include their acres of lakes under each of the various source categories that contribute to impairment. This means that a single lake acre could be counted several times if it is polluted by multiple sources.

Figure 5.12 shows the top pollutants and the percent of impaired lake acres affected by each type. Nutrients

FIGURE 5.13

Summary of use support in assessed rivers and streams

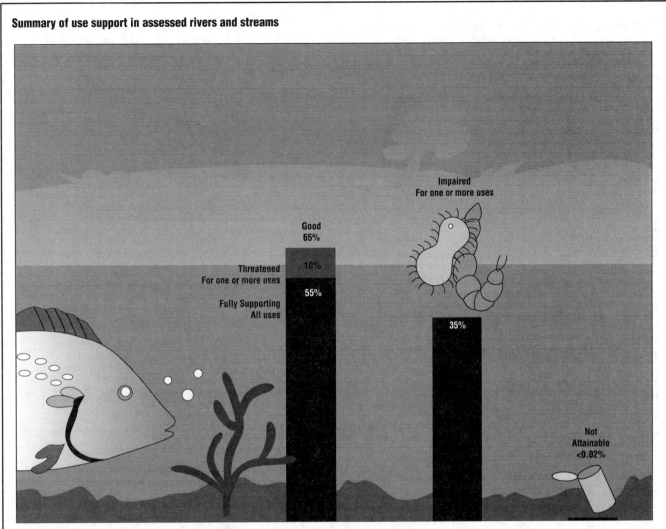

This figure presents the status of the assessed miles of rivers and streams. Of the more than 800,000 miles of rivers and streams assessed, 65% fully support their designated uses and 35% are impaired for one ore more uses. Ten percent of the assessed waters are fully supporting uses but threatened.

SOURCE: "Figure 3-2. Summary of Use Support in Assessed Rivers and Streams," in *National Water Quality Inventory: 1998 Report to Congress*, Environmental Protection Agency, Washington, DC, 2000

were the most prevalent, affecting 44 percent of impaired lake acres. Excessive nutrients stimulate the rapid growth of algae and aquatic plants, a process called eutrophication. When these plants and algae die, bacteria in the water decompose them, using oxygen in the process. As a result, fish populations that depend on an abundant supply of oxygen also die. Notice that oxygen-depleting substances affected 14 percent of impaired lakes. These two types of pollutants (nutrients and oxygen-depleting substances) are linked in the process just described. Agricultural runoff was the most extensive source of pollution, affecting 30 percent of impaired lake acres.

THE QUALITY OF U.S. RIVERS AND STREAMS

The United States has about 3.6 million miles of rivers and streams. In its 1998 *National Water Quality Inventory*

(2000) of U.S. rivers and streams, the EPA reported that all 50 states, 2 interstate river commissions, Puerto Rico, the District of Columbia, and 9 Native American tribes evaluated 23 percent of the nation's river and stream miles. Fifty-five percent of these miles fully supported their designated uses, 10 percent were threatened for one or more uses but currently supported their designated uses, and 35 percent were impaired. (See Figure 5.13.)

Causes and Sources of River and Stream Pollution

Pollutants such as pesticides or raw sewage can affect any stream or river. But according to the EPA's report, siltation, the smothering of riverbeds and streambeds by sediment (usually from soil erosion), was the most common pollutant. Pathogens (bacteria that cause serious health hazards), and nutrients (which cause rapid growth of

FIGURE 5.14

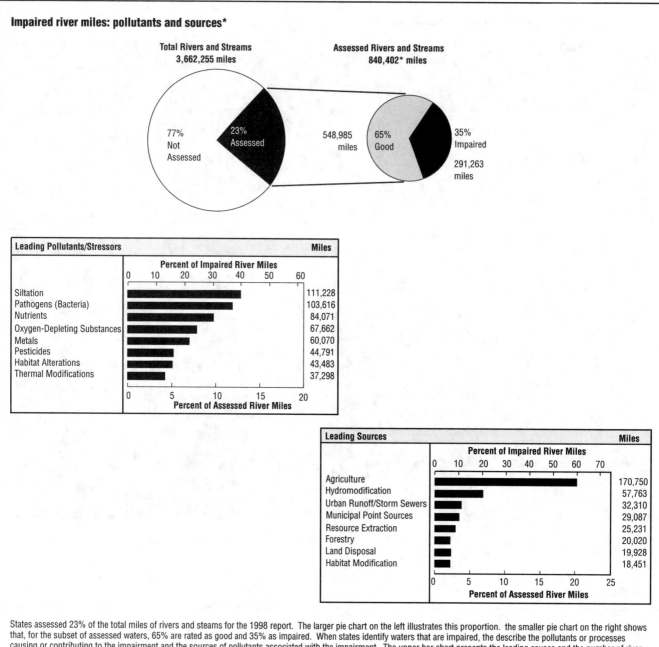

Impaired river miles: pollutants and sources*

States assessed 23% of the total miles of rivers and steams for the 1998 report. The larger pie chart on the left illustrates this proportion. the smaller pie chart on the right shows that, for the subset of assessed waters, 65% are rated as good and 35% as impaired. When states identify waters that are impaired, the describe the pollutants or processes causing or contributing to the impairment and the sources of pollutants associated with the impairment. The upper bar chart presents the leading causes and the number of river and stream miles impacted, and the lower bar chart presents the leading sources and the number of river and stream miles they impact. The percent scales on the upper and lower x-axis of the bar charts provide different perspectives on the magnitude of the impact of these pollutants and sources. The lower axis compares the miles impacted by the pollutant or source to the total assessed miles. The upper axis compares the miles impacted by the pollutant or source to the total impaired miles.

*Includes unknown and natural sources.

SOURCE: Adapted from "Figure 3-4. Leading POLLUTANTS in Impaired Rivers and Streams," and "Figure 3-5. Leading SOURCES of River and Stream Impairment," both in *National Water Quality Inventory: 1998 Report to Congress,* Environmental Protection Agency, Washington, DC, 2000

aquatic plant populations), were the second and third most common pollutants in impaired rivers. (See Figure 5.14.) Both siltation and nutrients usually come from nonpoint sources (those with no specific outlet or discharge point).

Agriculture was, by far, the leading source of pollution, affecting 60 percent of impaired river miles. Other major sources of pollution included hydromodification

(e.g., dredging, building dams), urban runoff/storm sewers, and municipal point sources. (See Figure 5.14.)

THE QUALITY OF U.S. WETLANDS

The EPA defines wetlands as areas inundated by water at a frequency or duration sufficient to support a prevalence of vegetation typically adapted for life in saturated soil conditions. Found throughout the United States, wetlands include swamps, marshes, bogs, and similar areas. Wetlands are recognized as some of the most unique and important areas of the earth because of their ability to support a wide variety of plant and animal life.

During the 1600s and 1700s, more than 200 million acres of wetlands existed in the area that now comprises the lower 48 states. Since then, wetlands have been drained, converted to farmland, and developed into cities. Less than 50 percent of the original wetlands remain. The three states that have sustained the greatest percentage of wetland loss are California (91 percent), Ohio (90 percent), and Iowa (89 percent).

The United States has about 274 million acres of wetlands. In its 1998 *National Water Quality Inventory* (2000) of U.S. wetlands, the EPA reported that only 4 percent of wetlands including Alaska and 9 percent of wetlands excluding Alaska were assessed. Since different methods were used to complete the assessments, and since the acreage assessed was so small, the EPA feels that it can draw only limited conclusions about water quality in wetlands. Some of these conclusions are that sediment deposits, the filling and draining of wetlands, and flow alterations of water in the wetlands appear to be widespread causes of their degradation. Additionally, sources of wetland degradation appear to include agriculture, hydromodification (e.g., dredging, building dams), and the general development of these areas.

In 1998 the Clinton Administration announced The Clean Water Action Plan, which, among other provisions, addressed wetlands both directly and indirectly. The Action Plan set a goal of increasing wetlands by 100,000 acres each year, beginning in 2005, by avoiding wetland losses and restoring wetland areas.

CHAPTER 6
POLLUTION OF GROUND WATER

Ground water lies beneath the earth's surface. It is found almost everywhere—beneath hills, mountains, plains, and even deserts; it may be close to the surface or many hundreds of feet below the surface. Approximately 96 percent of the earth's available fresh water reserve is stored in the ground as ground water. (See Figure 6.1.)

Ground water comes from water that cycles through the environment. The water cycle works like this: When rain falls or snow melts, some of this precipitation seeps into the soil. Plants take up water through their root systems and return moisture to the atmosphere via their leaves in a process called transpiration. Some water

FIGURE 6.1

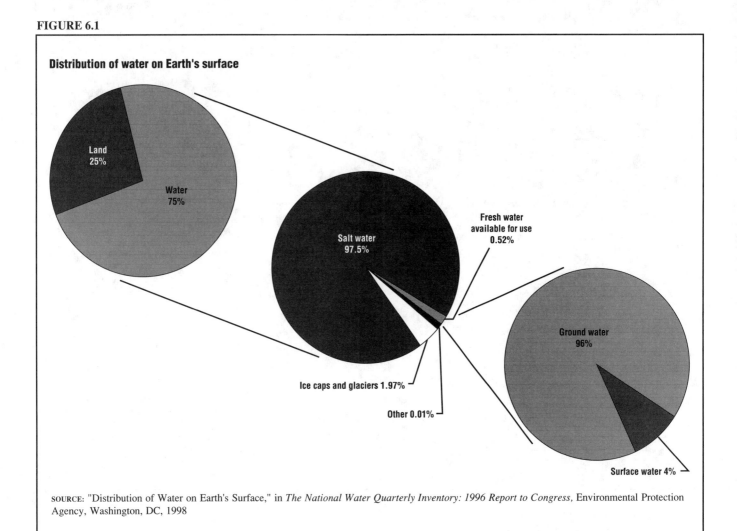

SOURCE: "Distribution of Water on Earth's Surface," in *The National Water Quarterly Inventory: 1996 Report to Congress,* Environmental Protection Agency, Washington, DC, 1998

FIGURE 6.2

The water cycle

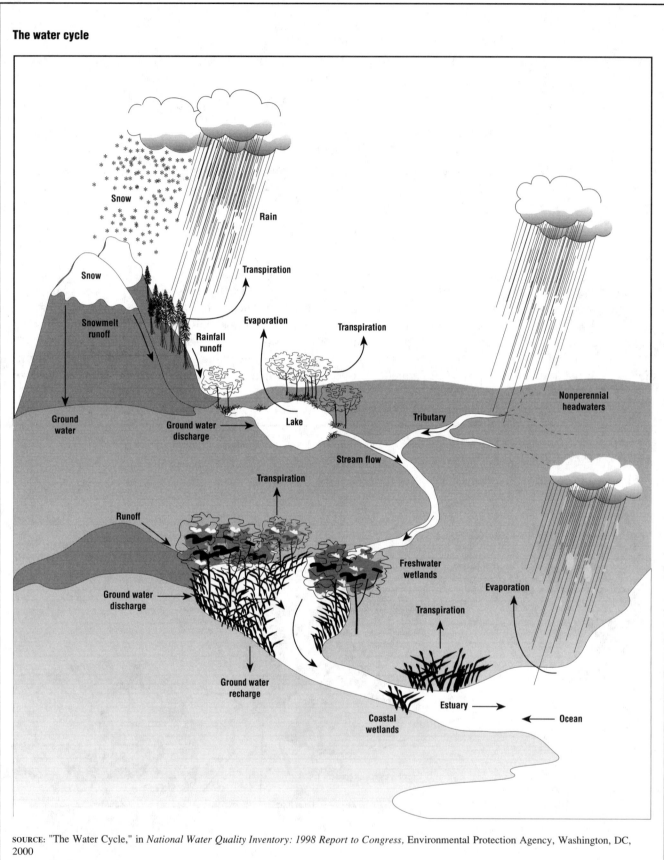

SOURCE: "The Water Cycle," in *National Water Quality Inventory: 1998 Report to Congress,* Environmental Protection Agency, Washington, DC, 2000

FIGURE 6.3

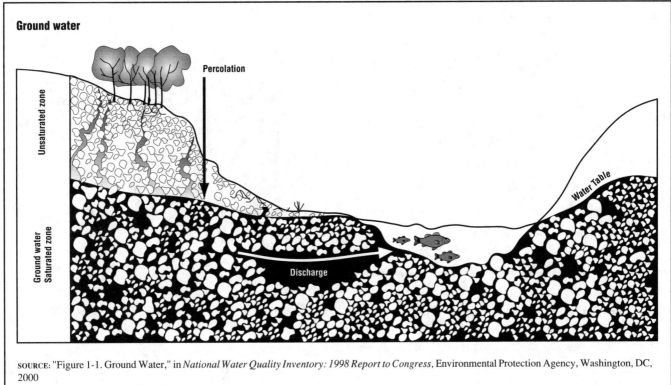

Ground water

Percolation

Unsaturated zone

Ground water Saturated zone

Discharge

Water Table

SOURCE: "Figure 1-1. Ground Water," in *National Water Quality Inventory: 1998 Report to Congress,* Environmental Protection Agency, Washington, DC, 2000

evaporates from the land and surface water, returning to the atmosphere again. And some precipitation runs off saturated land into rivers, streams, lakes, and the ocean. (See Figure 6.2.)

Water that seeps, or percolates, into the soil resides in two zones: the saturated zone and the unsaturated zone. (See Figure 6.3.) The unsaturated zone lies just beneath the surface of the land. Here, both air and water fill the spaces between particles of soil and rock. In most cases, the saturated zone lies beneath the unsaturated zone. The saturated zone lies in rock, and water fills all the spaces within and between particles of rock. Typical types of rock found in the saturated zone are permeable; that is, they have spaces that water can fill. These types of rock include sandstone, gravel, fractured limestone, and fractured granite. The water in this zone is termed ground water.

An aquifer is a saturated zone that contains enough water to yield significant amounts when a well is sunk. Aquifers vary from a few feet thick to tens or hundreds of feet thick. They can be located just below the earth's surface or thousands of feet beneath it, and can cover a few acres or many thousands of square miles. Any one aquifer may be a part of a large system of aquifers that feed into one another.

The water table is the level at which the unsaturated zone and the saturated zone meet. The water table is not fixed, but may rise or fall, depending on water availability. In areas where the climate is fairly consistent, the level of the water table may vary little; in areas subject to extreme flooding and drought, it may rise and fall substantially.

Sometimes ground water discharges into surface water, and, sometimes, surface water replenishes (recharges) ground water. Therefore, polluted ground water can contaminate surface water and polluted surface water can contaminate ground water. Ground water can become contaminated from the precipitation that recharges it as well.

FACTORS AFFECTING GROUND WATER POLLUTION

The process by which ground water becomes polluted depends on a variety of factors, such as:

- The mineral composition of the soil and rocks in the unsaturated zone. Heavy soil and organic materials lessen the potential for contamination.

- The presence or absence of biodegrading microbes in the soil.

- The amount of rainfall. Less rainfall results in less water entering the saturated zone and, therefore, lower quantities of contaminants.

- The evapotranspiration rate. This is the rate at which water is discharged into the atmosphere through evaporation from the soil, surface water, and plants. High rates reduce the amount of contaminated water reaching the saturated zone.

TABLE 6.1

Activities that can cause ground-water contamination

GROUND SURFACE	Infiltration of polluted surface water	De-icing salt use & storage
	Land disposal of wastes	Animal feedlots
	Stockpiles	Fertilizers & pesticides
	Dumps	Accidental spills
	Sewage sludge disposal	Airborne source particulates
ABOVE WATER TABLE	Septic tanks, cesspools, & privies	Underground pipeline leaks
	Holding ponds & lagoons	Artificial recharge
	Sanitary landfills	Sumps and dry wells
	Waste disposal in excavations	Graveyards
	Underground storage tank leaks	
BELOW WATER TABLE	Waste disposal in wells	Exploratory wells
	Drainage wells and canals	Abandoned wells
	Underground storage	Water-supply wells
	Mines	Ground-water withdrawal

SOURCE: "Table 1. Activities that can cause ground-water contamination," in *Citizen's Guide to Groundwater Protection,* U.S. Environmental Protection Agency, Washington, DC, 1990, updated 1999

FIGURE 6.4

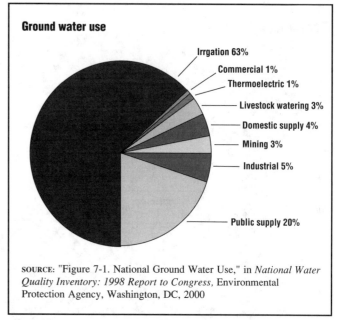

Ground water use

Irrgation 63%
Commercial 1%
Thermoelectric 1%
Livestock watering 3%
Domestic supply 4%
Mining 3%
Industrial 5%
Public supply 20%

SOURCE: "Figure 7-1. National Ground Water Use," in *National Water Quality Inventory: 1998 Report to Congress,* Environmental Protection Agency, Washington, DC, 2000

• The distance between the land surface where pollution occurs and the depth of the water table. The greater the distance, the greater the chance that the pollutants will biodegrade (break down) or will react with soil minerals.

To elaborate on this last point: Ground water can become polluted from activities occurring at the surface of the ground, within the ground above the water table, and within the ground below the water table. Table 6.1 shows the types of activities that can cause ground water contamination at each of these levels. Pollutants introduced onto or into the soil above the level of the ground water are likely to affect the ground water less than those pollutants introduced directly into the ground water, since as a pollutant moves through layers of soil it may become filtered, diluted, and decayed.

GROUND WATER USE

According to the latest data available from the U.S. Geological Survey (USGS), approximately 46 percent of the nation's population and 95 percent of rural residents depended on ground water as their primary source of drinking water in 1995. Of all the ground water used that year, 20 percent was used for the public water supply. Sixty-three percent, the largest share of ground water use, was for agricultural irrigation. (See Figure 6.4.)

SOURCES AND TYPES OF GROUND WATER POLLUTION

Waste was historically discarded in streets and waterways for centuries prior to the 1900s. By the 1920s, wastes were dumped into open pits or buried in containers that soon corroded. (See Figure 1.1.) Although landfill practices are more sophisticated today and protect ground water from pollutants, there is still some danger of chemicals leaching into the ground water from old landfill

areas. Additionally, many other practices place chemicals on the ground that can flow into surface waters or seep into ground water. For example, cities spray icy roads with salts and chemicals. Farmers use pesticides and fertilizers to help grow their crops and feed our population.

While the threat to surface waters from these practices became evident in the 1960s, no one suspected at that time that many of these pollutants would eventually work their way into the ground water, only to reappear in the drinking water, in the water used to raise food crops, or in fish and shellfish. It was thought that the soil provided a barrier or protective filter that neutralized the downward migration of pollutants from the land surface and prevented the ground water from becoming contaminated with them. The discovery of pesticides and other pollutants in ground water, however, demonstrated that human activities do influence ground water quality. Although the Clean Water Act of 1970 was considered the answer to many water problems, it did little to address ground water pollution problems.

Once it became apparent in the late 1970s and early 1980s that ground water was being contaminated, the questions of which waters were being polluted, the severity of contamination, and what should be done about it had to be addressed. Many government and private organizations are working to find the answers, but it is not an easy task. As with other types of pollution control, problems include lack of accurate data, inadequate reporting and measurement techniques, the determination of acceptable standards, illegal dumping, the designation of cleanup responsibilities, and, of course, funding.

From 1978 to 1995, the USGS assessed 25 of the most important regional aquifer systems in the United States as part of the Regional Aquifer-System Analysis

FIGURE 6.5

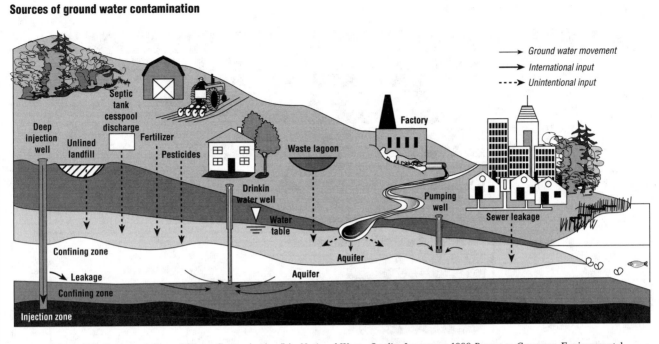

Sources of ground water contamination

SOURCE: "Figure 7-5. Sources of Ground Water Contamination," in *National Water Quality Inventory: 1998 Report to Congress,* Environmental Protection Agency, Washington, DC, 2000

(RASA) Program. After that time, Congress became concerned that efforts to evaluate these aquifers were declining, which led to a 1998 USGS report to Congress that outlined a strategy for addressing key issues about the nation's aquifers (*Strategic Directions for the U.S. Geological Survey Ground-Water Resources Program: A Report to Congress*, USGS, Washington, DC, November 1998). The National Research Council (NRC) concurred, stated that there was little ongoing assessment of America's ground water resources, and concluded that the regional ground water assessment activity of the nature proposed by the USGS should be pursued (*Investigating Groundwater Systems on Regional and National Scales*, NRC, Washington, DC, 2000).

The Environmental Protection Agency (EPA) reports that the quality of most available ground water in the United States is good. However, the USGS notes that ground water resources are at risk from overuse and contamination.

Figure 6.5 shows sources of ground water pollution. As part of preparing its *National Water Quality Inventory: 1998 Report to Congress* (Washington, DC, 2000), the EPA worked with the states to determine the 10 top sources that potentially threaten their ground water. Figure 6.6 shows the sources most frequently cited by states as a potential threat to ground water quality. Leaking underground storage tanks are the top potential source of pollution of ground water, followed closely by septic systems and landfills.

In its report, the EPA grouped similar sources of ground water contamination, and four broad categories emerged. The four categories that are the most important potential sources of ground water pollution are: (1) fuel storage practices, (2) waste disposal practices, (3) agricultural practices, and (4) industrial practices.

The EPA also noted in its report that 31 of 37 states identified the types of contaminants they found in their ground water. The states said that nitrates, metals, volatile (rapidly evaporating) and semi-volatile organic compounds, and pesticides were found most commonly.

Underground Storage Tanks

The EPA reported that leaking underground storage tanks (USTs) was the most frequently cited source of ground water contamination in 1998. (See Figure 6.6.) The EPA also reported that the most important category of potential ground water pollution in 1998 was fuel storage practices. While USTs can be used to store hazardous and toxic chemicals and diluted wastes, the great majority (an estimated 1.5 to 2 million) are used to store petroleum products such as gasoline, diesel fuel, and fuel oil. Although some are above ground, most are located beneath the thousands of service stations throughout the country.

Most underground storage tanks are made of steel, which eventually rusts and disintegrates, releasing the contents of the tanks into the ground. A pollutant in the ground is likely to pollute ground water. (See Figure 6.7.)

FIGURE 6.6

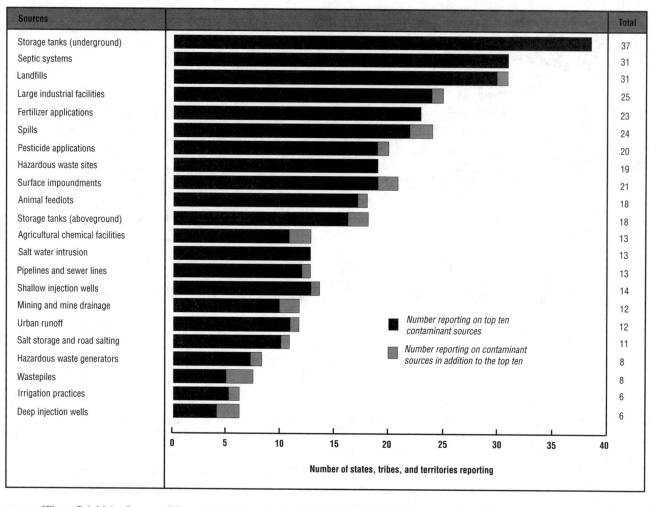

Major sources of ground water contamination

Sources		Total
Storage tanks (underground)		37
Septic systems		31
Landfills		31
Large industrial facilities		25
Fertilizer applications		23
Spills		24
Pesticide applications		20
Hazardous waste sites		19
Surface impoundments		21
Animal feedlots		18
Storage tanks (aboveground)		18
Agricultural chemical facilities		13
Salt water intrusion		13
Pipelines and sewer lines		13
Shallow injection wells		14
Mining and mine drainage		12
Urban runoff		12
Salt storage and road salting		11
Hazardous waste generators		8
Wastepiles		8
Irrigation practices		6
Deep injection wells		6

■ Number reporting on top ten contaminant sources

■ Number reporting on contaminant sources in addition to the top ten

Number of states, tribes, and territories reporting

SOURCE: "Figure 7-6. Major Sources of Ground Water Contamination," in *National Water Quality Inventory: 1998 Report to Congress,* Environmental Protection Agency, Washington, DC, 2000

One gallon of gasoline a day can contaminate 1 million gallons of water, or the amount of water needed for a community of 50,000 people. According to the EPA, "Leaking storage tanks may be causing the most serious risks to human health and the environment."

The average lifespan of a gasoline storage tank varies dramatically depending on where it is installed. In the Great Lakes region, a typical tank may begin to leak within seven years, while a tank may remain intact for well over 30 years in an arid region like Arizona. Of all the tanks currently in use, more than 1 million have been in place for more than 18 years. Some experts believe that many thousands of tanks are already leaking and many thousands more will leak in the near future.

To resolve the problem, all USTs must be dug up and replaced with tanks made of durable, non-corrosive materials. These tanks are extremely expensive; buying and

installing one new steel tank can cost more than $70,000. The major oil companies, which own thousands of tanks, know the chances of leakage are high and they can be held liable for cleanup procedures. They have developed programs to make more durable tanks and replace old ones. Owners of small gas stations who have only a few tanks sometimes gamble that their tanks will not leak and, if they do, the leaks will go undetected. Of course, if the gamble is lost, the costs can run into millions of dollars in fines, cleanup costs, and lawsuits.

Government regulations greatly reduced the options for most tank owners. In 1984 Congress amended the Resource Conservation and Recovery Act (RCRA) to deal with the construction, installation, and monitoring of underground tanks. In 1986 Congress established the Leaking Underground Storage Tank (LUST) program to enforce clean-ups. It established a trust fund, derived primarily from a 0.1 cent-per-gallon motor fuel tax from

1987 to 1995, which generated approximately $150 million per year, and was reinstated in the Taxpayer Relief Act of 1997, effective through March 2005.

In 1988 the EPA issued "comprehensive and stringent" rules requiring devices to detect leaks, modification of tanks to prevent corrosion, regular monitoring, and immediate cleanup of leaks and spills. Older tanks had to be upgraded, replaced, or closed by December 22, 1998. Many small UST owner/operators, "Mom and Pop" gasoline stations, could not afford the cost of replacements and the liability insurance for storage tanks, resulting in the closing of many smaller, independently-owned operations.

Currently, owners of USTs must determine at least every 30 days whether their USTs and piping are leaking by using proper release detection methods. Figure 6.8 shows an example of a tank with proper monitoring systems. Since leaked petroleum produces vapors, the vapor monitoring well samples vapors in the soil gas surrounding the UST. The interstitial monitoring detects leaks in the space between the UST and a second barrier. And a ground water monitoring well checks the water table near the UST for the presence of leaked petroleum.

The EPA estimates that since the federal government's UST program began, nearly 1.2 million of the 2.1 million tanks subject to regulation have been closed. Through September 2000, 412,000 leaks of contaminants were identified, at least 302,000 cleanups were begun, and at least 192,000 cleanups were completed. In roughly 95 percent of the cases, the EPA or the states have been successful in getting the responsible party to perform the cleanup.

Septic Systems and Sewage Disposal

SEPTIC TANKS. The EPA reported that septic systems were the second most frequently cited sources of ground water contamination in 1998. (See Figure 6.6.) Additionally, the EPA reported that the second most important category of potential ground water pollution in 1998 was waste disposal practices.

Septic systems are designed to hold solids and release fluids and wastewaters into constructed leach beds and then into the soil. Bacteria and other natural processes occurring in the leach beds and the soil degrade pollutants in the wastewaters over time. However, if septic systems are poorly constructed, improperly used or maintained, or abandoned, these processes may not occur in full, and the ground water may become contaminated. Typical contaminants from septic systems include bacteria, viruses, nitrates from human waste, phosphates from detergents, and chemicals from household cleaners.

Approximately 20 million Americans, living mostly in rural areas, use individual sewage-disposal systems (septic tanks). These systems are the main source of disease-causing bacteria and nitrates in polluted ground water in

FIGURE 6.7

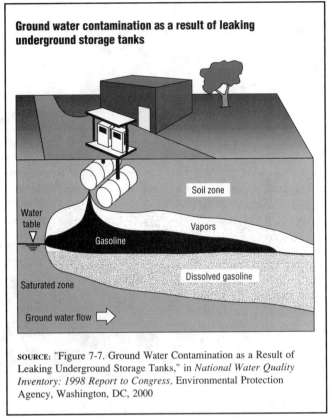

Ground water contamination as a result of leaking underground storage tanks

Soil zone

Water table

Vapors

Gasoline

Dissolved gasoline

Saturated zone

Ground water flow

SOURCE: "Figure 7-7. Ground Water Contamination as a Result of Leaking Underground Storage Tanks," in *National Water Quality Inventory: 1998 Report to Congress,* Environmental Protection Agency, Washington, DC, 2000

rural areas. Septic tanks discharge between 820 and 1,450 billion gallons of waste into the ground each year.

WASTEWATER TREATMENT FACILITIES. Although waters that are safe for fishing and swimming have doubled since the enactment of the Clean Water Act, sewage remains one of the nation's greatest problems. Treatment of wastewater is inconsistent, even within a given sewage system.

Wastewater is the water that flows through sewer systems from the sinks, toilets, showers, and bathtubs of American homes and businesses. Some wastewater systems are combined systems; that is, water from both storm sewers and sanitary sewers merge before the wastewater reaches the treatment facility. Therefore, wastewater contains human waste, food waste from garbage disposals in homes and restaurants, and the various chemicals that Americans pour down their drains at home and at work. It may also contain sand and gravel from storm sewers.

There are two basic stages in the treatment of wastewater: primary treatment and secondary treatment. Figure 6.9 depicts primary treatment. The wastewater (influent) first flows through screens that hold back large items, such as rags, sticks, or the teddy bear that a child may have successfully flushed down the toilet. The influent then goes to a grit chamber, where cinders, sand, and small stones settle to the bottom. Smaller suspended solids settle out in the sedimentation tank. These collected solids are called

FIGURE 6.8

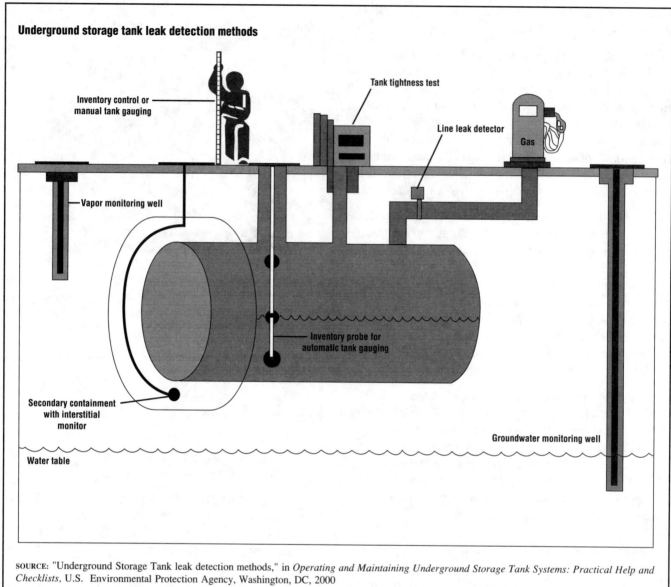

Underground storage tank leak detection methods

SOURCE: "Underground Storage Tank leak detection methods," in *Operating and Maintaining Underground Storage Tank Systems: Practical Help and Checklists*, U.S. Environmental Protection Agency, Washington, DC, 2000

sludge, a watery, black mud that is aerated, baked, and decomposed. Sludge must be deposited in landfills, incinerated, dumped, or disposed of in some other manner.

After primary treatment, the treated wastewater (effluent) still contains organic matter, primarily from human feces. During secondary treatment, aerobic bacteria in the wastewater digest the organics when the wastewater is mixed with air. (See Figure 6.10.) Generally, the effluent from secondary treatment is then treated with chlorine to kill pathogens, and the treated water is discharged to surface water near the treatment plant.

Figure 6.11 shows an overview of the wastewater treatment process. It also shows that tertiary treatment (advanced waste treatment) may be necessary to remove heavy metals, chemical compounds, and toxic substances from the wastewater.

FIGURE 6.9

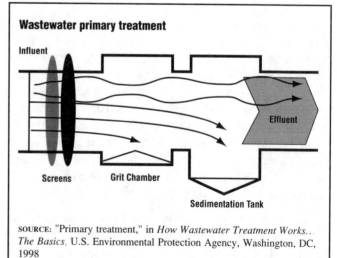

Wastewater primary treatment

SOURCE: "Primary treatment," in *How Wastewater Treatment Works... The Basics*, U.S. Environmental Protection Agency, Washington, DC, 1998

Due to provisions of the Clean Water Act, thousands of municipalities have received federal funds to construct or expand wastewater treatment facilities to prevent or reduce the discharge of pollutants to rivers, lakes, and streams. However, it is estimated that $139.5 billion is still needed to construct or improve wastewater treatment facilities to correct current water quality and public health problems.

Landfills and Hazardous Waste Sites

LANDFILLS. Landfills were the third most frequently cited sources of ground water contamination in 1998. (See Figure 6.6.) The EPA also reported that the second most important category of potential ground water pollution in 1998 was waste disposal practices.

Materials that are commonly discarded in landfills include plastics, metals, sludge, low-level radioactive waste, wood, brick, cellulose (plant matter), petroleum compounds, ceramics, synthetics, polypropylene, and ash. In the past, landfills were generally located on land considered to have no other use—abandoned sand and gravel pits, old strip mines, marshlands, and sinkholes. In many instances, the water table was at or very near the surface, and the potential for ground water contamination was high. (Figure 6.5 shows an unlined landfill as one source of ground water contamination.)

Early environmental regulation aimed at reducing air and surface-water pollution called for disposing of solid wastes underground. Many of the disposal sites were nothing more than large holes in the ground, and chemicals and bacteria seeped through the earth into underground aquifers. The leachate (the liquid that percolates through the waste materials) from landfills contains contaminants that can easily pollute ground water. Although regulations have changed dramatically, past practices continue to cause a threat to ground water. Some studies estimate that 75 percent of all active and inactive landfill sites are leaking contaminants into the ground water.

There have been attempts to identify and classify the thousands of landfills, or dumps, that are spread all over the country, but the lists are incomplete. It is the responsibility of each state to count its own dumps and report on their compliance with federal pollution standards. In 1993 new standards went into effect for landfills. The 20,000 landfills that had operated in the 1970s had shrunk to 2,216 in 1999, at least in part because of the new rules. (See Table 2.4 in Chapter 2.)

HAZARDOUS WASTE SITES. Some materials that have been regularly deposited in landfills for many years are now known to be hazardous to human health. The majority of those sites considered dangerous contain industrial chemical wastes. Some are municipal dumps, where high concentrations of pesticides and hazardous household cleaning solvents are present. In many areas, the extent of

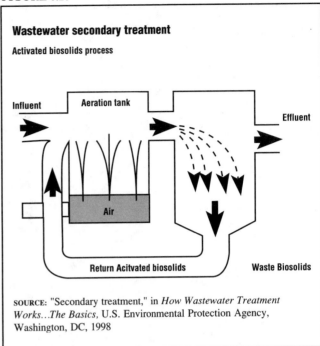

FIGURE 6.10

Wastewater secondary treatment

Activated biosolids process

Influent

Aeration tank

Effluent

Air

Return Acitvated biosolids

Waste Biosolids

SOURCE: "Secondary treatment," in *How Wastewater Treatment Works...The Basics,* U.S. Environmental Protection Agency, Washington, DC, 1998

the problem is only now becoming apparent. In remote areas, for example, dumping was often permitted. Today, as new suburban communities spread out from the cities, these sites have become serious contamination problems since people now live so close by.

When a site is found to be so badly contaminated with hazardous waste that it represents a serious threat to human health (for example, contamination of ground water used for drinking), it is placed on the National Priorities List, commonly known as "Superfund," making it eligible for federal intervention and cleanup assistance.

The EPA reported in 1995 that approximately 73 million people lived fewer than four miles from at least one Superfund site, and much debate has occurred about the extent to which these sites pose health risks to those residents. The EPA found that one-third of the sites studied posed serious health risks to nearby residents, primarily through ground water (*Superfund—Information on Current Health Risks*, 1995).

Ground water monitoring is the primary method of detecting contamination at hazardous waste sites. Monitoring systems consist of a number of wells placed around a waste facility, as shown in Figure 6.12. Data taken from those wells can indicate whether contamination is occurring at the site.

Of the total 1,789 hazardous waste sites on the National Priorities List in 1998, about 73 percent have already contaminated ground water, and another 22 percent could contaminate ground water in the future. (See Figure 6.13.) In addition, about 32 percent of the sites have already

FIGURE 6.11

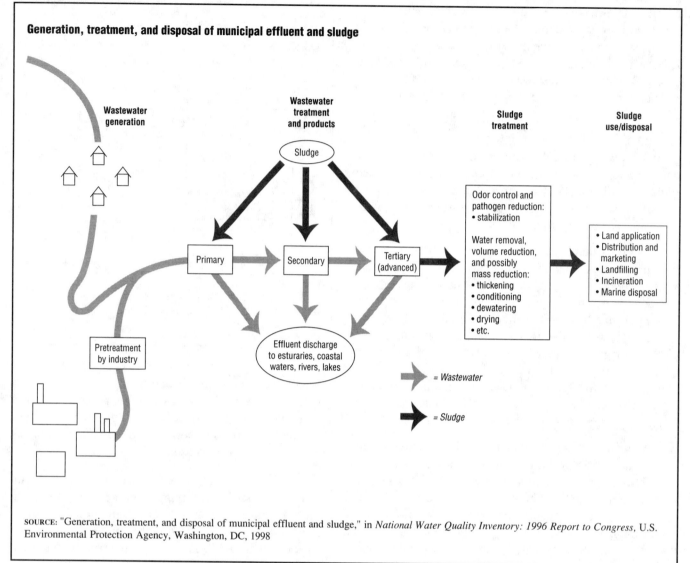

Generation, treatment, and disposal of municipal effluent and sludge

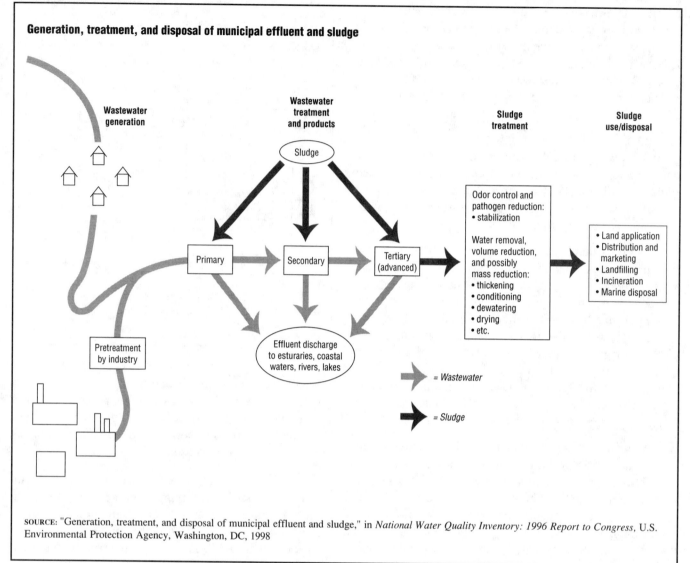

SOURCE: "Generation, treatment, and disposal of municipal effluent and sludge," in *National Water Quality Inventory: 1996 Report to Congress,* U.S. Environmental Protection Agency, Washington, DC, 1998

tainted drinking water sources, with another 56 percent potentially capable of contaminating drinking water.

Pesticides, Herbicides, and Fertilizers

The EPA reported that fertilizer applications and pesticide applications were the fifth and seventh (respectively) most frequently cited sources of ground water contamination in 1998. (See Figure 6.6.) The EPA also reported that the third most important category of potential ground water pollution in 1998 was agricultural practices.

PESTICIDES. The ancient Greeks were the first documented users of pesticides. A pesticide is a chemical used to kill insects or other pests (such as fungi) harmful to cultivated plants. Pliny the Elder (C.E. 23–79) reported using common compounds such as arsenic, sulfur, caustic soda, and olive oil to protect crops. The Chinese later used similar substances to repel insects and retard the growth of fungi on plants. Such inorganic (non-carbon-based) pesticides were used until the 1900s. They were then banned

because they persist in the environment for long periods, and they harm or kill many forms of life, including humans.

The invention of DDT (dichloro-diphenyl-trichloroethane, a powerful organic [carbon-based] insecticide) in 1939 marked a revolution in the war against pests. DDT was effective, relatively inexpensive, and apparently safe—a miracle chemical that promised a world without insects and with unprecedented crop yields. In 1948 Swiss researcher Paul Müller received a Nobel Prize for its discovery. Convinced that chemicals were the modern wave of the future, farmers began using pesticides intensively and began to accept chemicals as essential to agriculture.

The use of organic pesticides came with problems, however. Like inorganic pesticides, they harmed or killed many forms of life and persisted in the environment. Often, insects became immune to their effects. In 1947 Congress passed the Federal Insecticide, Fungicide, and Rodenticide Act (FIFRA), which requires all pesticides

FIGURE 6.12

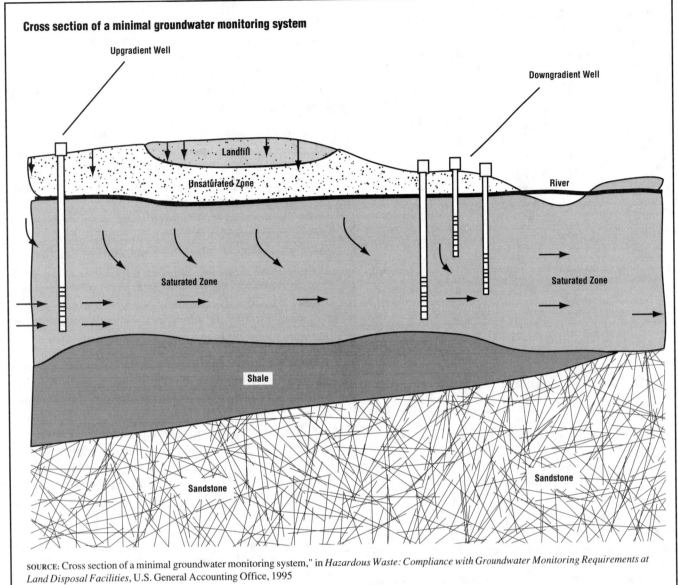

Cross section of a minimal groundwater monitoring system

Upgradient Well

Downgradient Well

Landfill

Unsaturated Zone

River

Saturated Zone

Saturated Zone

Shale

Sandstone

Sandstone

SOURCE: Cross section of a minimal groundwater monitoring system," in *Hazardous Waste: Compliance with Groundwater Monitoring Requirements at Land Disposal Facilities*, U.S. General Accounting Office, 1995

sold or distributed in the U.S. (including imported pesticides) to be registered by the EPA. Even if manufacture and use in the United States is permitted, each pesticide must be re-registered every five years and may be banned if information has emerged that it is exceptionally harmful. DDT and many other pesticides have been banned in the United States.

Today, farmers apply about 1.1 billion pounds of pesticides per year to their crops. Seventy-five percent of pesticide use is in industrialized countries. In the United States, pesticide use in agriculture has approximately tripled since 1965.

The discovery of certain pesticides in underground drinking water many years after their being banned challenged long-held notions about agricultural chemicals. Farmers had thought pesticides either evaporated or

degraded into harmless substances. Now farmers were confronted with the possibility that they may have poisoned their own drinking water. Many experts believe this is the tip of the iceberg, as increasing evidence of pesticides in the air, water, and food chain is being found. The EPA currently lists 55 possible carcinogens (cancer-causing substances) being used on U.S. food crops.

In recent years, improved safety testing has prompted tougher standards for a new generation of pesticides. The best of the new pesticides can be used in minute quantities and cause few health problems. They are, however, more expensive than older types of pesticides. Many farmers continue to use the older pesticides, especially in developing countries. DDT is now banned in most industrialized countries, but it is still used in developing nations, where many farmers see it as an inexpensive way to control

FIGURE 6.13

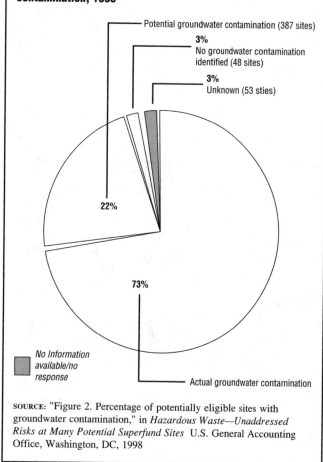

Percentage of potentially eligible sites with groundwater contamination, 1998

Potential groundwater contamination (387 sites)

3%
No groundwater contamination identified (48 sites)

3%
Unknown (53 sties)

22%

73%

No Information available/no response

Actual groundwater contamination

SOURCE: "Figure 2. Percentage of potentially eligible sites with groundwater contamination," in *Hazardous Waste—Unaddressed Risks at Many Potential Superfund Sites* U.S. General Accounting Office, Washington, DC, 1998

pounds per year of the seven agricultural herbicides from 1964 to 1994. Six of these chemicals (all except acetochlor) were found in samples taken from shallow ground water, which had been recharged within the past 10 years. Samples found atrazine, metolachlor, prometon, and simazine most frequently, with atrazine the most commonly reported chemical, especially in agricultural areas. (See Figure 6.15.)

However, results of the study revealed that more than 98 percent of the samples had concentrations of less than one microgram per liter of each herbicide. These data confirmed that fewer than 0.1 percent of the sites did not meet the standards necessary for safe drinking water; most did meet the standards. Although these results show that most aquifers were not contaminated with troublesome levels of herbicides, the USGS pointed out that the conclusions of the report do not fully reflect the overall health risks of herbicide use because data were collected on only seven herbicides. Additionally, the USGS noted that they did not know what the additive effects of mixtures of these chemicals were on human and aquatic health.

FERTILIZERS. Fertilizer is a substance that is spread on or through the soil to enrich it with nutrients for plant growth. Fertilizers include manure and synthetic chemical mixtures. From 1950 to 1984, fertilizer use contributed to the increase in the world's food production at a rate of 7 percent per year. Since 1984, however, these increases have dropped to less than 2 percent annually. As the world adds another 90 million people per year, the need for food supplies expands, yet the growth in world fertilizer use has actually slowed.

In the United States, the high cost of fertilizer, coupled with new methods to more precisely measure the fertilizer needs of various crops, is discouraging excessive use of chemical fertilizers. Farmers have found that the "little bit" extra that they might once have used is lost in nutrient runoff and adds to stream pollution in agricultural areas. The major factor, however, is the decreasing response of crops to fertilizer. During the 1960s, an additional ton of fertilizer applied on a farm in the U.S. cornbelt boosted output by 20 tons. Today, another ton may boost output by only a few tons. Crops are apparently approaching the limits of photosynthetic efficiency (maximum possible yield).

ANIMAL WASTE. Animal agriculture, the production of livestock and poultry, is important to the economic well-being of the United States, producing $98.8 billion per year in farm revenue. In addition to providing food for Americans, the industry also contributes to the stability of many rural communities.

Livestock includes cattle (beef, dairy, and veal), swine, poultry (chickens and turkeys), and sheep and lambs. The U.S. Department of Agriculture (USDA) reports that markets for these meats have changed in

pests. Nonetheless, even the new formulations are not entirely safe, especially for wildlife.

As an alternative to pesticide use and abuse, many scientists and the federal government encourage the practice of Integrated Pest Management (IPM). This method combines biological controls (such as natural predators of pests), certain agricultural practices (such as planting rotation and diversification), and genetic manipulation (such as the use of pest-resistant crop varieties) with a modest use of chemicals. Rather than attempting the impossible task of eliminating pests, the goal is to strike a sustainable, profitable balance with nature. IPM is becoming increasingly common in the United States and in many parts of the world.

HERBICIDES. Herbicides are chemicals used to kill weeds. In *Distribution of Major Herbicides in Ground Water of the United States* (1999), the USGS reported on a study it conducted in the early-to-mid 1990s in which it measured the presence of seven herbicides in ground water samples throughout the United States. The herbicides studied included seven high-use herbicides: atrazine, alachlor, cyanazine, simazine, prometon, acetochlor, and metolachlor. Figure 6.14 shows the use in

FIGURE 6.14

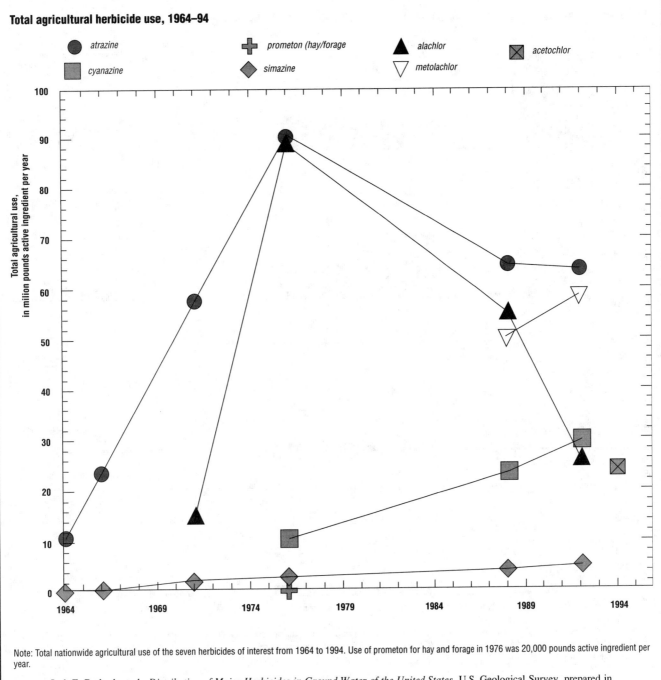

Total agricultural herbicide use, 1964–94

- ● atrazine
- ■ cyanazine
- ✚ prometon (hay/forage
- ◆ simazine
- ▲ alachlor
- ▽ metolachlor
- ⊠ acetochlor

Note: Total nationwide agricultural use of the seven herbicides of interest from 1964 to 1994. Use of prometon for hay and forage in 1976 was 20,000 pounds active ingredient per year.

SOURCE: Jack E. Barbash et al., *Distribution of Major Herbicides in Ground Water of the United States,* U.S. Geological Survey, prepared in cooperation with the U.S. Environmental Protection Agency, Sacramento, CA, 1999

recent decades, with Americans eating less beef since the 1970s and more poultry. (See Table 6.2.) Livestock consumption has grown elsewhere in the world, because of the growing population and livestock's increasing affordability in many parts of the world. The United States has become the largest exporter of meat in the world.

Concern over pollution resulting from intensive livestock and poultry production has increased in recent years. Nationwide, about 130 times more animal waste is produced than human waste. The livestock of some large

farming operations produce as much waste as a town or city. This huge volume of waste threatens surface and ground water quality. Figure 6.6 shows that waste from animal feedlots was cited as the tenth major source of ground water contamination in 1998.

As animal production is increasingly concentrated in larger operations and in certain areas of the country, traditional animal management practices may not be adequate to prevent ground water contamination. Typically, animals are tightly confined, often indoors on slatted metal floors,

FIGURE 6.15

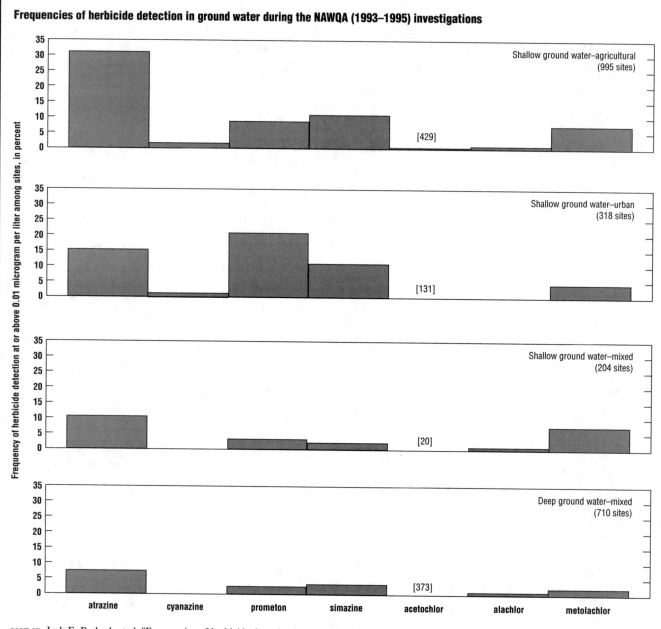

Frequencies of herbicide detection in ground water during the NAWQA (1993–1995) investigations

SOURCE: Jack E. Barbash et al.,"Frequencies of herbicide detection in ground water during the NAWQA (1993–1995) investigations," in *Distribution of Major Herbicides in Ground Water of the United States,* U.S. Geological Survey, prepared in cooperation with the U.S. Environmental Protection Agency, Sacramento, CA, 1999

beneath which their feces are flushed. Animal waste contains potential ground water pollutants such as organic matter, sediments, pathogens, heavy metals, hormones, antibiotics, and nitrates. Rainwater, snowmelt, or irrigation water transports these pollutants through the soil to the ground water or into rivers, lakes, and coastal waters.

From 1996 through 1998, the federal government provided more than $384 million in assistance to producers for animal waste management. (Figure 6.16 shows the share of assistance provided by various federal agencies.) The USDA administers several major programs to provide financial and technical assistance to producers for managing animal wastes. The nation's federal and state regulatory systems for protecting environmental health have, however, largely been unable to keep pace with the rapid growth of large farms.

Surface Impoundments

The EPA reported that the fourth most important category of potential ground water pollution in 1998 was industrial practices. Additionally, the EPA reported that surface impoundments were the ninth most frequently cited source of ground water contamination in 1998. (See Figure 6.6.)

TABLE 6.2

Red meat and poultry (boneless, trimmed equivalent), per capita consumption, 1909–99

	Red meat					Poultry		
Year	Beef	Veal	Pork	Lamb	Total	Chicken	Turkey	Total
					Pounds			
Averages								
1909-19	44.7	4.7	40.0	4.1	93.5	10.2	0.9	11.1
1920-29	39.0	5.3	41.8	3.6	89.6	10.1	1.1	11.1
1930-39	37.0	5.3	38.2	4.5	85.0	9.9	1.5	11.4
1940-49	44.6	6.6	45.2	4.2	100.6	13.3	2.6	15.8
1950-59	52.8	5.7	45.4	2.8	106.7	16.3	4.1	20.5
1960-69	69.2	3.4	46.9	2.8	122.3	22.6	6.0	28.6
1970-79	80.9	2.0	45.0	1.5	129.5	28.4	6.8	35.2
1980-89	71.7	1.3	47.7	1.0	121.8	36.3	9.9	46.2
1990-99	63.9	0.8	48.1	0.9	113.7	48.5	14.1	62.6

SOURCE: Adapted from "Red meat, poultry, and fish (boneless, trimmed equivalent): Per capita consumption," Per Capita Food Consumption Data System, U.S. Department of Agriculture, Economic Research Service, Washington, DC [Online] http://www.ers.usda.gov/Data/FoodConsumption/Spreadsheets/mtpcc.xls [accessed on October 15, 2001]

FIGURE 6.16

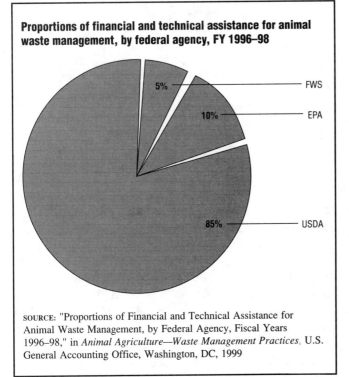

Proportions of financial and technical assistance for animal waste management, by federal agency, FY 1996–98

SOURCE: "Proportions of Financial and Technical Assistance for Animal Waste Management, by Federal Agency, Fiscal Years 1996–98," in *Animal Agriculture—Waste Management Practices*, U.S. General Accounting Office, Washington, DC, 1999

FIGURE 6.17

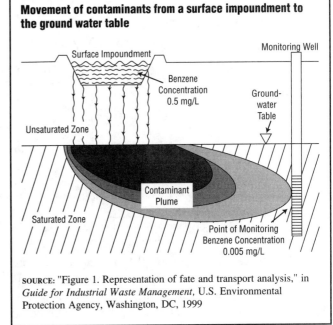

Movement of contaminants from a surface impoundment to the ground water table

SOURCE: "Figure 1. Representation of fate and transport analysis," in *Guide for Industrial Waste Management*, U.S. Environmental Protection Agency, Washington, DC, 1999

Surface impoundments are pits, lagoons, and ponds, usually human-made, that receive treated or untreated wastes directly from the discharge point or are used to store chemicals for later use, to wash or treat ores, or to treat water for further use. Most are small, less than one acre, but some industrial and mining impoundments may be as large as 1,000 acres.

Most impoundments are not lined with a synthetic or impermeable natural material, such as clay, to prevent liquids from leaching into the ground. This is particularly important, since about 87 percent of the impoundments

are located over aquifers currently used as sources of drinking water. Only 2 percent are located in areas where there is no ground water or where the ground water is too salty for use. About 70 percent of the sites are located over very permeable aquifers that can allow contaminants entering their waters to spread rapidly. Ground water protection has rarely, if ever, been considered during the site selection of impoundments.

Figure 6.17 shows an illustration of a surface impoundment with a benzene contaminant in its waters. The illustration shows how contaminated fluids from the surface impoundment move through the unsaturated zone. The rate of movement of the pollutants depends on the

FIGURE 6.18

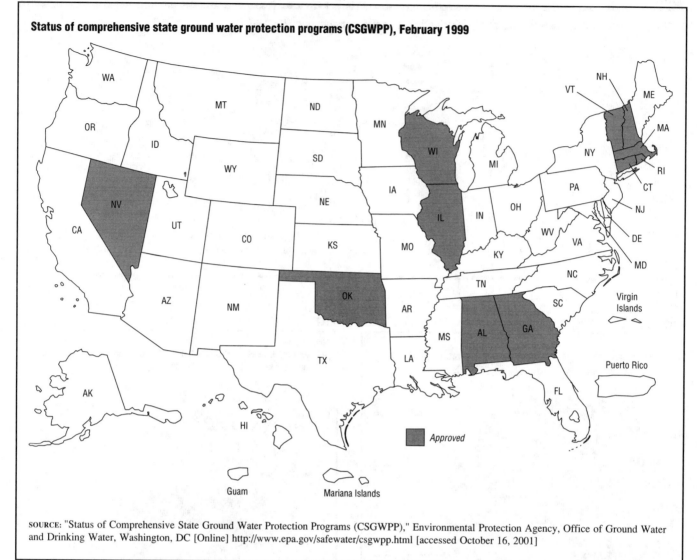

Status of comprehensive state ground water protection programs (CSGWPP), February 1999

□ Approved

SOURCE: "Status of Comprehensive State Ground Water Protection Programs (CSGWPP)," Environmental Protection Agency, Office of Ground Water and Drinking Water, Washington, DC [Online] http://www.epa.gov/safewater/csgwpp.html [accessed October 16, 2001]

type of geological material below the impoundment. More rapid movement occurs through coarse-textured materials such as sand and gravel than through fine-textured materials such as silt and clay. Additionally, clays retard pollutant movement to the water table because they tend to attract them. That is, the pollutants stick to the clay particles. If not retarded in their movement to the water table, pollutants form an area of contamination (contaminant plume) in the ground water and can contaminate nearby wells.

THE CLEANUP AND PROTECTION OF GROUND WATER

Cleaning up the nation's ground water is expensive. The costs for cleaning up typical ground water contamination from a chemical landfill are estimated at $5 to $10 million per site.

In allocating limited resources, cleanup decisions are based on a cost/benefit analysis that considers such fac-

tors as the extent of the problem, the potential health effects, and the alternatives, if any. If the pollution is localized, it may be more practical to simply shut down the contaminated wells and find water elsewhere. Cleanup options range from "capping" a section of an aquifer with a layer of clay that prevents more pollution, to more complex (and expensive) methods such as pumping out and treating the water and then returning it to the aquifer. Where radioactive or hazardous materials have permeated the soil and contaminated ground water, both the water and soil may need to be treated.

The States' Role

Since the 1980s, the individual states have conducted extensive activities to protect ground water. Studies by the National Conference of State Legislatures indicated that all 50 states have enacted legislation with ground water management provisions since that time. Additionally, under the Clean Water Act, the EPA has provided nearly

TABLE 6.3

Federal Laws administered by EPA affecting ground water

Federal Laws Administered by EPA Affecting Ground Water

Clean Water Act (CWA)
Ground water protection is addressed in Section 102 of the CWA, providing for the development of federal, state, and local comprehensive programs for reducing, eliminating, and preventing ground water contamination.

Safe Drinking Water Act (SDWA)
Under the SDWA, EPA is authorized to ensure that water is safe for human consumption. To support this effort, SDWA gives EPA the authority to promulgate Maximum Contaminant Levels (MCLs) that define safe levels for some contaminants in public drinking water supplies. One of the most fundamental ways to ensure consistently safe drinking water is to protect the source of that water (i.e., ground water). Source water protection is achieved through four programs: the Wellhead Protection Program (WHP), the Sole Source Aquifer Program, the Underground Injection Control (UIC) Program, and, under the 1996 Amendments, the Source Water Assessment Program.

Resource Conservation and Recovery Act (RCRA)
The intent of RCRA is to protect human health and the environment by establishing a comprehensive regulatory framework for investigating and addressing past, present, and future environmental contamination or ground water and other environmental media. In addition, management of underground storage tanks is also addressed under RCRA.

Comprehensive Environmental, Response, Compensation, and Liability Act (CERCLA)
CERCLA provides a federal "Superfund" to clean-up soil and ground water contaminated by uncontrolled or abandoned hazardous waste sites as well as accidents, spill, and other emergency releases of pollutants and contaminants into the environment. Through the Act, EPA was given power to seek out those parties responsible for any release and assure their cooperation in the clean-up. The program is designed to recover costs, when possible, from financially viable individuals and companies when the clean-up is complete.

Federal Insecticide, Fungicide, and Rodenticide Act (FIFRA)
FIFRA protects human health and the environment from the risks of pesticide use by requiring the testing and registration of all chemicals used as active ingredients of pesticides and pesticide products. Under the Pesticide Management Program, States and Tribes wishing to continue use of chemicals of concern are required to prepare a prevention plan that targets specific areas vulnerable to ground water contamination.

SOURCE: Federal Laws Administered by EPA Affecting Ground Water," in *Safe Drinking Water Act, Section 1429 Ground Water Report to Congress*, Environmental Protection Agency, Office of Water, Washington, DC, 1999

$80 million since 1985 to all the states to develop statewide ground water strategies. These programs are called Comprehensive State Ground Water Protection Programs (CSGWPPs) and consist of a set of six strategic activities. The goal of these activities is to foster the protection of ground water through a coordinated operation of all relevant federal, state, and local programs within a state. Figure 6.18 shows which states had approved CSG-WPPs as of February 1999.

The Federal Role

Many federal laws administered by the EPA help protect ground water. Table 6.3 lists most of these laws and describes each. Additional laws include those described below.

The Superfund Amendments and Reauthorization Act of 1986 (SARA) amended CERCLA, the Comprehensive Environmental, Response, Compensation, and Liability Act. SARA made additions and changes to CERCLA based on the EPA's experience in administering the complex Superfund program during its first six years. SARA also required the cleanup of hazardous wastes that can seep into the ground water. SARA included a provision that cities and industry build better-managed and better-constructed landfills for hazardous materials so that the ground water will not be polluted in the future.

The Toxic Substances Control Act (TSCA) of 1976 was enacted by Congress to give the EPA the ability to track the 75,000 industrial chemicals currently produced or imported into the U.S., including those with a potential to contaminate ground water.

In August 1993 the Oil Pollution Act of 1990 went into effect. The law, which was passed in response to the 1989 *Exxon Valdez* oil spill in Alaska, requires companies involved in storing and transporting petroleum to have standby plans for cleaning up spills on land or in water. A result of the law has been a resurgence of interest in and a new market for innovative methods for oil-spill cleanup.

CHAPTER 7
HAZARDOUS WASTE

WHAT IS HAZARDOUS WASTE?

Solid waste is garbage, trash, and construction and demolition debris. It also includes semisolids, liquids, and gases from mining, agricultural, commercial, and industrial activities. Hazardous waste is dangerous solid waste. Figure 7.1 lists and describes the characteristics that identify waste as being hazardous.

Because of its dangerous characteristics, hazardous waste requires special care when being stored, transported, or discarded. The Environmental Protection Agency (EPA), under the Resource Conservation and Recovery Act (RCRA) and its amendments, ensures that hazardous waste is managed in an environmentally safe manner from generation to disposal.

Contamination of the air, water, and soil with hazardous waste can frequently lead to serious health problems. The Environmental Protection Agency (EPA) estimates that roughly 1,000 cases of cancer annually can be linked to hazardous waste exposure, as can some degenerative diseases, mental retardation, birth defects, and chromosomal changes. While most scientists agree that exposure to high doses of hazardous waste is dangerous, there is less agreement on the danger of exposure to low doses.

INDUSTRIAL HAZARDOUS WASTE

Only 2 to 4 percent of all waste generated in the United States is hazardous waste. The chemical industry, petroleum refiners, and the metal processing industry produce 90 percent of hazardous waste, and the remaining 10 percent comes from a variety of sources such as photo labs, service stations, dry cleaners, body shops, printers, laboratories, and private homes.

Industrial wastes are usually a combination of compounds, one or more of which may be hazardous. For example, used pickling solution from a metal processor may contain acid, a hazardous waste, along with water and other nonhazardous compounds. (Pickling is a chemical method of cleaning metal and removing rust during processing.) A mixture of waste produced regularly as a result of industrial processes is called a waste stream, and it generally consists of diluted rather than full-strength

FIGURE 7.1

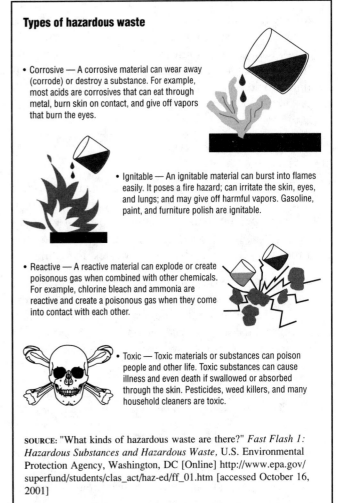

Types of hazardous waste

- Corrosive — A corrosive material can wear away (corrode) or destroy a substance. For example, most acids are corrosives that can eat through metal, burn skin on contact, and give off vapors that burn the eyes.

- Ignitable — An ignitable material can burst into flames easily. It poses a fire hazard; can irritate the skin, eyes, and lungs; and may give off harmful vapors. Gasoline, paint, and furniture polish are ignitable.

- Reactive — A reactive material can explode or create poisonous gas when combined with other chemicals. For example, chlorine bleach and ammonia are reactive and create a poisonous gas when they come into contact with each other.

- Toxic — Toxic materials or substances can poison people and other life. Toxic substances can cause illness and even death if swallowed or absorbed through the skin. Pesticides, weed killers, and many household cleaners are toxic.

SOURCE: "What kinds of hazardous waste are there?" *Fast Flash 1: Hazardous Substances and Hazardous Waste*, U.S. Environmental Protection Agency, Washington, DC [Online] http://www.epa.gov/ superfund/students/clas_act/haz-ed/ff_01.htm [accessed October 16, 2001]

compounds. Often the hazardous components are suspended or dissolved in a mixture of dirt, oil, or water.

HOUSEHOLD HAZARDOUS WASTE

Household hazardous waste (HHW) consists of the residue of many common consumer products that can result in the release of potentially toxic substances. Because of the relatively low amount of hazardous substances in individual products, HHW is not regulated as a hazardous waste. Examples of HHW include nail polish remover, toilet and drain cleaners, chlorine bleach, pesticides, small batteries, automotive oil and batteries, and oil-based paints and thinners.

The National Solid Waste Management Association reports that HHW comprises less than 1 percent of municipal solid waste. The EPA reports that the average household discards approximately four to five pounds of HHW per person per year. Batteries outnumber all other components of HHW. However, by weight, paint, stain, and varnish are the greatest components, followed by batteries and automotive products.

Since 1980 some 4,600 HHW collection programs have been organized. Most of these have been one-day programs in which residents bring all household products containing hazardous materials to a collection point to be discarded. Every state has at least one such program. In addition, many municipalities now maintain permanent locations for drop-off of HHW. A small number of residential curbside recycling programs collect certain HHW items, such as oil and batteries.

METHODS OF MANAGING HAZARDOUS WASTE

In North America, 96 percent of all hazardous waste is treated and disposed of on the site at which it is produced. Four percent is treated and disposed of by commercial waste service companies. A variety of techniques exist for safely managing hazardous wastes, including:

- Reduction—Waste generators change their manufacturing processes and materials in order to produce less hazardous waste. For example, a food packaging plant might replace solvent-based adhesives, which result in hazardous waste, with water-based adhesives, which result in non-hazardous waste.

- Recycling—Some waste materials become raw material for another process or can be recovered, reused, or sold.

- Treatment—A variety of chemical, biological, and thermal processes can be applied to neutralize or destroy toxic compounds. For example, microorganisms or chemicals can remove hazardous hydrocarbons from contaminated water.

- Land disposal—State and federal regulations require the pre-treatment of most hazardous wastes before they can be discarded in landfills. These treated materials can only be placed in specially designed land disposal facilities.

- Injection wells—Hazardous waste may be injected under high pressure deep underground in wells thousands of feet deep.

- Incineration—Hazardous waste can be burned. However, as waste is burned, hot gases are released into the atmosphere, carrying toxic materials not consumed by the flames. In 1999 the Clinton Administration imposed a ban on new hazardous waste incinerators.

GOVERNMENT REGULATION

The Resource Conservation and Recovery Act (RCRA)

The Resource Conservation and Recovery Act (RCRA), first enacted by Congress in 1976 and expanded by amendments in 1980, 1984, 1992, and 1996, was designed to manage the disposal, incineration, treatment, and storage of waste in landfills, surface impoundments, waste piles, tanks, and container storage areas. It regulates the production and disposal of hazardous waste, and provides guidelines and mandates to improve waste disposal practices. The EPA also has the authority under the RCRA to require businesses with hazardous waste operations to take corrective action to clean up the waste they have released into the environment.

The RCRA imposes design and maintenance standards for waste disposal facilities, such as the installation of liners to prevent waste from migrating into ground water. Land disposal facilities in operation after November 1980 are regulated under the act and are required to meet RCRA standards or close. Owners of facilities that ceased operation prior to November 1980 are required to clean up any hazardous waste threats their facilities still pose. Abandoned sites and those that owners cannot afford to clean up under the RCRA are usually referred to the national Superfund program.

CERCLA and the Superfund

The Comprehensive Environmental Response, Compensation, and Liability Act of 1980 (CERCLA) established the Superfund program to pay for cleaning up highly contaminated hazardous waste sites that had been abandoned or where a sole responsible party could not be identified. A $1.6 billion five-year program, Superfund was focused initially on cleaning up leaking dumps that jeopardized ground water.

During the original mandate of Superfund, only six sites were cleaned up. When the program expired in 1985, many observers viewed it as a billion-dollar fiasco rampant with scandal and mismanagement. Nonetheless, the negative publicity surrounding the program increased public awareness of

FIGURE 7.2

Types of environmental and public health risks addressed at Superfund sites

Contaminated air

Direct contact with hazardous waste

Contaminated drinking water

Fire or explosion hazard

The food chain

Contaminated ground water

Contaminated soil

Contaminated surface water

SOURCE: Adapted from "Types of Environmental and Public Health Risks Addressed at Superfund Sites," in *Superfund: Program Management*, U.S. General Accounting Office, Washington, DC, 1992

the magnitude of the cleanup job in America. Consequently, in 1986 and 1990, Superfund was reauthorized.

THE NATIONAL PRIORITIES LIST. CERCLA requires the government to maintain a list of hazardous waste sites that pose the highest potential threat to human health and the environment. This list is known as the National Priorities List (NPL) and is a published list of hazardous waste sites in the country that are being cleaned up under the Superfund program. Figure 7.2

TABLE 7.1

Percentage of potentially eligible sites contributing to specified adverse conditions and percentage of sites for which conditions' presence is uncertain

Conditions resulting from contamination at 1,789 potentially eligible sites	Number of potentially eligible sites with condition	Percentage of potentially eligible sites with condition	Percentage of potentially eligible sites for which presence of condition is uncertain
Workers/visitors may have direct contact with contaminants	981	55	21
Trespassers may come into direct contact with contaminants	969	54	20
Fences/barriers/signs are erected to keep residents or others out of contaminated areas	618	35	19
Residents/community have concerns about contamination or potential health effects caused by this site	548	31	35
Fish could be unsafe to eat	486	27	29
Institutional restrictions are necessary because of site's contamination[1]	410	23	46
Residents/others should avoid exposure to contaminated dust on some days	355	20	23
Sources of drinking water permanently changed[2]	215	12	20
Obnoxious odors are present	194	11	24
Residents advised not to use wells	150	8	20
Fish, plants, or animals are sick/dying	143	8	33
Residents, workers, etc. use water (for bathing, landscaping, etc.) that fails to meet the water quality standards	102	6	29
Recreation (e.g., fishing, swimming) is stopped or restricted	85	5	23
Residents advised to use filtered water	75	4	21
Residents advised to use bottled water	72	4	20
Residents advised not to let children play/dig in their yards	55	3	20
Crops are irrigated with contaminated water	52	3	29
Livestock drink contaminated water	44	3	28

[1]Institutional restrictions include limitations on uses of a property such as deed restrictions that limit a property to industrial use or legal limits placed on the depth of a well at a site.
[2]For example, by connecting residents to municipal water supplies in place of well water.

SOURCE: "Percentage of Potentially Eligible Sites Contributing to Specified Adverse Conditions and Percentage of Sites for Which Conditions' Presence is Uncertain," in *Hazardous Waste: Unaddressed Risks at Many Potential Superfund Sites,* U.S. General Accounting Office, Washington, DC, 1998

shows the types of environmental risks addressed at NPL (Superfund) sites.

In August 1998 the U.S. General Accounting Office (GAO) noted in its report *Hazardous Waste: Unaddressed Risks at Many Potential Superfund Sites* that the contamination at many potentially eligible NPL sites was resulting in a number of adverse conditions. Table 7.1 shows the percentage of sites at that time that experienced or contributed to the specific conditions listed on the left of the table.

The GAO also noted in its report that the states varied in their abilities to fund cleanup activities of NPL sites if the responsible parties were not willing or able to pay for these actions. State officials from about 25 percent of the states listed in Table 7.2 responded that their states' ability to fund these efforts was excellent or good, and more than 50 percent said that their states' abilities to fund these cleanups was poor or very poor.

As of November 2001, the NPL listed 1,227 final sites (which does not include deleted sites and proposed sites). Most were general sites, such as landfills used by manufacturers and municipal landfills. Some were federal sites, including those for the disposal of nuclear materials from bombs or U.S. Air Force bases that did not properly dispose of fuels and other dangerous materials.

Many of the sites are still years away from being cleaned up. Current estimates indicate that cleanups are expected to cost the federal government about $300 billion and the private sector hundreds of billions more.

Figure 7.3 shows a comparison of the cleanup progress of hazardous waste sites on the NPL over a seven-year period. As of September 2000, approximately 50 percent of NPL sites were classified as completions compared to approximately 12 percent in 1993. According to the EPA, more than three times as many Superfund sites were cleaned up between 1993 and 2000 than in all of the prior years of the program combined. Figure 7.4 shows the anticipated completion totals from 1999 to 2010. The EPA estimates that 85 percent of the NPL sites will be cleaned up by 2008. Figure 7.5 shows that completion for the remaining 15 percent of the sites may take well beyond 2008.

FUNDING FOR SUPERFUND. Funding for the Superfund program is derived from taxes on crude oil and certain chemicals, and by environmental taxes on corporations. It is also financed by appropriations made to the EPA from U.S. general revenues. In fiscal year (FY) 2002, the Superfund program will represent about 16.4 percent of the EPA's budget, about $1.2 billion. (See Table 7.3.) In total, the EPA requested $7.3 billion for FY 2002,

TABLE 7.2

Assessments of states' financial capabilities to clean up potentially eligible sites

State[1]	State officials' assessment of state's financial capability to clean up potentially eligible sites
Alabama	Very poor
Alaska	Excellent
Arizona	Excellent
Arkansas	Good
California	Fair
Colorado	Very poor
Connecticut	Poor
Delaware	Excellent
Florida	Fair
Georgia	Poor
Hawaii	Fair
Illinois	Fair
Indiana	Very poor
Iowa	Very poor
Kansas	Very poor
Kentucky	Good
Louisiana	Poor
Maine	Poor
Maryland	Other[2]
Massachusetts	Fair
Michigan	Excellent
Minnesota	Good
Mississippi	Very poor
Montana	Very poor
Nebraska	Very poor
Nevada	Poor
New Hampshire	Poor
New Jersey	Good
New Mexico	Very poor
North Carolina	Poor
North Dakota	Poor
Ohio	Very poor
Oklahoma	Very poor
Oregon	Fair
Pennsylvania	Excellent
Rhode Island	Poor
South Carolina	Good
South Dakota	Other[2]
Tennessee	Poor
Texas	Poor
Vermont	Poor
Washington	Fair
West Virginia	Other[2]
Wisconsin	Excellent

[1] State officials in Idaho, New York, Missouri, Utah, Virginia, and Wyoming declined to participate in our telephone survey.
[2] "Other" indicates that the respondent was uncertain about the state's financial capability.

SOURCE: "Assessments of States' Financial Capabilities to Clean Up Potentially Eligible Sites," in *Hazardous Waste: Unaddressed Risks at Many Potential Superfund Sites,* U.S. General Accounting Office, Washington, DC, 1998

FIGURE 7.3

Measuring the progress of site remediation at sites on the National Priorities List, September 2000 and January 1993

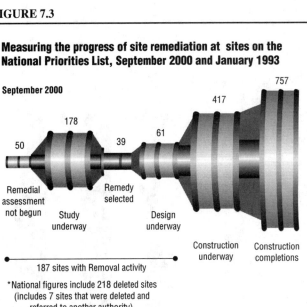

187 sites with Removal activity

*National figures include 218 deleted sites (includes 7 sites that were deleted and referred to another authority), 59 proposed sites, and 1,232 final NPL sites.

Total FY 2000 NPL Sites = 1509*

Legend: By September 2000, 50 Remedial Assessments had not begun, 178 sites had studies underway, 39 had the remedy selected, 61 had the design process underway, construction had begun with 417 sites and 757 sites had construction completed.

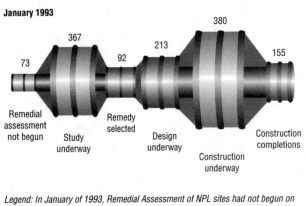

Legend: In January of 1993, Remedial Assessment of NPL sites had not begun on 73 sites, 367 sites had studies underway, 92 had the remedy selected, 213 had the design process underway, construction had begun with 380 sites, and 155 sites had construction completed.

SOURCE: "Figure 1. Measuring the Progress of Site Remediation at NPL Sites," in *Superfund Cleanup Figures,* Environmental Protection Agency, Washington, DC, [Online] http://www.epa.gov/superfund/action/process/mgmtrpt.htm [accessed October 16, 2001]

6 percent less than FY 2001 funding. (Figure 7.6 shows EPA funding by major categories since FY 1983.)

In addition to funding cleanup of NPL sites through the Superfund program, the EPA is authorized to compel parties responsible for creating hazardous pollution, such as waste generators, waste haulers, site owners, or site operators, to clean up the sites. If these parties cannot be found or if a settlement cannot be reached, the Superfund program finances the cleanup. After completing a cleanup, the EPA can take action against the responsible parties to recover costs and replenish the fund. The average cost of cleanup is about $30 million, large enough to make it worthwhile for parties to pursue legal means to spread the costs among large numbers of responsible parties. Many cleanups involve dozens of parties.

FIGURE 7.4

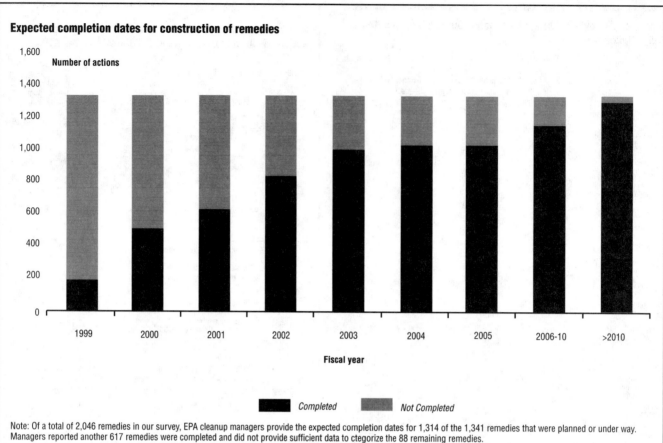

Expected completion dates for construction of remedies

Note: Of a total of 2,046 remedies in our survey, EPA cleanup managers provide the expected completion dates for 1,314 of the 1,341 remedies that were planned or under way. Managers reported another 617 remedies were completed and did not provide sufficient data to ctegorize the 88 remaining remedies.

SOURCE: "Expected Completion Dates for Construction of Remedies," in *Superfund: Half the Sites Have All Cleanup Remedies in Place or Completed,* U.S. General Accounting Office, Washington, DC, 1999

FIGURE 7.5

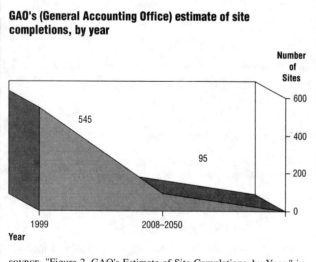

GAO's (General Accounting Office) estimate of site completions, by year

SOURCE: "Figure 2. GAO's Estimate of Site Completions, by Year," in *Superfund: Information on the Program's Funding and Status,* U.S. General Accounting Office, Washington, DC, 1999

Disputes have arisen between industries and cities over who is responsible for a cleanup, and numerous lawsuits have been filed by industries against cities over responsibility for what is usually a huge expense. Many businesses and municipalities may be unable to assume such expense. The EPA reports that the government currently collects only one-fifth of the cleanup costs that could be recovered from polluters under the Superfund law. According to the EPA, in many cases, the polluters have disappeared or are unable to pay. In other cases, the agency lacks the staff or evidence to proceed with lawsuits.

BROWNFIELDS

Brownfields are former industrial sites that are moderately contaminated but that can be redeveloped for commercial or residential use. The EPA defines Brownfields as abandoned, idled, or underused industrial or commercial sites where expansion or redevelopment is complicated by real or perceived environmental contamination. Real estate developers generally perceive Brownfields as inappropriate sites for redevelopment. There are nearly 450,000 Brownfields in the United States, concentrated mostly in the Northeast and Midwest.

Most Brownfield sites are not as contaminated as is generally thought. In fact, fewer than 1 percent are listed on the NPL and will require federal Superfund action. State and federal governments have strong motivations to want developers to clean up Brownfields to restore the environment, reuse abandoned sites, revitalize cities, create jobs, and generate municipal tax revenues.

In 1997 President Bill Clinton signed the Taxpayer Relief Act, which included new tax incentives to spur the cleanup and redevelopment of Brownfields. This Act enabled taxpayers to consider any qualified environmental remediation expenditure as a tax deduction in the year paid rather than spreading the cost over many tax years.

In the FY2002 national budget, President George W. Bush requested $97 million to clean up Brownfields that have development potential. The House and Senate have recommended $95 million. Brownfields reclamation is one of the Bush Administration's environmental priorities.

ENVIRONMENTAL JUSTICE— AN EVOLVING ISSUE

Environmental justice concerns stem from the claim that racial minorities are disproportionately subject to pollution hazards. The environmental justice movement gained national attention in 1982 when a demonstration took place to protest the building of a hazardous waste landfill in Warren County, North Carolina, a county with a predominantly African American population. A resulting 1983 congressional study found that in three out of four landfill areas surveyed, African Americans made up the majority of the population living nearby. In addition, at least 26 percent of the population in those communities was living below the poverty level. In 1987 the United Church of Christ published a nationwide study, *Toxic Waste and Race in the United States,* and reported that race was the most significant factor among the variables tested in determining locations of hazardous waste facilities.

In 1990 an EPA report (*Environmental Equity: Reducing Risk for All Communities*) concluded that racial minorities and low-income people bear a disproportionate burden of environmental risk. These groups were exposed to lead, air pollutants, hazardous waste facilities, contaminated fish, and agricultural pesticides in far greater frequencies than the general population. In 1994 President Clinton issued Executive Order 12898 (*Federal Actions to Address Environmental Justice in Minority Populations and Low-Income Populations*), which required federal agencies to develop a comprehensive strategy for including environmental justice factors in their decision-making.

Unlike earlier findings, however, a 1995 U.S. General Accounting Office report (*Hazardous and Nonhazardous Wastes: Demographics of People Living Near Waste Facilities,* Washington, DC) found that minorities and

TABLE 7.3

EPA major appropriations account, FY1999, FY2000, FY2001 and FY2002 actions

(in millions of dollars)

Account	FY1999 P.L. 105-276	FY2000 P.L. 106-74	FY2001 P.L. 106-377	FY2002 Request	FY2002 House-Passed	FY2002 Senate-Passed
Operating Programs						
Science and Technology	640.0	645.0	695.5	640.5	680.4	665.7
Environmental Programs and Management	1,848.0	1,895.3	2,087.9	1,973.0	2,014.8	2,062.0
Office of Inspector General	31.2	32.4	34.0	34.0	34.0	34.0
Buildings and Facilities	57.0	62.46	23.9	25.3	25.3	25.3
Oil Spill Response	15.0	14.9	15.0	15.0	15.0	15.0
Superfund	1,500.0	1,400.0	1,268.1	1,270.0	1.270.0	1,274.6
Leaking Underground Storage Tank Trust Fund	72.5	69.8	72.1	71.9	79.2	72.0
State and Tribal Assistance Grants	3,406.8	3,466.7	3,640.3	3,288.7	3,433.9	3,603.0
EPA Total	**7,590.4**	**7,591.7**	**7,828.9**	**7,316.6**	**7,545.4**	**7,751.6**

Note: In FY2000, the conferees elected to fund the National Institutes of Environmental Health Sciences (NIEHS) and the Agency for Toxic Substances and Disease Registry (ATSDR) – a total of $130 million – independent of the Superfund appropriation. The FY2002 Superfund request does not include funding for these two agencies, now funded separately.

SOURCE: "Table 1. EPA Major Appropriations Accounts: FY1999, FY2000, FY2001 and FY2002 Actions," in *Environmental Protection Agency: FY 2002 Budget Issues,* Congressional Research Service, Washington, DC, 2001

low-income people were not disproportionately represented near the majority of nonhazardous landfills. The data showed that people living near municipal landfills were likely to have poverty rates similar to or lower than rates in the rest of the country. (See Figure 7.7.) In fact, median household income was as likely to be higher than the national average as it was to be lower than the national average. (See Figure 7.8.) The study suggested that the results differed from prior studies because the various studies used differing methods.

Kennedy Heights Lawsuit

In 1997 residents of Kennedy Heights, a Houston, Texas, neighborhood of about 1,400 residents, complained about a variety of illnesses such as cancer, tumors, lupus (an autoimmune disease), and rashes. Their homes had been built three decades prior atop abandoned oil pits, and residents believed oil sludge from the pits had seeped into their water supply. Some tests of the municipal water found traces of crude oil. Kennedy Heights attracted

FIGURE 7.6

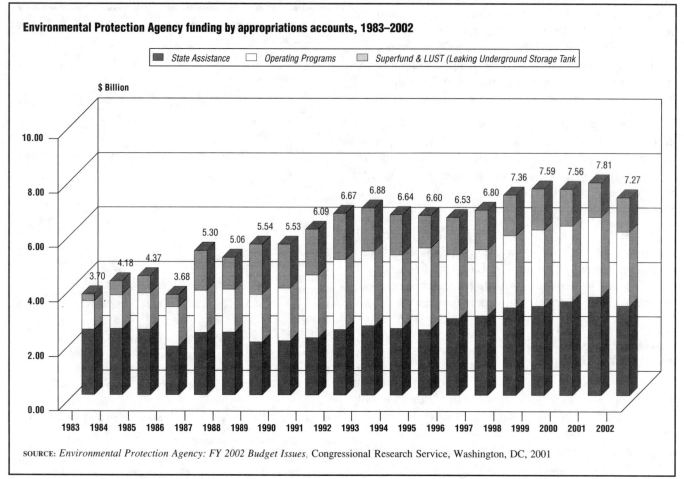

Environmental Protection Agency funding by appropriations accounts, 1983–2002

■ State Assistance   □ Operating Programs   ▨ Superfund & LUST (Leaking Underground Storage Tank

SOURCE: *Environmental Protection Agency: FY 2002 Budget Issues,* Congressional Research Service, Washington, DC, 2001

ever-wider attention because of accusations of environmental racism. Homeowners, who were predominantly African American, were not told the property sat on an oil dump abandoned in the 1920s. Chevron Oil Company, which acquired the property from Gulf Oil, denied that contamination could have caused any illness. The homes lost virtually all their resale value because of the claims.

In 2000 Chevron and the Kennedy Heights homeowners reached a $12.7 million settlement. Of this settlement award, $7.6 million was to be divided among 2,000 homeowners and $5.1 million was to be paid to John O'Quinn, the famed Houston personal injury attorney representing them. However, the residents felt that this settlement was far less than the $500 million settlement O'Quinn promised. More than 100 residents subsequently sued the attorney, claiming legal malpractice in his representation of them. As of October 2001 the lawsuit had been sent to arbitration by a Texas district judge.

State Actions

Some states and communities have stepped in to ensure that racial minorities do not suffer disproportionately from environmental problems. Table 7.4 shows the states that have enacted or introduced environmental jus-

tice legislation. Furthermore, lawsuits have occurred where discrimination is suspected. For example, in *James M. Seif v. Chester Residents Concerned Citizens et al.* (1998), residents of Chester, Pennsylvania, argued that the Pennsylvania Department of Environmental Protection violated Title IV of the Civil Rights Act of 1964 by issuing a solid waste permit for a facility in the minority community. Although the case was dismissed when the treatment facility withdrew its application, the action demonstrated the possibility of claiming discrimination under Title IV.

LAND DISPOSAL AND GROUND WATER CONTAMINATION

Ground water is a major source of drinking water for many parts of the nation. If not properly constructed, land disposal facilities for hazardous waste may leak contaminants into the underlying ground water. The RCRA imposes control over such facilities to minimize their adverse environmental impacts. The EPA implements the RCRA and requires that owners/operators of hazardous waste sites install wells to monitor the ground water under their facilities. Figure 6.12 shows a cross-section of a ground water monitoring system.

FIGURE 7.7

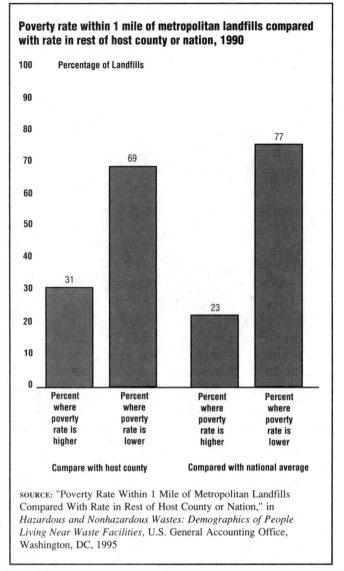

Poverty rate within 1 mile of metropolitan landfills compared with rate in rest of host county or nation, 1990

SOURCE: "Poverty Rate Within 1 Mile of Metropolitan Landfills Compared With Rate in Rest of Host County or Nation," in *Hazardous and Nonhazardous Wastes: Demographics of People Living Near Waste Facilities,* U.S. General Accounting Office, Washington, DC, 1995

FIGURE 7.8

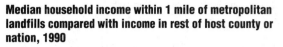

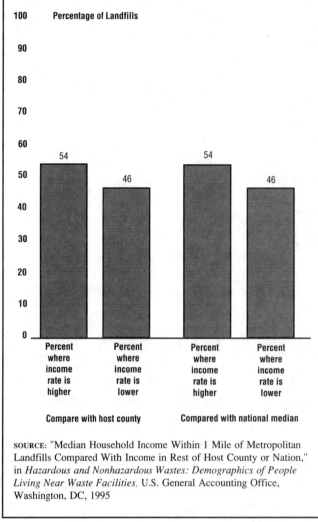

Median household income within 1 mile of metropolitan landfills compared with income in rest of host county or nation, 1990

SOURCE: "Median Household Income Within 1 Mile of Metropolitan Landfills Compared With Income in Rest of Host County or Nation," in *Hazardous and Nonhazardous Wastes: Demographics of People Living Near Waste Facilities,* U.S. General Accounting Office, Washington, DC, 1995

By 1995, 1,209 hazardous waste land disposal facilities nationwide were subject to ground water monitoring requirements. Texas and Ohio had the greatest number of facilities subject to requirements (130 and 76, respectively). About 77 percent of the facilities require only one monitoring well; due to hydro-geological conditions, some facilities require from 2 to 17 monitoring wells.

Most hazardous waste land disposal facilities have released contaminants into the ground water since they began receiving hazardous waste. Of the 1,209 hazardous waste land disposal facilities reviewed in 1994 by the U.S. General Accounting Office, 74 percent had experienced a release. (See Figure 7.9.) Of all facilities subject to ground water monitoring by the EPA, 54 percent were cited for ground water violations. The most common violations were sampling and analysis violations, followed by an inadequate number of monitoring wells. (See Figure 7.10.) The reasons why facilities have not complied with regulations varied. The most frequently cited reason was

disagreement over the technical/administrative requirements. Recalcitrance (resistance to authority) was the second most common explanation.

RADIOACTIVE WASTE

What is Radioactivity?

Radioactivity is the spontaneous emission of energy and/or high-energy particles from the nucleus of an atom. One type of radioactivity is produced naturally and is emitted by radioactive isotopes (or radioisotopes), such as radioactive carbon (carbon-14) and radioactive hydrogen (H-3 or tritium). The energy and high-energy particles that radioactive isotopes emit include alpha rays, beta rays, and gamma rays.

Isotopes are atoms of an element that have the same number of protons but different numbers of neutrons in their nuclei. For example, the element carbon has 12

TABLE 7.4

State action on environmental justice, 2001

	Enacted legislation	Introduced legislation
Alabama		X
Arizona		X
Arkansas	X	
California		X
Colorado		X
Connecticut		X
Florida	X	
Georgia		X
Illinois		X
Louisiana	X	
Maryland	X	
Massachusetts		X
Michigan	X	
Minnesota		X
Mississippi		X
Missouri		X
New Mexico		X
New York	X	
North Carolina	X	
Oregon		X
Rhode Island	X	
South Carolina		X
Tennessee	X	
Texas		X
Virginia	X	
Washington		X

SOURCE: Adapted from "New Developments in Environmental Justice," *NCSL Legisbrief,* National Conference of State Legislatures, Denver, CO, August/September 1999, updated September 2001 by author's personal communication with Sia Davis of NCSL

FIGURE 7.9

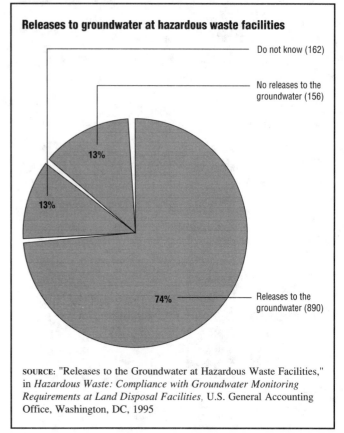

Releases to groundwater at hazardous waste facilities

Do not know (162)

No releases to the groundwater (156)

13%

13%

74%

Releases to the groundwater (890)

SOURCE: "Releases to the Groundwater at Hazardous Waste Facilities," in *Hazardous Waste: Compliance with Groundwater Monitoring Requirements at Land Disposal Facilities,* U.S. General Accounting Office, Washington, DC, 1995

protons and 12 neutrons comprising its nucleus. One isotope of carbon, C-14, has 12 protons and 14 neutrons in its nucleus.

Radioisotopes (such as C-14) are unstable isotopes and their nuclei decay, or break apart, at a steady rate. Decaying radioisotopes produce other isotopes as they emit energy and/or high-energy particles. If the newly formed nuclei are radioactive too, they emit radiation and change into other nuclei. The final products in this chain are stable, nonradioactive nuclei.

Radioisotopes reach our bodies daily, emitted from sources in outer space, and from rocks and soil on earth. Radioisotopes are also used in medicine and provide useful diagnostic tools. Figure 7.11 notes the sources of radiation.

Decades after the discovery of radiation at the turn of the century by Antoine Henri Becquerel, Marie Curie, and Pierre Curie, other scientists determined that they could unleash energy by "artificially" breaking apart atomic nuclei. Such a process is called nuclear fission. Scientists learned that they could produce the most energy by bombarding nuclei of an isotope of uranium called uranium 235 (U-235). The fission of U-235 releases several neutrons, which can penetrate other U-235 nuclei. In this way, the fission of a single U-235 atom can begin a cascading chain of nuclear reactions, as shown in Figure 7.12. If this series of reactions is regulated to occur slowly, as it is in nuclear power plants, the energy emitted can be captured for a variety of uses, such as generating electricity. (See Figure 7.13 for the process through which raw uranium becomes electricity.) If this series of reactions is allowed to occur all at once, as in a nuclear (atomic) bomb, the energy emitted is explosive. (Plutonium-239 can also be used to generate a chain reaction similar to that of U-235.)

A Culture of Secrecy

As scientists raced to develop an atomic bomb during World War II (1939–45), wartime concern for national security led to a "culture of secrecy" that became characteristic of agencies dealing with nuclear power. On July 16, 1945, the first bomb, "Trinity," was exploded above ground in Alamogordo, New Mexico. A few weeks later, two nuclear bombs were dropped on Japan. World War II ended and the nuclear age began.

In 1948 the Atomic Energy Commission warned that then-existing disposal practices for nuclear materials would result in contamination of the environment. The commission's advice was dismissed, in part because of the expense of improving disposal methods. By the 1950s, there was already evidence that the commission's advice should have been heeded. Officials at the Hanford, Washington, nuclear facility discovered that high-level waste had corroded the

FIGURE 7.10

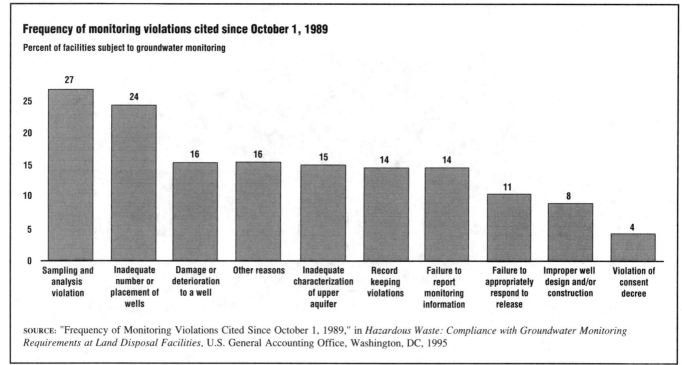

Frequency of monitoring violations cited since October 1, 1989

Percent of facilities subject to groundwater monitoring

SOURCE: "Frequency of Monitoring Violations Cited Since October 1, 1989," in *Hazardous Waste: Compliance with Groundwater Monitoring Requirements at Land Disposal Facilities,* U.S. General Accounting Office, Washington, DC, 1995

tanks in which it was contained, and radioactive waste was leaking into the soil and ground water. A number of similar events occurred in subsequent years.

In 1993 U.S. Energy Secretary Hazel O'Leary disclosed that since the late 1940s, the United States nuclear establishment had conducted hundreds of unannounced atomic tests (from 1948 to 1952), experimented with human subjects on the effects of plutonium, often without their knowledge or approval, and dumped tons of toxic waste across the United States. Secretary O'Leary revealed that of 925 nuclear tests, 204 had been secret, and that the government was storing 33.5 metric tons of plutonium in six U.S. locations.

Although nuclear waste management received little attention from government policymakers for three decades after the development of the atomic bomb in 1945, considerably more attention has focused on nuclear waste as a national and worldwide issue since the 1970s. In fact, during the 1990s, the Department of Energy (DOE) spent hundreds of millions of dollars to treat, store, and dispose of radioactive wastes generated at over 50 of its nuclear facilities around the country.

RADIOACTIVE WASTE DISPOSAL

The nuclear energy process produces five basic types of radioactive waste.

- Uranium mill tailings are sand-like wastes produced in uranium refining operations that emit low levels of radiation.

- Low-level waste contains varying lesser levels of radioactivity, and includes trash, contaminated clothing, and hardware.

- Spent fuel is "used" reactor fuel that will be classified as waste if not reprocessed to recover usable uranium and plutonium, which can be used again as nuclear reactor fuel.

- High-level waste is the by-product of a reprocessing plant. These wastes contain highly toxic and extremely dangerous fission products that require great care in disposal.

- Transuranic wastes are 11 man-made radioactive elements with an atomic number (number of protons) greater than that of uranium (92) and therefore beyond ("trans-") uranium ("-uranic") on the periodic chart of the elements. Their half-lives, the time it takes for half the radioisotopes present in a sample to decay to non-radioactive elements, are thousands of years. They are found in trash (such as protective clothing, tools, glassware, and equipment) produced mainly by nuclear weapons plants and are therefore a part of the nuclear waste problem that must be directly resolved by the government.

The end of the Cold War has brought the problem of military nuclear waste to the forefront. Both the United States and Russia have agreed to begin to destroy many of their nuclear weapons. In fact, in November 2001 President Bush and President Vladimir Putin of Russia pledged

FIGURE 7.11

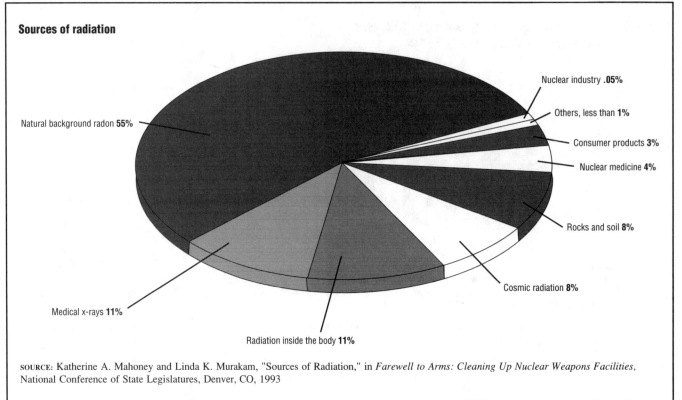

Sources of radiation

Natural background radon **55%**

Nuclear industry **.05%**

Others, less than **1%**

Consumer products **3%**

Nuclear medicine **4%**

Rocks and soil **8%**

Cosmic radiation **8%**

Medical x-rays **11%**

Radiation inside the body **11%**

SOURCE: Katherine A. Mahoney and Linda K. Murakam, "Sources of Radiation," in *Farewell to Arms: Cleaning Up Nuclear Weapons Facilities*, National Conference of State Legislatures, Denver, CO, 1993

to slash the number of long-range nuclear weapons by two-thirds—to the lowest level in three decades.

Destroying nuclear weapons is an involved and lengthy process that will likely take many decades to complete. The highly toxic and extremely dangerous fission wastes produced by this process will likely have to be stored for extended periods of time and then eventually be moved to permanent storage facilities. Many facilities scattered across the United States will play a role in dismantling the American nuclear arsenal.

Uranium Mill Tailings

Uranium mill tailings are the earthen residues, usually in the form of fine sand, that remain after mining and extracting uranium from ores. These wastes emit low levels of radiation, mostly radon, which can contaminate water and air. Most tailing sites are west of the Mississippi River, primarily in Utah, Colorado, New Mexico, and Arizona.

Prior to the early 1970s, the tailings were believed to have such low levels of radiation that they were not harmful to humans. Miners, many of whom were Native Americans, received little protection from the radiation. Now, many of these workers are reporting very high rates of cancer. Tailings were also left in scattered piles without posted warnings or safeguards, exposing anyone who came near. Some tailings were deposited in landfills, and homes were built on top of them. Authorities now recog-

FIGURE 7.12

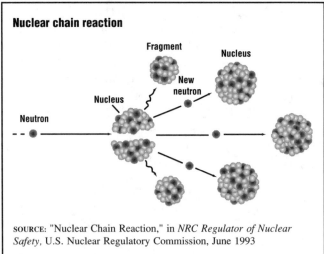

Nuclear chain reaction

Fragment

Nucleus

New neutron

Nucleus

Neutron

SOURCE: "Nuclear Chain Reaction," in *NRC Regulator of Nuclear Safety*, U.S. Nuclear Regulatory Commission, June 1993

nize that mill tailing handling and disposal must be properly managed to control radiation exposure.

Proper management of uranium mill tailings is particularly important because they are generated in relatively large volumes—about 10 to 15 million tons annually. About 15 percent of the radioactivity is removed during the milling process, while the remainder (85 percent) stays in the tailings. Radium-226, the major radioactive waste product, retains its radioactivity for thousands of years and produces two potentially hazardous radiation

FIGURE 7.13

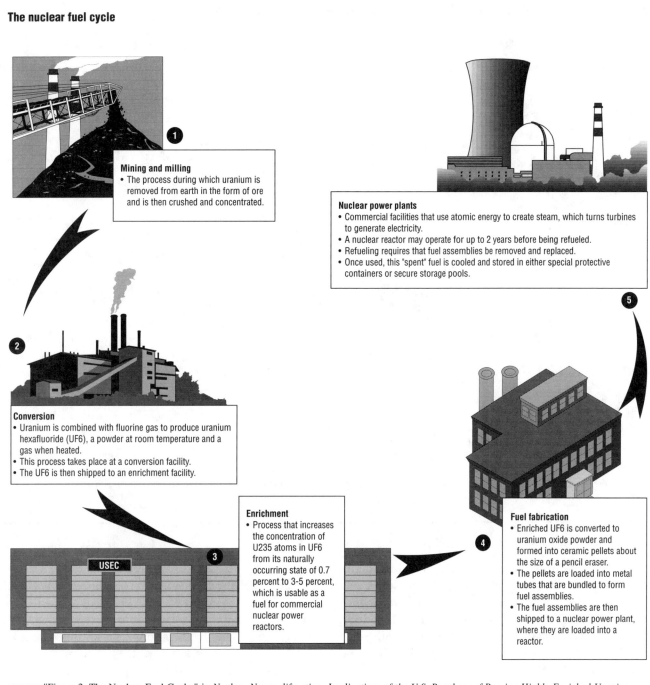

The nuclear fuel cycle

① Mining and milling
- The process during which uranium is removed from earth in the form of ore and is then crushed and concentrated.

Nuclear power plants
- Commercial facilities that use atomic energy to create steam, which turns turbines to generate electricity.
- A nuclear reactor may operate for up to 2 years before being refueled.
- Refueling requires that fuel assemblies be removed and replaced.
- Once used, this "spent" fuel is cooled and stored in either special protective containers or secure storage pools.

② Conversion
- Uranium is combined with fluorine gas to produce uranium hexafluoride (UF6), a powder at room temperature and a gas when heated.
- This process takes place at a conversion facility.
- The UF6 is then shipped to an enrichment facility.

③ Enrichment
- Process that increases the concentration of U235 atoms in UF6 from its naturally occurring state of 0.7 percent to 3-5 percent, which is usable as a fuel for commercial nuclear power reactors.

④ Fuel fabrication
- Enriched UF6 is converted to uranium oxide powder and formed into ceramic pellets about the size of a pencil eraser.
- The pellets are loaded into metal tubes that are bundled to form fuel assemblies.
- The fuel assemblies are then shipped to a nuclear power plant, where they are loaded into a reactor.

SOURCE: "Figure 2. The Nuclear Fuel Cycle," in *Nuclear Nonproliferation: Implications of the U.S. Purchase of Russian Highly Enriched Uranium*, U.S. General Accounting Office, Washington, DC, 2000

conditions—gamma radiation and the emission of gaseous radon. Results of research studies show a causal relationship between these radioactive elements and leukemia and lung cancer.

In response to growing concern, Congress passed the Uranium Mill Tailing Radiation Control Act of 1978 to regulate mill tailing operations. The law called for the cleanup of abandoned mill sites, primarily at federal expense, although owners of still-active mines were financially responsible for their own cleanup.

Low-Level Waste

Low-level radioactive waste decays in 10 to 100 years. Until the 1960s, the United States dumped low-level wastes into the ocean. The first commercial site to house such waste was opened in 1962, and by 1971 six sites were licensed for disposal. The volume of low-level

FIGURE 7.14

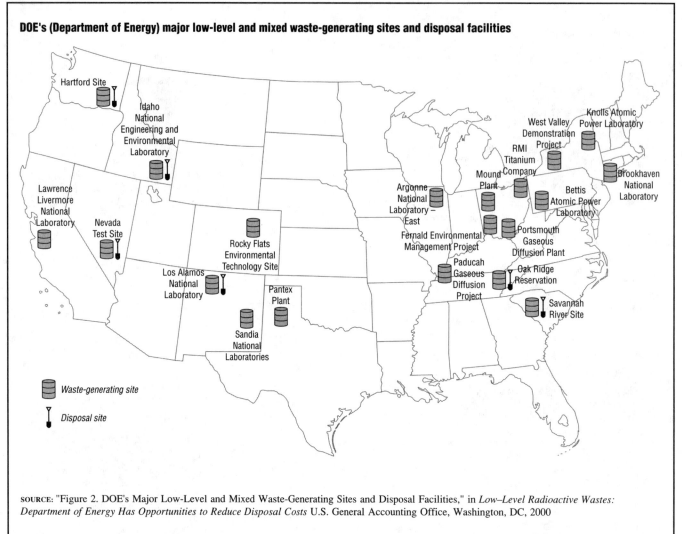

DOE's (Department of Energy) major low-level and mixed waste-generating sites and disposal facilities

SOURCE: "Figure 2. DOE's Major Low-Level and Mixed Waste-Generating Sites and Disposal Facilities," in *Low–Level Radioactive Wastes: Department of Energy Has Opportunities to Reduce Disposal Costs* U.S. General Accounting Office, Washington, DC, 2000

waste increased during the initial years of commercially generated waste disposal (1963–80) until the Low-Level Radioactive Waste Policy Act of 1980, and its amendments in 1985. At that time, approximately 3.25 million cubic feet of radioactive wastes were disposed. Since then, the volume has declined to under 1 million cubic feet per year.

By 1979 only three commercial low-level waste sites were still operating—Richland (Hanford), Washington; Beatty, Nevada; and Barnwell, South Carolina. The facility at Beatty, Nevada, closed permanently in 1982. In response to the threatened closing of the South Carolina site, Congress called for the establishment of a national system of such facilities under the Low-Level Radioactive Waste Policy Act. Every state was to be responsible for finding a low-level disposal site for wastes generated within its borders by 1986. It also gave states the right to bar low-level wastes if they were engaged in regional compacts for waste disposal. The disposal of high-level wastes remained a federal responsibility.

As of 2000, the Department of Energy (DOE) was operating six low-level and mixed radioactive waste disposal facilities. (Mixed waste is low-level waste that also contains nonradioactive hazardous wastes such as lead.) Figure 7.14 shows the location of these sites, along with DOE's 20 major radioactive waste-generating sites.

The amount and types of radioactive waste that each radioactive waste disposal facility receives depends on its size, location, and physical characteristics. For example, facilities located in wet climates where the water table is high, such as at the Savannah River (Georgia) and Oak Ridge (Tennessee) sites, must store radioactive wastes aboveground. Such facilities are expensive to build and have a relatively small capacity. Other sites, such as those in remote locations with drier climates and deep water tables, are able to use low-cost open trenches for radioactive waste disposal. Table 7.5 shows the volumes of wastes produced by the DOE's 20 major radioactive waste-generating sites as of 1999.

TABLE 7.5

Past and future disposal volumes of low-level and mixed wastes for DOE's (Department of Energy) 20 major waste generating sites, 1999 statistics

Volume in cubic meters

DOE site	Low-level waste			Mixed waste			Total
	Disposal completed	Disposal planned	Total	Disposal completed[a]	Disposal planned	Total	
Argonne National Laboratory East, IL	886	623	**1,509**	25	62	87	**1,596**
Bettis Atomic Power Laboratory, PA	12,254	3,642	**15,896**	Less than 1	27	27	**15,923**
Brookhaven National Laboratory, NY	1,403	b	**1,403**	20	b	20	**1,423**
Fernald Environmental Management Project, OH	439,017	2,173,271	**2,612,288**	5,011	14,855	19,866	**2,632,154**
Hanford Site, WA[c]	495,049	128,707	**623,756**	182	72,589	72,771	**696,527**
INEEL, ID	98,500	26,000	**124,500**	82	1,440	1,522	**126,022**
Knolls Atomic Power Laboratory, NY	5,763	6,267	**12,030**	Less than 1	81	81	**12,111**
Lawrence Livermore National Laboratory, CA	5,641	6,350	**11,991**	1,959	1,217	3,176	**15,167**
Los Alamos National Laboratory, NM	223,400	273,000	**496,400**	b	b	b	**496,400**
Mound Plant, OH	54,798	103,321	**158,119**	Less than 1	19	19	**158,138**
NTS, NV[d]	243,000	119,983	**362,983**	270	Less than 1	270	**363,253**
Oak Ridge Reservation, TN	4,253	579,191	**583,444**	20,526	114,471	134,997	**718,441**
Paducah Gaseous Diffusion Plant, KY	b	11,000	**11,000**	b	5,600	5,600	**16,600**
Pantex Plant, TX	3,070	b	**3,070**	213	b	213	**3,283**
Portsmouth Gaseous Diffusion Plant, OH	978	14,387	**15,365**	2,033	8,717	10,750	**26,115**
RMI Titanium Company, OH	44	10,477	**10,521**	Less than 1	735	735	**11,256**
Rocky Flats Environmental Technology Site, CO	9,424	157,436	**166,860**	16,499	45,146	61,645	**228,505**
Sandia National Laboratories, NM	2,047	4,220	**6,267**	29	660	689	**6,956**
Savannah River Site, SC	353,911	407,000	**760,911**	0	6,216	6,216	**767,127**
West Valley Demonstration Project, NY	11,988	56,634	**68,622**	4	283	287	**68,909**
Total	**1,965,426**	**4,081,509**	**6,046,935**	**46,853**	**272,118**	**318,971**	**6,365,906**

Note: The volumes of wastes in this table were provided by the 20 sites in 1999.

[a] Since Hanford and NTS have the only disposal facilities for on-site mixed wastes and currently cannot dispose of mixed wastes from other sites, any other sites that disposed of mixed wastes did so at a commercial facility.

[b] Information was not readily available from this site.

[c] The quantities for Hanford include only DOE wastes; they exclude Department of Defense wastes disposed of at the site.

[d] The amounts disposed of at NTS are approximate. In addition, the total volume of low-level and mixed wastes that could be disposed of at NTS depends on future decisions on regulatory, technical, or management issues (e.g., final negotiated soil cleanup levels, funding gaps in site baseline budgets, etc.).

SOURCE: "Table 3. Past and Future Disposal Volumes of Low-Level and Mixed Wastes for DOE's 20 Major Waste -Generating Sites," in *Low–Level Radioactive Wastes: Department of Energy Has Opportunities to Reduce Disposal Costs* U.S. General Accounting Office, Washington, DC, 2000

COMPACTS. The 1980 Low-Level Radioactive Waste Policy Act and its amendments encouraged states to organize themselves into compacts to develop new radioactive waste facilities. As of 2001, Congress had approved 10 such compacts serving 44 states. Figure 7.15 shows the organization of states into compacts and the six unaffiliated states, Puerto Rico, and the District of Columbia.

No compact or state has, however, successfully developed a new disposal facility for low-level wastes. California had planned a facility, but the land could not be obtained. At this writing, California faces a lawsuit from other compact members for not living up to its responsibilities as host of the compact for the first 30 years. In a similar situation in 2000, a federal court ruled that

Nebraska was legally liable for shirking its responsibilities as the host state for a Midwestern low-level radioactive waste compact.

Compacts and unaffiliated states have confronted significant barriers to developing disposal sites, including public health and environmental concerns, antinuclear sentiment, substantial financial requirements, political issues, and "not in my backyard" campaigns by citizen activists.

STORAGE AND TRANSPORT PROBLEMS. Developing storage areas for hazardous waste is difficult for many reasons. One reason is that regulatory requirements mandate a buffer zone of land surrounding each site, which,

FIGURE 7.15

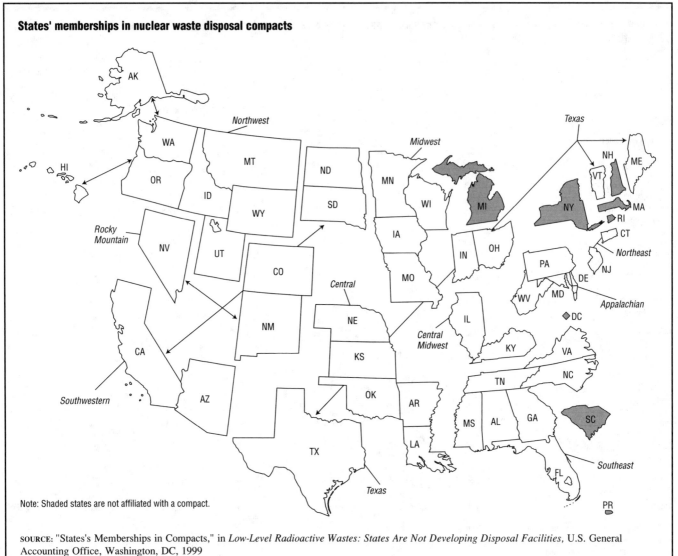

States' memberships in nuclear waste disposal compacts

Note: Shaded states are not affiliated with a compact.

SOURCE: "States's Memberships in Compacts," in *Low-Level Radioactive Wastes: States Are Not Developing Disposal Facilities,* U.S. General Accounting Office, Washington, DC, 1999

along with the storage area, requires constant monitoring and limited land-use applications for at least a century. Larger sites collectively reduce the total number of acres required because they only need one buffer zone, but smaller and more numerous local facilities reduce the probability of transportation accidents. Other storage problems include the degradation of the packages that contain stored waste. Depending on the environment, degradation can occur from temperature fluctuations, corrosion, and containers becoming brittle.

Spent Fuel and High-Level Waste

Spent fuel, the used uranium that has been removed from a nuclear reactor, is far from being completely "spent." It contains highly penetrating and toxic radioactivity and requires isolation from living things for thousands of years. It still contains significant amounts of uranium, as well as plutonium, created during the nuclear fission process. Spent fuel is a disposal problem for

nuclear power plants that will be decommissioned before the projected availability of a long-term, high-level waste disposal repository for this waste. Figure 7.16 shows the locations of spent nuclear fuel and high-level radioactive waste destined for disposal. Unless a temporary site becomes available, commercial and government nuclear reactor facilities have the following options:

• Leave the fuel on site.

• Use on-site casks (large barrel-like containers) for storage. This is not an option for hot fuel—fuel that has been out of the core of the reactor for less than five years.

• Ship the spent fuel to France for reprocessing. France, which is heavily dependent on nuclear power, has developed the technology to reprocess spent fuel, something not available in the United States. In a controversial action, spent nuclear fuel from the defunct

FIGURE 7.16

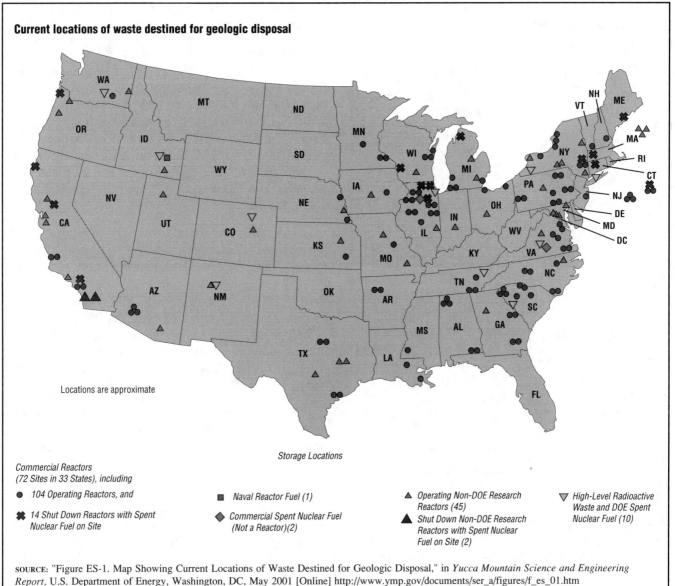

Current locations of waste destined for geologic disposal

Locations are approximate

Storage Locations

Commercial Reactors
(72 Sites in 33 States), including

● *104 Operating Reactors, and*

✖ *14 Shut Down Reactors with Spent*
Nuclear Fuel on Site

■ *Naval Reactor Fuel (1)*

◆ *Commercial Spent Nuclear Fuel*
(Not a Reactor)(2)

▲ *Operating Non-DOE Research*
Reactors (45)

▲ *Shut Down Non-DOE Research*
Reactors with Spent Nuclear
Fuel on Site (2)

▽ *High-Level Radioactive*
Waste and DOE Spent
Nuclear Fuel (10)

SOURCE: "Figure ES-1. Map Showing Current Locations of Waste Destined for Geologic Disposal," in *Yucca Mountain Science and Engineering Report,* U.S. Department of Energy, Washington, DC, May 2001 [Online] http://www.ymp.gov/documents/ser_a/figures/f_es_01.htm [Accessed 9/27/2001]

Shoreham plant was shipped to France in 1993 for reprocessing at a cost of $74 million to utility customers. Nuclear watchdog groups, including the Friends of the Earth and the Union of Concerned Scientists, oppose sending nuclear fuel abroad because they fear the possibility of theft or accidental spread of nuclear materials. The safe transport of spent fuel is primarily a federal responsibility. The U.S. Department of Transportation (DOT) and the Nuclear Regulatory Commission (NRC) are responsible for packaging regulations, container safety, regulations regarding sabotage, escorts, routing, and employee training.

• Continue to operate the unit. Some plants might not be decommissioned, as originally planned, but would continue to operate and keep any spent fuel onsite.

• Ship the fuel to a monitored retrievable storage facility, if one is available.

DISPOSAL OF RADIOACTIVE WASTE

The Nuclear Energy Agency (NEA) of the Organization for Economic Cooperation and Development (OECD) is an international group established in 1958 and comprised of 27 countries, including the United States. Its purpose is to help member nations maintain and develop safe, environmentally friendly, and economical use of nuclear energy for peaceful purposes. One area of competence of the NEA is radioactive waste management.

In a recent publication, *Geologic Disposal of Radioactive Waste in Perspective* (2000), the NEA notes that there has been little fundamental change in the basic technology

FIGURE 7.17

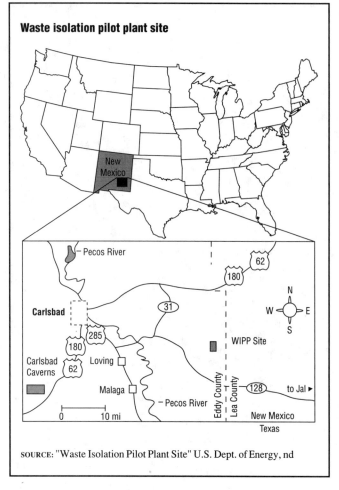

Waste isolation pilot plant site

Pecos River

62

180

Carlsbad

31

N
W   E
S

285

WIPP Site

180

Carlsbad
Caverns   62

Loving

Malaga

128   to Jal ▶

Pecos River

0   10 mi

Eddy County

Lea County

New Mexico
Texas

SOURCE: "Waste Isolation Pilot Plant Site" U.S. Dept. of Energy, nd

of geologic (underground) repositories (waste disposal sites) in the past ten years. However, the book notes that there has been significant progress in the development of what is termed robust engineered barrier systems.

Robust engineered barrier systems combine multiple physical barriers with chemical controls and provide a high level of long-term containment for radioactive waste. An example of a robust engineered barrier system would place radioactive waste, which had been chemically treated for long-term storage, into steel drums. The drums would be placed in a concrete container. Many of these drum-filled concrete containers, surrounded with special chemically treated backfill material, would be placed in a larger concrete container deep in the ground. The rock surrounding this large concrete container would have low ground water flow. The multiple barriers, chemical conditions, and geologic conditions under which the wastes are stored ensure that the wastes dissolve slowly and pose little danger to the ground water.

Geologic Repositories in the United States

In the United States, the government is focusing on two locations as geologic repositories: the Waste Isolation

Pilot Plant (WIPP) in southeastern New Mexico for transuranic (defense) waste and Nevada's Yucca Mountain for nuclear power plant waste.

THE WASTE ISOLATION PILOT PLANT (WIPP). The Waste Isolation Pilot Plant (WIPP) became the world's first deep depository for nuclear waste when it received its first shipment on March 26, 1999. The large facility near Carlsbad, New Mexico, is restricted to defense or transuranic waste. WIPP is 655 meters below the surface, in the salt beds of the Salado Formation, and is intended to house up to 6.25 million cubic feet of transuranic waste for more than 10,000 years. Figure 7.17 shows the location of the site.

More than 99 percent of transuranic waste is temporarily stored in drums at nuclear defense sites in California, Colorado, Idaho, Illinois, Nevada, New Mexico, Ohio, Tennessee, South Carolina, and Washington. As transuranic waste is transported to the WIPP, it is tracked by satellite and moved at night when traffic is light. It can be transported only in good weather and must be routed around major cities. Figure 7.18 shows transport routes from the 10 sites temporarily storing and currently producing transuranic waste to the WIPP facility.

By the beginning of the twenty-first century, about 61 million Americans lived within 50 miles of a military nuclear waste storage site. By the time the WIPP has been in operation for 10 years, that number should drop to 4 million. By 2035, barring court challenges, almost 40,000 truckloads of nuclear waste will have been transported across the country to the WIPP.

YUCCA MOUNTAIN. The centerpiece of the federal government's geologic disposal plan for spent fuel and high-level waste is the Yucca Mountain site in Nevada. (See Figure 7.19.) The Nuclear Waste Policy Act of 1982 required the Secretary of Energy to investigate the site and, if it is suitable, to recommend to the president that the site be established. The investigation of Yucca Mountain has taken a long time. The DOE's 1998 objective was to begin disposing of waste in the repository in 2010, 12 years later than originally expected.

It is not clear whether the Yucca Mountain site is suitable. It is located near volcanic and earthquake activity, and local Native American tribes are contesting rights to the land. Additionally, the proposed repository sits above an aquifer that is an important resource for the area surrounding Yucca Mountain. If the site is found to be acceptable, the president approves it, and a recommendation goes to Congress, the state of Nevada is expected to file a notice of disapproval.

In order for the Yucca Mountain Repository to be built, the DOE must satisfactorily demonstrate to the Nuclear Regulatory Commission (NRC) that the

FIGURE 7.18

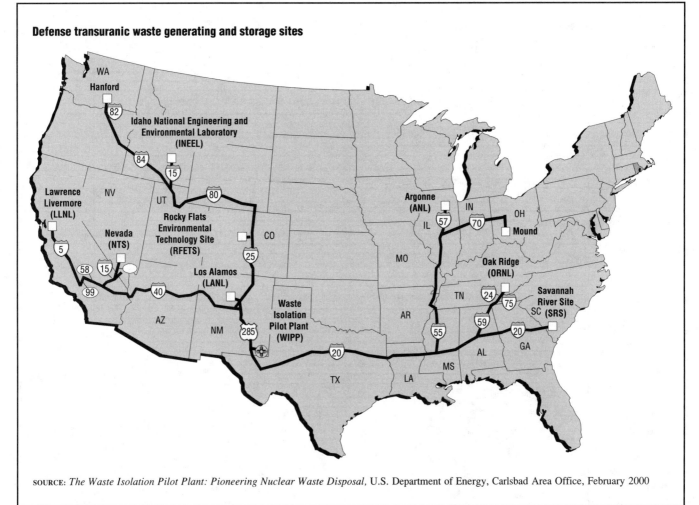

Defense transuranic waste generating and storage sites

SOURCE: *The Waste Isolation Pilot Plant: Pioneering Nuclear Waste Disposal*, U.S. Department of Energy, Carlsbad Area Office, February 2000

combination of the site and the repository design complies with the standards set forth by the EPA. The EPA's standard is based on a new approach of using numerical probabilities to establish requirements for containing radioactivity within the repository. Their quantitative terms are:

- Cumulative releases of radioactivity from a repository must have a likelihood of less than one chance in ten of exceeding limits established in the standard and a likelihood of less than one chance in 1,000 of exceeding ten times the limits for a period of 10,000 years.

- Exposures of radiation to individual members of the public for 1,000 years must not exceed specified limits.

- Limits are placed on the concentration of radioactivity for 1,000 years after disposal from the repository to a nearby source of ground water that (1) currently supplies drinking water for thousands of persons, and (2) is irreplaceable.

- Prescribed technical or institutional procedures or steps must provide confidence that the containment requirements are likely to be met.

Crisis in the Nuclear Power Industry

The long delay in providing a disposal site for nuclear wastes, coupled with the accelerated pace at which nuclear plants are being retired, has created a crisis in the nuclear power industry. Several aging plants are being maintained—at a cost of $20 million a year for each reactor— simply because there is no place to send the waste once the plants are decommissioned. Under the Nuclear Waste Policy Act of 1982, the DOE was scheduled to begin picking up waste on January 31, 1998. Nuclear power plants have been paying one-tenth of one cent per kilowatt-hour produced by the reactors to finance a waste repository.

In February 1999 the DOE announced that because it was unable to receive nuclear waste for permanent storage, it would take ownership of the waste and pay temporary storage costs with money the utilities have paid to develop the permanent repository. The waste will stay where it currently is being stored.

Both the Senate and the House have passed legislation to build a temporary repository in Nevada. The Clinton Administration, however, opposed the temporary site,

FIGURE 7.19

Location of Yucca Mountain Site

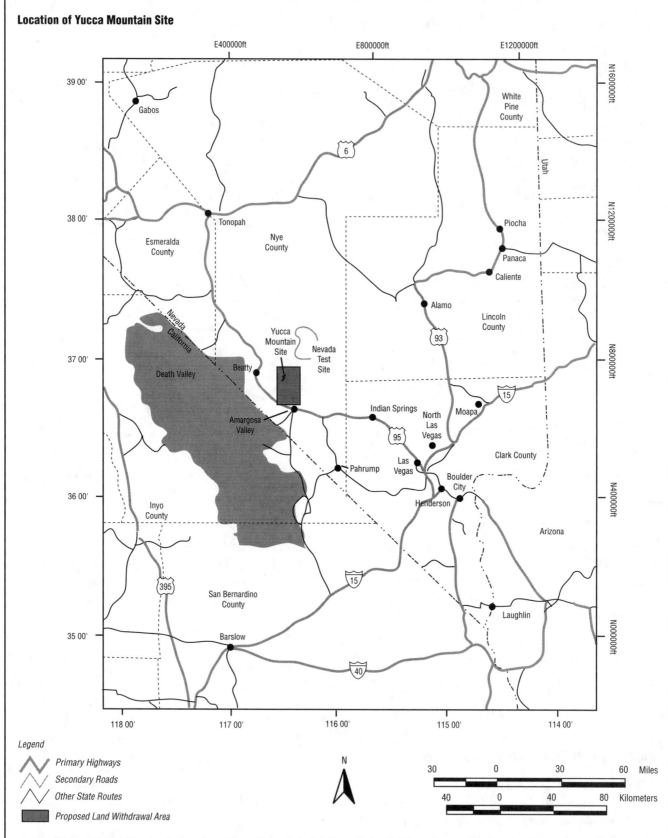

Legend

Primary Highways

Secondary Roads

Other State Routes

Proposed Land Withdrawal Area

N

| 30 | 0 | 30 | 60 | Miles |

| 40 | 0 | 40 | 80 | Kilometers |

SOURCE: "Figure 1-5. Map Showing the Location of Yucca Mountain in Relation to Major Highways; Surrounding Counties, Cities, and Towns in Nevada and California; the Nevada Test Site; and Death Valley National Park," in *Yucca Mountain Science and Engineering Report*, U.S. Department of Energy, Washington, DC, May 2001

claiming that it had not been proven safe and would deflect funds and engineering talent needed to build the permanent facility. Even without the expense of temporary storage, the nuclear waste fund (from the 1 cent per 10 kilowatt-hours of nuclear power generated by the utilities) is many billions short of what Yucca Mountain is expected to cost.

According to the NRC, which licenses nuclear power plants, almost all nuclear plants will soon reach their capacity for storing their spent nuclear waste for several reasons.

- There is a backlog of nuclear waste. At least 35,000 metric tons of nuclear waste is sitting in what are called "spent fuel pools" at 70 nuclear energy plants around the country. (There were 104 nuclear reactors in the United States in 1999, down from 112 in 1990.) By 2010, the earliest feasible date for opening the Yucca Mountain repository, the total waste is expected to reach 60,000 metric tons.

- Many nuclear plants are shutting down well ahead of schedule because of premature aging and high maintenance and repair costs. Although the NRC licenses power plants to operate for 40 years, they do not last that long. The average life of the more than 20 reactors that have been shut down has been about 13 years.

- The nation's power system has been restructured from a regulated industry to one driven by competition. As many as 26 U.S. nuclear power plants are vulnerable to shutdown because production costs are higher than the projected market prices of electricity.

TRANSPORTING RADIOACTIVE WASTE

Since the beginning of this country's nuclear program, there have been more than 2,500 shipments of spent fuel and many more shipments of low-level waste. However, shipments of radioactive waste increased in 1999 when the Waste Isolation Pilot Plant (WIPP) began operation and will rise dramatically when Yucca Mountain opens.

Transportation of nuclear waste is of particular concern to states and Native American reservations along the main transportation routes to possible disposal sites. Several transportation organizations are actively preparing for potential shipments across country. Under the Hazardous Materials Transportation Act of 1975, the DOT and the NRC share responsibility for regulating standards of safety for packaging and transport of hazardous materials by any mode in interstate and foreign commerce.

Spent nuclear fuel and radioactive wastes are solid material shipped in large, heavy metal containers called casks, which are designed to shield radiation and withstand severe accidents without releasing their toxic contents. Such fuel is usually transported by truck or rail. Casks, which are regulated by the NRC, have multiple layers of walls. Each container can hold fourteen 55-gallon drums. A satellite tracking system maintains constant contact with the trucks, and drivers are tested for safety and trained in emergency response.

INTERNATIONAL APPROACHES TO HIGH-LEVEL WASTE DISPOSAL

In 1998 nuclear power generated 16 percent of the world's electricity and 19 percent of America's electricity. Governments, scientists, and engineers around the world generally believe that deep geologic disposal, such as that in operation at the WIPP and proposed for Yucca Mountain, offers the best option for isolating highly radioactive waste. According to the NEA of the OECD, in *Geologic Disposal of Radioactive Waste in Perspective* (2000), several countries have made significant progress toward implementation of geologic disposal, but the rate of progress has been slower than expected. Additionally, some countries have experienced serious setbacks in the implementation of their plans because of political, public, and regulatory issues.

A few countries have implemented geologic disposal of many types of radioactive waste. The United States opened the first (and only) deep geologic repository for long-lived nuclear wastes in the world at the WIPP in 1999. The only other geologic disposal sites are in Germany, Sweden, Finland, and Norway, but these sites accept only low and medium-level radioactive wastes. Germany has operated a deep repository in a salt dome at Morsleben since 1981, although it is not accepting waste at this time. Sweden has operated a repository in caverns at the Forsmark nuclear site since 1988. Finland began operation of a repository in caverns at the Olkiluoto nuclear site in 1992 and at the Loviisa site in 1998. Norway began operation of a waste site in caverns at the Himdalen facility in 1999.

Other sites for deep geologic repositories for long-lived nuclear wastes are in the planning stages in Finland and Sweden. Planning in Belgium, France, and Japan is on track but far from implementation. The Yucca Mountain site will likely be the second long-lived nuclear waste deep geologic repository in the world.

In 1993 the United Kingdom opened a nuclear fuel reprocessing plant, one of only two in the world (the other is in France) that reprocesses used fuel from nuclear power generators around the world.

CHAPTER 8

PUBLIC OPINION AND ENVIRONMENTAL POLICY

Although most Americans are concerned about the environment, their involvement in environmentalism appears to have dropped between the early 1990s and the early 2000s. In 1991 a Gallup Poll asked people whether they thought of themselves as environmentalists. Seventy-eight percent said they were environmentalists, while only 19 percent indicated they were not. Ten years later, in 2001, the Gallup organization asked people whether they thought of themselves as active participants in the environmental movement, sympathetic towards the movement but not active, neutral, or unsympathetic towards the environmental movement. Eighteen percent said they were active participants, 50 percent reported that they were sympathetic but not active, 25 percent were neutral, and 5 percent were unsympathetic. Although 68 percent of those surveyed appeared interested in environmental issues, only 18 percent were acting on their interest. (See Table 8.1.)

MOOD OF THE NATION

The 2001 Gallup survey found that only 25 percent of Americans felt the nation has made a great deal of progress in dealing with environmental problems in the past few decades. This number was down from 36 percent in 1999, but was considerably higher than the result of 14 percent in 1990. However, the percentage of Americans who felt that we had made only some progress (rather than a great deal) remained relatively stable throughout the decade, and was at about 64 percent in 2001. (See Table 8.2.)

When asked if they thought the federal government was doing too much, too little, or about the right amount to protect the environment, only 11 percent of people polled felt that the government was doing too much. Fifty-five percent felt the government was doing too little, and 31

TABLE 8.1

Levels of participation in and sympathy for the environmental movement, 2000–01

Question: Thinking specifically about the environmental movement, do you think of yourself as — an active participant in the environmental movement, sympathetic towards the movement, but not active, neutral, or unsympathetic towards the environmental movement?

	Active participant %	Sympathetic, but not active %	Neutral %	Unsympathetic %	No opinion %
2001 Mar 5-7	18	50	25	5	2
2000 Apr -9	16	55	23	5	1

Note: Data based on telephone interviews with a randomly selected national sample of 1,060 Americans, 18 years and older. Margin of error is +/− 3 percentage points.

SOURCE: Riley E. Dunlap and Lydia Saad, *Only One in Four Americans Are Anxious About the Environment,* The Gallup Organization, Princeton, NJ, April 16, 2001 [Online] http://www.gallup.com/poll/releases/pr010416.asp [accessed October 2, 2001]

TABLE 8.2

Opinion on progress in dealing with environmental problems, selected years, 1990–2001

How much progress have we made in dealing with environmental problems in the past few decades — say since 1970? Would you say we have made a great deal of progress, only some progress, or hardly any progress at all?

	A great deal of progress	Only some progress	Hardly any progress at all	No opinion
2001 Mar 5-7	25	64	9	2
2000 Apr 3-9	26	64	9	1
1999 Apr 13-14	36	55	8	1
1995 Apr 17-19	24	61	14	1
1991 Apr 11-14	18	61	19	1
1990 Apr 5-8	14	63	21	2

Note: 2001 data based on telephone interviews with a randomly selected national sample of 506 Americans, 18 years and older. Margin of error is +/− 5 percentage points.

SOURCE: Riley E. Dunlap and Lydia Saad, *Only One in Four Americans Are Anxious About the Environment,* The Gallup Organization, Princeton, NJ, April 16, 2001 [Online] http://www.gallup.com/poll/releases/pr010416.asp [accessed October 2, 2001]

TABLE 8.3

Opinion on amount of effort put into protecting the environment, March 2001

Question: For each of the following, please say whether you think they are doing too much, too little, or about the right amount in terms of protecting the environment. How about — ?

2001 Mar 5-7	Too much %	Too little %	About the right amount %	No opinion %
A. The federal government	11	55	31	3
B. U.S. corporations	4	68	23	5
C. The American people	2	65	30	3

Note: Data based on telephone interviews with a randomly selected national sample of 1,060 Americans, 18 years and older. Margin of error is +/– 3 percentage points.

SOURCE: Riley E. Dunlap and Lydia Saad, *Only One in Four Americans Are Anxious About the Environment,* The Gallup Organization, Princeton, NJ, April 16, 2001 [Online] http://www.gallup.com/poll/releases/pr010416.asp [accessed October 2, 2001]

TABLE 8.4

Attitudes concerning the priority of various environmental problems, October 2000

MEAN ON A SCALE OF 1 (LOW PRIORITY) TO 10 (HIGH PRIORITY)

Water pollution	8.4	Ozone depletion	7.4
Air pollution	8.0	Pesticides and herbicides	7.3
Recycling more material	7.9	Hormone disrupting chemicals	7.3
Depletion of forest lands	7.7	Endangered species	7.1
Alternative fuels for automobiles	7.5	Global warming	7.0
Garbage and landfills	7.4		

Note: Results are from a survey conducted October 20-23, 2000. Telephone interviews were conducted among a representative random sample consisting of 1,005 adults (age 18+) residing within the continental U.S. Some questions were asked of a split sample consisting of approximately 500 respondents. The margin of sampling error at a 95 percent confidence interval is ±3.1 percentage points for the full sample and ±4.4 for the split sample.

SOURCE: "Priority of Environmental Problems," in *The Wirthlin Report: Current Trends in Public Opinion From Wirthlin Worldwide,* vol. 10, no. 8, Wirthlin Worldwide, McLean, VA, November 2000

percent thought that it was doing about the right amount. (See Table 8.3.) Additionally, most Americans thought other sectors of society were not concerned enough about environmental problems. Sixty-five percent thought the American public was doing too little about the environment. Criticism of American business and industry was high, with 68 percent of those surveyed responding that U.S. corporations are doing too little to protect the environment.

In an October 2000 survey conducted by Wirthlin Worldwide, a Virginia-based marketing research and consulting company, Americans rated what they felt were the most important environmental problems. Water pollution, air pollution, and recycling more material ranked highest, with concerns over hormone-disrupting chemicals, endangered species, and global warming ranking the lowest. Garbage and landfills rated 7.4 out of 10 on their level of concern, where 10 indicates the highest priority. (See Table 8.4.)

Similarly, in the 2001 Gallup survey, Americans rated their environmental concerns. (See Table 8.5.) As with the Wirthlin survey, water pollution and air pollution ranked highest, and soil pollution was also a pressing concern. (Gallup did not include recycling on their list.) Urban sprawl, global warming, and acid rain ranked lowest on the Gallup list of concerns.

When Wirthlin survey respondents were asked which industries were "causers" or "solvers" of environmental problems, the chemical, oil, and gas industries were ranked worst as causers of pollution. The computer and natural gas industries ranked best. However, the 2000 scores for the top-ranked computer and natural gas industries were lower than in the past, indicating that they are no longer seen as "solvers" of environmental problems but "causers." (See Table 8.6.)

Roper Starch Worldwide, in a 1998 study ("The Power of Two: Conservation and Corporate Environmental Responsibility," *The Public Pulse*), reported that Americans looked favorably on corporations that undertake environmental improvement measures. Seventy-eight percent said they had more positive feelings about corporations associated with environmental groups. Three in four claimed they would be more likely to buy such a corporation's products, and two in five said they might invest in a company that partners with an environmental group.

Environmental Organizations

Results from a 1999 survey conducted by Wirthlin Worldwide revealed sources of information about environmental health risks. Americans generally viewed environmental watchdog groups as more credible than private industries. However, the respondents rated the Environmental Protection Agency as having higher credibility than environmental groups, and statements from independent scientists or medical doctors were ranked most credible. (See Table 8.7.)

A MISINFORMED PUBLIC—THE NINTH ANNUAL NATIONAL REPORT CARD

The National Environmental Education and Training Foundation (NEETF), a private non-profit organization, was chartered by Congress to serve as a link between the public and private sectors to facilitate partnerships in support of environmental education. NEETF annually commissions Roper Starch Worldwide to conduct surveys of the American people, which provide the data for the *National Report Card on Environmental Attitudes, Knowledge, and Behaviors.* To date, nine annual report cards have been published.

The latest version of the report card was published in 2001. The data for this report were collected in 2000.

TABLE 8.5

Degree of worry about environmental problems, 1989, 2000, and 2001

	Percent who worry "a great deal"		
	2001	2000	1989
Pollution of drinking water	64	72	—
Pollution of rivers, lakes, and reservoirs	58	66	72
Contamination of soil and water by toxic waste	58	64	69
Contamination of soil and water by radioactivity from nuclear facilities	49	52	54
Air pollution	48	59	63
The loss of natural habitat for wildlife	48	51	58
Damage to the Earth's ozone layer	47	49	51
The loss of tropical rain forests	44	51	42
Ocean and beach pollution	43	54	60
Extinction of plant and animal species	43	45	—
Urban sprawl and loss of open spaces	35	42	—
The "greenhouse effect" or global warming	33	40	35
Acid rain	28	34	41

Note: Data based telephone interviews with a randomly selected national sample of 1,060 Americans 18 years and older. Respondents were given a list of 13 problems and asked to indicate the degree to which they worry about each one. Margin of error is +/– 3 percentage points.

SOURCE: Riley E. Dunlap and Lydia Saad, *Only One in Four Americans Are Anxious About the Environment,* The Gallup Organization, Princeton, NJ, April 16, 2001 [Online] http://www.gallup.com/poll/releases/pr010416.asp [accessed October 2, 2001]

TABLE 8.6

Views on various industries' environmental performance, selected years 1993–2000

	INDUSTRY	1993 score*	1997 score*	1998 score*	2000 score*
Best	Computers	25	11	15	-4
	Natural gas	11	-9	7	-8
	Electrical utilities	n/a	n/a	-11	-10
	Furniture	-29	-19	-15	-18
	Forest/paper products	-28	-36	-34	-24
	Nuclear power	-42	-50	-43	-31
	Steel	n/a	-40	-21	-36
	Plastics	-38	-36	-35	-37
	Fast food	-69	-43	-45	-41
	Automotive	n/a	-50	-56	-49
	Oil/gasoline	-59	-69	-65	-57
Worst	Chemicals	-59	-75	-71	-69

* difference score = % who say this industry has SOLVED environmental problems minus % who say this industry has CAUSED environmental problems. Higher scores are better. "NEITHER" responses are not reflected in the scores.

Note: 2000 results are from a survey conducted October 20-23, 2000. Telephone interviews were conducted among a representative random sample consisting of 1,005 adults (age 18+) residing within the continental U.S. Some questions were asked of a split sample consisting of approximately 500 respondents. The margin of sampling error at a 95 percent confidence interval is ±3.1 percentage points for the full sample and ±4.4 for the split sample.

SOURCE: "Industry Environmental Scorecard," in *The Wirthlin Report: Current Trends in Public Opinion From Wirthlin Worldwide,* vol. 10, no. 8, Wirthlin Worldwide, McLean, VA, November 2000

TABLE 8.7

Opinion on reliability of various sources about environmental health risks, 1999

(MEAN RATING, WHERE 7=VERY RELIABLE, 1=NOT AT ALL RELIABLE)

5.6	A statement from an independent scientist or medical doctor
5.3	The U.S. Environmental Protection Agency
5.0	An environmental watchdog group
4.9	An independently published story
4.2	News reports in the media
4.1	A local government agency
3.9	Friends and neighbors
3.9	A statement from a scientist or medical doctor who works for the company/industry in question
3.5	Web sites on the Internet
3.2	A spokesperson for the company or industry in question

Note: Data contain selected results from two different surveys conducted June 4-7, 1999 and October 22-26, 1999. Interviews were conducted by telephone with representative random samples consisting, respectively, of 1,004 and 1,023 adults (age 18+) residing within the continental United States. The margin of sampling error for each sample is ±3 percentage points in 95 out of 100 cases.

SOURCE: "Reliability of Sources About Environmental Health Risks," in *The Wirthlin Report: Current Trends in Public Opinion From Wirthlin Worldwide,* vol. 9, no. 9, Wirthlin Worldwide, McLean, VA, November 1999

Researchers conducted telephone interviews of 1,505 Americans, 18 years of age and older, asking them about their beliefs on environmental issues and questioning respondents about their knowledge on such matters.

Two out of three adults failed a simple test on environmental knowledge. (See Table 8.8.) For example, only one in three knew that the burning of fossil fuels—coal, natural gas, and oil—produces most of the country's electricity. Half the public thought electricity was produced mostly by waterpower (as at the Hoover Dam, for example), which actually accounts for just 12 percent of U.S. energy. Such misunderstandings, shown throughout this test, may explain why lawmakers often find it difficult to engage the general public in issues such as global warming and the maintenance of air quality. Table 8.9 shows how the American public scored on various subjects.

The 2001 *National Report Card* (2000 NEETF/Roper Survey) showed that the public, despite considerable ignorance of issues, clearly ranks laws for the protection of water and air as some of the most important among environmental protection laws. Seventy percent of respondents felt that laws and regulations for water pollution have not gone far enough, and 63 percent felt this way about air pollution laws and regulations. (See Figure 8.1.)

The *National Report Card* also revealed that Americans stated they engaged in certain environmental activities. When asked how often they performed eight activities that benefit the environment, a majority of Americans said they performed four of them "frequently." As Figure 8.2 shows, 85 percent of those surveyed noted that they try to conserve electricity, 61 percent try to conserve water, 59 percent recycle, and 54 percent try to reduce the amount of trash and garbage they create. The proportion of respondents saying they try to conserve

TABLE 8.8

National environmental report card
Subject: Environmental knowledge
Student: The American public

Grade		Percent of total sample receiving grade	Percent of men receiving grade	Percent of women receiving grade
A (11 or 12 correct)	Pass	11	15	6
B (10 correct)	Pass	10	14	7
C (9 correct)	Pass	11	14	8
D (8 correct)	Fail	13	13	13
F (7 or fewer)	Fail	55	45	65
Overall percentage passing		32	43	21

SOURCE: "Figure 18: National Environmental Report Card," in *The Ninth Annual National Report Card on Environmental Attitudes, Knowledge, and Behaviors,* The National Environmental Education & Training Foundation and Roper Starch Worldwide, Washington, DC, May 2001

TABLE 8.9

Percentage answering environmental knowledge questions correctly, 1997 and 2000

Content of Environmental Knowledge Question	2000 %	1997 %
The most common source of water pollution	28	23
How most electricity in the U.S. is generated	33	33
Definition of biodiversity	41	40
The primary benefit of wetlands	53	53
Protection provided by ozone in upper atmosphere	54	57
Disposal of nuclear waste in the U.S.	57	58
Recognition of a renewable resource	65	66
The largest source of carbon monoxide (air pollution) in U.S.	65	69
Knowledge about materials considered hazardous waste	67	67
Name of the primary federal agency that works to protect environment	72	74
The most common reason for extinction of animal and plant species	74	73
Where most household garbage ends up	85	83

SOURCE: "Figure 19: Percentage Answering Knowledge Questions Correctly," in *The Ninth Annual National Report Card on Environmental Attitudes, Knowledge, and Behaviors,* The National Environmental Education & Training Foundation and Roper Starch Worldwide, Washington, DC, May 2001

water, reduce the amount of garbage they produce, purchase biodegradable or recyclable products, avoid using chemicals in their yard or garden, or use alternative transportation is lower than in the past two years, however.

In trying to explain this decline in environmentally-conscious behaviors, the Roper researchers uncovered a relationship between environmental knowledge and engagement in environmentally-related activities. Correlation studies showed that as overall environmental knowledge increased, the likelihood of participation in several environmental activities also increased. This trend was most evident for turning off lights when not in use, recycling newspapers, cans, and glass, and avoiding the use of chemicals in the yard. It is likely, then, that increasing the environmental knowledge of the U.S. populace would increase overall involvement in environmental activities, and respondents support the idea of environmental education. Ninety-five percent of adults believe environmental education should be taught in schools. (See Table 8.10.)

NEETF and Roper Starch found that Americans also seemed hopeful about the future of the environment in 2000. Most believed that technology would help solve environmental problems. (See Figure 8.3.)

PROTECTING THE ENVIRONMENT VS. ECONOMIC GROWTH

In a 1998 report on the environmental attitudes of Americans, Wirthlin Worldwide concluded that environmental support in the United States generally moves in accord with the economy. Wirthlin compared U.S. unemployment rates to data they collected on environmental support among Americans. They found a statistically significant inverse relationship between the unemployment

level and support for environmental protection—that is, when unemployment rises, environmental support falls. The report concluded, "When consumer confidence reflects a good economy, public concern for social issues is heightened, and pro-environmental sentiments run high. But when the economy is bad, the environment tends to fall to the back burner." ("Environmental Support Systems Amid Economic Uncertainty," *The Wirthlin Report 8,* no. 9, September 1998, p. 1.)

All nine NEETF/Roper surveys (*National Report Card*) agree with the conclusions of the 1998 Wirthlin Worldwide report. They found that the majority of Americans believe that environmental protection and economic development go hand in hand. According to these reports, most Americans do not believe that they must choose between environmental protection and economic development, but feel they can find a balance between the two. If forced to choose, however, 71 percent of the public in the 2000 survey chose to make the environment a priority. This percentage remained relatively stable over the previous four years. (See Figure 8.4.)

When asked to weigh the benefit of protecting the environment at the expense of economic growth, Gallup's 2001 survey produced somewhat weaker pro-environment results. (Note: The Gallup data were collected in 2001 and the NEETF/Roper data were collected in 2000.) The Gallup data showed that 57 percent of respondents thought that the environment should be given priority over the economy, even if that prioritization risked curbing economic growth. Just 33 percent thought economic growth should be given priority, even if the environment suffered to some extent. This pro-environment viewpoint

FIGURE 8.1

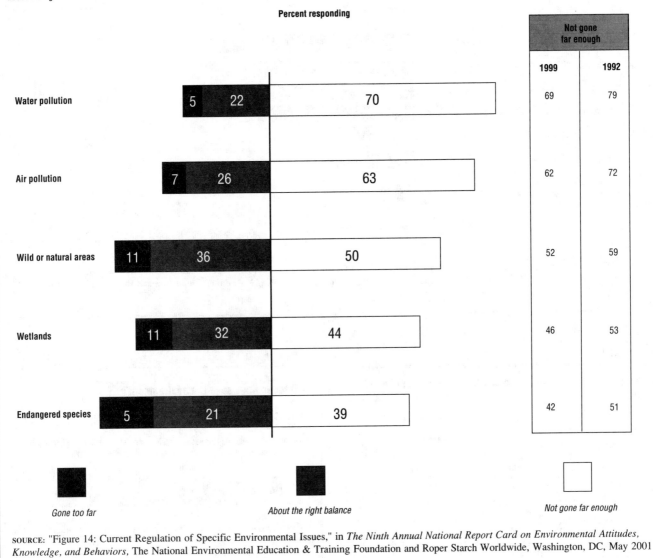

Current regulation of specific environmental issues

Question: Thinking now about some specific areas, at the present time, do you think laws and regulations for (INSERT ISSUE) have gone too far, not far enough, or have struck about the right balance?

Percent responding

	Gone too far	About the right balance	Not gone far enough	Not gone far enough 1999	Not gone far enough 1992
Water pollution	5	22	70	69	79
Air pollution	7	26	63	62	72
Wild or natural areas	11	36	50	52	59
Wetlands	11	32	44	46	53
Endangered species	5	21	39	42	51

Gone too far   About the right balance   Not gone far enough

SOURCE: "Figure 14: Current Regulation of Specific Environmental Issues," in *The Ninth Annual National Report Card on Environmental Attitudes, Knowledge, and Behaviors*, The National Environmental Education & Training Foundation and Roper Starch Worldwide, Washington, DC, May 2001

has ranged between 57 and 71 percent since it was first measured in 1984, and the March 2001 figure of 57 percent is the lowest the number has been in that time. (See Table 8.11.)

Wirthlin Worldwide collected similar data in its November 2000 report. Figure 8.5 shows that 66 percent of respondents felt environmental standards could not be too high, and continuing improvements must be made regardless of cost.

Even when faced with a specific instance in which they must weigh economic versus environmental issues, more Americans choose a pro-environment position. The 2001 Gallup Poll surveyed Americans regarding their approval or disapproval of President George W. Bush's

non-adherence to the Kyoto international treaty, which sets voluntary limits on the production of carbon dioxide and other global warming-related gases. Bush feels that the treaty places more of an economic burden on the U.S. than other countries. As shown in Table 8.12, 41 percent of those polled approve of Bush's actions in this matter, and 48 percent disapprove.

How Reliable Are Polls on Environmental Issues?

Some experts suggest that opinion polls are unreliable guides to how voters feel about environmental issues. Although polls of Americans indicate that concern for environmental issues is great, some observers suggest that people often claim in polls that they are interested in environmental reform, giving the pollster the answer they

FIGURE 8.2

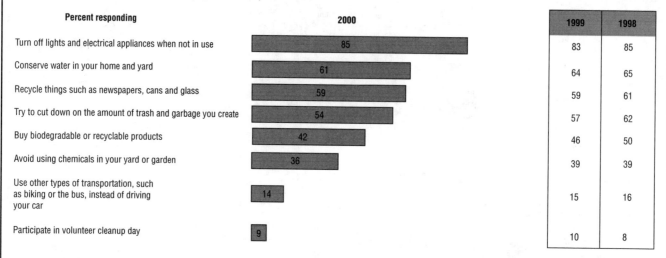

Environmental activities performed frequently in day-to-day life, 1998–2000

Question: Now I would like to ask you about some of the things you may do in your day-to-day life. For each of the following things, would you pleae tell me whether you never do it, sometimes do it, or frequently do it. (First/Next)...(Ask about each)

Percent responding

	2000	1999	1998
Turn off lights and electrical appliances when not in use	85	83	85
Conserve water in your home and yard	61	64	65
Recycle things such as newspapers, cans and glass	59	59	61
Try to cut down on the amount of trash and garbage you create	54	57	62
Buy biodegradable or recyclable products	42	46	50
Avoid using chemicals in your yard or garden	36	39	39
Use other types of transportation, such as biking or the bus, instead of driving your car	14	15	16
Participate in volunteer cleanup day	9	10	8

SOURCE: "Figure 20: Environmental Activities Performed Frequently in Day-to-Day Life," in *The Ninth Annual National Report Card on Environmental Attitudes, Knowledge, and Behaviors,* The National Environmental Education & Training Foundation and Roper Starch Worldwide, Washington, DC, May 2001

TABLE 8.10

Awareness and opinion of environmental education in schools, 1997 and 2000

	Percent responding					
	Yes		No/Depends		Don't know	
	2000	1997	2000	1997	2000	1997
Do you think environmental education should be taught in schools?	95	94	3	4	2	2
Do the schools in your community have environmental education?	50	51	9	9	41	40

SOURCE: "Figure 1: Awareness and Opinion of Environmental Education in Schools," in *The Ninth Annual National Report Card on Environmental Attitudes, Knowledge, and Behaviors,* The National Environmental Education & Training Foundation and Roper Starch Worldwide, Washington, DC, May 2001

FIGURE 8.3

Will technology save the environment?

Technology will find a way of solving environmental problems

Question: Please indicate (for each of the following statements) whether you strongly agree, mostly agree, mostly disagree, or strongly disagree.

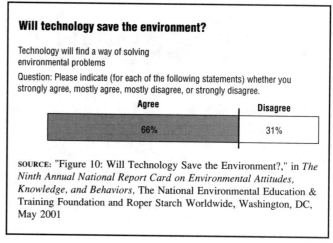

Agree	Disagree
66%	31%

SOURCE: "Figure 10: Will Technology Save the Environment?," in *The Ninth Annual National Report Card on Environmental Attitudes, Knowledge, and Behaviors,* The National Environmental Education & Training Foundation and Roper Starch Worldwide, Washington, DC, May 2001

---

think he or she wants to hear, when in actuality respondents may be more interested in economic growth.

THE ANTI-REGULATORY MOVEMENT

Over the past decade and a half, dissatisfaction with government regulation has grown. In 1994 the newly elected Republican-controlled Congress attempted to strike down a wide variety of federal regulations, including environmental regulations they considered overly burdensome. Bills were introduced to relax regulations under the Clean Water Act, Endangered Species Act, the Super-

fund Toxic Waste Clean-up Program, the Safe Drinking Water Act, and other environmental statutes. Although much of that legislation ultimately failed to pass, budget cuts resulted in a lack of enforcement of many statutes.

Several factors contributed to this reaction to federal regulation. During the early days of the environmental era, the United States was experiencing a post-World War II (1939-45) economic boom, leading Americans to regard regulatory costs as sustainable. But during the 1970s and 1980s, economic growth slowed, wages stagnated, and Americans became uncertain about the future. An increasing number of Americans started to question the costs of environmental protection. The return of a

FIGURE 8.4

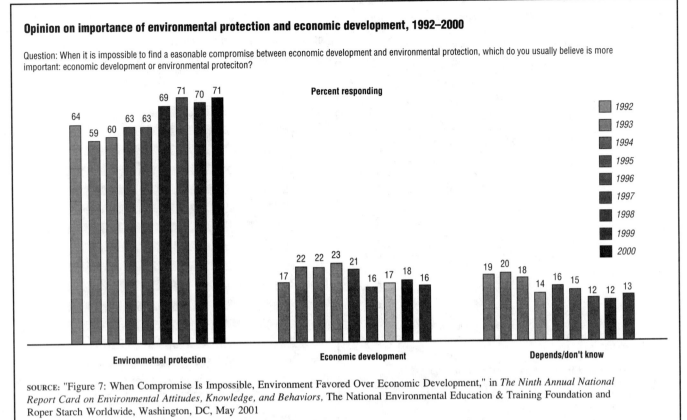

Opinion on importance of environmental protection and economic development, 1992–2000

Question: When it is impossible to find a easonable compromise between economic development and environmental protection, which do you usually believe is more important: economic development or environmental proteciton?

SOURCE: "Figure 7: When Compromise Is Impossible, Environment Favored Over Economic Development," in *The Ninth Annual National Report Card on Environmental Attitudes, Knowledge, and Behaviors,* The National Environmental Education & Training Foundation and Roper Starch Worldwide, Washington, DC, May 2001

vigorous economy in recent years has revived the American commitment to environmental issues, but not to the levels that some environmentalists had hoped. Most recently, the economy has taken a downturn, which may cause Americans to place environmental issues on the back burner once again.

Private property use has also played a very important role in the anti-regulatory movement. The Endangered Species Act and the wetlands provisions of the Clean Water Act spurred a grass-roots "private property rights" movement. Many people became concerned about legislation that would allow the government to "take" or devalue properties without compensation. For example, if federal regulations prohibited a landowner from building a beach house on his own private property, which happened to be protected land, the owner wanted the government to compensate him for devaluing the land. In addition, some observers believe that regulation of the waste industry, among others, has accomplished its goals and that it is time to relax control in favor of economic growth.

COMPARATIVE RISK ASSESSMENT—HOW CLEAN IS CLEAN?

Many Americans believe that pollution control budgets are too high in comparison to threats to the environment. They also believe that when pollution occurs,

governments overreact on the theory that the safest thing to do is clean up everything completely. This is no longer considered practical by many Americans, especially as regulatory agencies begin focusing on smaller and smaller pollution sources. Instead of responding immediately to every potential threat, many experts believe there needs to be a pause for evaluation. Such an approach is termed comparative risk assessment.

Comparative risk assessment differs from the scientific discipline of quantitative risk assessment and cost-benefit analysis that some congressmen advocate. Comparative risk assessment factors in more subjective criteria than does quantitative risk assessment. Comparative risk assessment works like this: A committee of citizens looks into potential pollution problems, reviewing pertinent scientific information—including risk assessments and cost-benefit analyses—about the hazards, and then ranks the perils to a city's health, natural surroundings, and general quality of life. In short, comparative risk assessment asks communities to decide for themselves what environmental problems to take most seriously by factoring in both scientific evidence and quality-of-life concerns that cannot be economically quantified. A number of states have launched comparative risk assessment projects. Critics of this approach fear it will be used as a way to cloud issues and hold up progress.

TABLE 8.11

Opinion about priority level of the environment and the economy, selected years, 1984–2001

Question: With which one of these statements about the environment and the economy do you most agree: protection of the environment should be given priority, even at the risk of curbing economic growth (or) economic growth should be given priority, even if the environment suffers to some extent?

	Protection of the environment %	Economic growth %	Equal priority (vol.) %	No opinion %
2001 Mar 5-7	57	33	6	4
2000 Apr 3-9	67	28	2	3
2000 Jan 13-16	70	23	—	7
1999 Apr 13-14	67	28	—	5
1999 Mar 12-14	65	30	—	5
1998 Apr 17-19	68	24	—	8
1997 Jul 25-27	66	27	—	7
1995 Apr 17-19	62	32	—	6
1992 Jan 5-Mar 31	58	26	8	8
1991 Apr	71	20	—	9
1990 Apr	71	19	—	10
1984 Sep	61	28	—	11

Note: (vol.) = Volunteered response. 2001 data based on telephone interviews with a randomly selected national sample of 1,060 Americans, 18 years and older. Margin of error is +/– 3 percentage points.

SOURCE: Riley E. Dunlap and Lydia Saad, *Only One in Four Americans Are Anxious About the Environment,* The Gallup Organization, Princeton, NJ, April 16, 2001 [Online] http://www.gallup.com/poll/releases/pr010416.asp [accessed October 2, 2001]

LITIGATION AND ENVIRONMENTAL POLICY

Courts have been an important forum for developing environmental policy because they allow citizens to challenge complex environmental laws and to affect the decision-making process. Individuals and groups can sue after a regulation has been enacted, if an agency fails to enforce a policy, or if they feel the legislature is unsympathetic to their cause. Just the threat of litigation has changed policy within agencies enforcing environmental laws.

An environmental law can be challenged on grounds that it violates the Constitution of the United States. Successful challenges can force the legislature to bring the law into constitutional compliance. A lawsuit can also be filed based on harm to a person, property, or an economic interest, such as major claims involving asbestos, lead, or loss of private property. Lawsuits have also prompted legislation, such as the federal Superfund law and the Toxic Substances Control Act, requiring agencies to control pollutants.

NORTH AMERICAN AGREEMENT ON ENVIRONMENTAL COOPERATION (NAAEC)

In 1993 the United States, Canada, and Mexico signed the North American Agreement on Environmental Cooperation (NAAEC), the environmental side

FIGURE 8.5

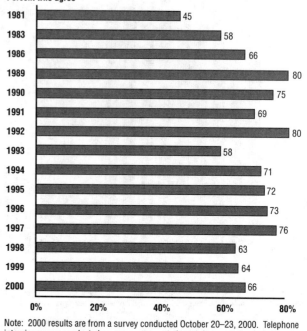

Opinion on importance of environmental standards regardless of cost, selected years 1981–2000

Statement: "Environmental standards cannot be too high, and continuing improvements must be made regardless of cost"

Percent who agree

Year	Percent
1981	45
1983	58
1986	66
1989	80
1990	75
1991	69
1992	80
1993	58
1994	71
1995	72
1996	73
1997	76
1998	63
1999	64
2000	66

Note: 2000 results are from a survey conducted October 20–23, 2000. Telephone interviews were conducted among a representative random sample consisting of 1,005 adults (age 18+) residing within the continental U.S. Some questions were asked of a split sample consisting of approximately 500 respondents. The margin of sampling error at a 95% confidence interval is 63.1 percentage points for the full sample and 64.4 for the split sample.

SOURCE: "Environmentalism Barometer," in *The Wirthlin Report: Current Trends in Public Opinion From Wirthlin Worldwide,* vol. 10, no. 8, Wirthlin Worldwide, McLean, VA, November 2000

agreement to the North American Free Trade Agreement (NAFTA), to discourage countries from weakening environmental standards to encourage trade. Other countries may become members of the NAAEC, and a country may withdraw from the agreement and still remain a NAFTA member.

A member country can be challenged in two ways under the NAAEC if one of its states fails to enforce environmental laws. First, a nongovernmental agency, such as the Sierra Club or Audubon Society, may petition the commission. This alerts the public to the violation. Second, a member country can initiate proceedings against another member country showing a "persistent pattern of failure ... to enforce its environmental law" that can be directly linked to goods and services traded between the parties. If the conflict is not resolved through initial consultations, arbitration may be required and fines levied for failure to cooperate. If fines are not paid, a complaining party may suspend NAFTA benefits in an amount not exceeding the assessment.

EXPOSING POLLUTERS TO PUBLIC PRESSURE

The Clinton Administration expanded "right to know" initiatives, which are environmental programs designed to inhibit pollution, not with legislation and regulation, but by exposing polluters to pressure from a well-informed public. One of these initiatives is the Sector Facility Indexing Project (SFIP), which was initiated by the EPA in early 1995. SFIP provides data on the Internet in one location (http://www.epa.gov/oeca/sfi/) about 621 facilities in five industries: automobile, steel, metals, oil refining, and papermaking. In June 2001, data for 253 major federal facilities in the United States were added to SFIP. The environmental profiles of facilities include inspections, noncompliance, enforcement, pollution releases, and pollution spills. SFIP also includes information on the location of each facility and the population of the surrounding area.

TABLE 8.12

Opinion on President Bush's decision for the U.S. not to adhere to the Kyoto treaty, April 2001

Question: President Bush recently announced that the United States will not adhere to the Kyoto international treaty, which sets voluntary limits on the production of carbon dioxide and other global warming-related gases. Bush said that the treaty places too much of an economic burden on the U.S. while demanding little of developing countries. Do you approve or disapprove of Bush's decision for the U.S. not to adhere to the Kyoto treaty?

	Approve	Disapprove	No opinion
2001 Apr 6-8	41%	48%	11%

Note: Data based on telephone interviews with a randomly selected national sample of 519 Americans, 18 years and older. Margin of error is +/– 5 percentage points.

SOURCE: Riley E. Dunlap and Lydia Saad, *Only One in Four Americans Are Anxious About the Environment*, The Gallup Organization, Princeton, NJ, April 16, 2001 [Online] http://www.gallup.com/poll/releases/pr010416.asp [accessed October 2, 2001]

IMPORTANT NAMES AND ADDRESSES

Environmental Defense National Headquarters
257 Park Ave. South
New York, NY 10010
(212) 505-2100
FAX (212) 505-2375
http://www.edf.org

Environmental Industry Associations
4301 Connecticut Ave., NW, #300
Washington, DC 20008
(202) 244-4700
FAX (202) 966-4818
http://www.envasns.org

Foodservice and Packaging Institute, Inc.
150 S. Washington St., Suite 204
Falls Church, VA 22046
(703) 538-2800
FAX (703) 538-2187
http://www.fpi.org

Friends of the Earth
025 Vermont Ave. NW
Washington, DC 20005
(202) 783-7400
FAX (202) 783-0444
(877) 843-8687
http://www.foe.org

Glass Packaging Institute
515 King St., Suite 420
Alexandria, VA 22314
(703) 684-6359
FAX (703) 684-6048
http://www.gpi.org

Greenpeace USA
702 H St., NW, Suite 300
Washington, DC 20001
(202) 462-1177
FAX (202) 462-4507
http://www.greenpeace.org

Izaak Walton League of America
707 Conservation Ln.
Gaithersburg, MD 20878
(301) 548-0150
FAX (301) 548-0146
(800) 453-5463
http://www.iwla.org

League of Women Voters
1730 M St., NW, Suite 1000
Washington, DC 20036-4508
(202) 429-1965
FAX (202) 429-0854
http://www.lwv.org

National Audubon Society
700 Broadway
New York, NY 10003
(212) 979-3000
FAX (212) 979-3188
http://www.audubon.org

National Consumers League
1701 K. St., NW, Suite 1200
Washington, DC 20006
(202) 835-3323
FAX (202) 835-0747
http://www.nclnet.org

Natural Resources Defense Council
40 West 20th St.
New York, NY 10011
(212) 727-2700
http://www.nrdc.org

Sierra Club
85 Second St., Second Flr.
San Francisco, CA 94105-3441
(415) 977-5500
FAX (415) 977-5799
http://www.sierraclub.org

Steel Recycling Institute
680 Andersen Dr.
Pittsburgh, PA 15220-2700
FAX (412) 922-3213

(800) 876-7274
http://www.recycle-steel.org

U.S. Department of Energy (DOE)
1000 Independence Ave., SW
Washington, DC 20585
FAX (202) 586-4403
(800) DIAL-DOE
http://www.energy.gov

U.S. Environmental Protection Agency Headquarters (EPA)
Ariel Rios Building
1200 Pennsylvania Ave., NW
Washington, DC 20460
(202) 260-2090
http://www.epa.gov

U.S. Fish and Wildlife Service
1849 C St., NW
Washington, DC 20240
(202) 208-5634
http://www.fws.gov

U.S. Geological Survey National Center
12201 Sunrise Valley Dr.
Reston, VA 20192
(703) 648-4000
(888) 275-8747
http://www.usgs.gov

U.S. Nuclear Regulatory Commission (NRC)
Office of Public Affairs
Mail Stop O-2A13
Washington, DC 20555
(301) 415-8200
(800) 368-5642
http://www.nrc.gov

Worldwatch Institute
1776 Massachusetts Ave., NW
Washington, DC 20036-1904
(202) 452-1999
FAX (202) 296-7365
http://www.worldwatch.org

RESOURCES

The U.S. Environmental Protection Agency (EPA) is the most significant source of information on solid waste and pollution in America. The EPA is responsible for keeping statistics on pollution, educating the American people about pollution and environmental issues, and making sure that environmental regulations are obeyed. The EPA's *Let's Reduce and Recycle: Curriculum for Solid Waste Awareness* (1990) is a valuable teaching guide to introduce students to recycling and environmental pollution awareness. *The Plain English Guide to the Clean Air Act* (1993) offers a basic introduction to the Clean Air Act and the problems of air pollution. It is available on the Internet on the EPA website at www.epa.gov, and is updated regularly. The report *Municipal Solid Waste in the United States: 1999 Facts and Figures* (2000) is part of a series of reports that characterizes municipal solid waste in the U.S. The 1999 report provides a historical database for a 39-year characterization of the materials and products in the municipal waste stream. *National Air Quality and Emissions Trends Report, 1999* (2001) is the 27th annual report on air pollution trends in the United States. The *National Water Quality Inventory: 1998 Report to Congress* (2000) is the 12th biennial report to both Congress and the public about the quality of our nation's surface and ground water. The *1999 Toxics Release Inventory* (2001) is a publicly available database containing information on toxic chemical releases and other waste management activities.

The U.S. Geological Survey (USGS) provides scientific information to help describe and understand the earth; minimize loss of life and property from natural disasters; manage water, energy, and biological and mineral resources; and enhance and protect the quality of life. Its report *Distribution of Major Herbicides in Ground Water of the United States* (1999) was compiled in conjunction with the EPA and describes chemical contamination of American ground water.

The now-defunct Office of Technology Assessment (OTA), a branch of the United States Congress, provided studies on scientific problems facing the United States. The OTA's *Wastes in Marine Environments* (1987), *Bioremediation for Marine Oil Spills* (1991), and *Acid Rain and Transported Air Pollutants: Implications for Public Policy* (1984) are useful resources. OTA publications are still available from the U.S. Government Printing Office.

Other government publications helpful in the study of garbage and pollution include the U.S. Department of Energy's (DOE) *Yucca Mountain Science and Engineering Report* (2001), *The Waste Isolation Pilot Plant: Pioneering Nuclear Waste Disposal* (2000), and *Alternatives to Traditional Transportation Fuels* (1999). The Bureau of Justice Statistics of the U.S. Department of Justice published *Federal Enforcement of Environmental Laws, 1997* (1999) on environmental crime. *Superfund: Half the Sites Have All Cleanup Remedies in Place or Completed* (1999), *Superfund: Information on the Program's Funding and Status* (1999), *Indoor Pollution—Status of Federal Research Activities* (1999), *Solid Waste: State and Federal Efforts to Manage Nonhazardous Waste* (1995), *Animal Agriculture—Waste Management Practices* (1999), and *Hazardous and Nonhazardous Wastes: Demographics of People Living Near Waste Facilities* (1995) were all published by the U.S. General Accounting Office (GAO). The mission of the GAO is to ensure the executive branch's accountability to Congress under the Constitution and the government's accountability to the American people.

The Environmental Industry Associations, the waste management industry's trade association, provides many helpful brochures and booklets on waste management, including the timeline *Garbage Then and Now*.

The Natural Resources Defense Council (NRDC), a private environmental research organization, published *Testing the Waters: A Guide to Water Quality at Vacation*

Beaches (2001) on the condition of the nation's recreational beaches.

Wirthlin Worldwide, a private research and consulting firm in McLean, Virginia, publishes a monthly summary of trends in public opinion called the *Wirthlin Report*. The November 1999 and November 2000 issues are of particular interest to those studying the issues of garbage and pollution.

BioCycle, a journal of composting and recycling, provides information on waste disposal in its annual "State of Garbage in America" survey. The most recent version was published in two parts, in the April and November 2000 issues.

The National Conference of State Legislatures' *Legisbrief*, "New Developments in Environmental Justice" (1999), surveyed state enforcement of environmental laws, and "Lead Hazard Disclosures in Real Estate Transactions" (1997) provided data on states with lead disclosure laws. The National Conference of State Legislatures' staff updated both data sets for use in this book.

Roper Starch conducts an annual study for the National Environmental Education and Training Foundation. The most recent is the *Ninth Annual National Report Card on Environmental Knowledge, Attitudes, and Behaviors* (2001).

John C. Ryan and Alan Thein Durning, of Northwest Environmental Watch, published *Stuff—The Secret Lives of Everyday Things* (1997), on consumption in the United States.

Susan Strasser's *Waste and Want—A Social History of Trash* (Henry Holt and Company, New York, 1999) is a thorough and entertaining look at the treatment and role of garbage through history. It provides background on the history of solid waste.

The surveys of the Gallup Organization are a good resource to gauge public opinion on many different issues, including the environment.

Information Plus sincerely thanks all of the organizations listed above for the valuable information they provide.

INDEX

Page references in italics refer to photographs. References with the letter t following them indicate the presence of a table. The letter f indicates a figure. If more than one table or figure appears on a particular page, the exact item number for the table or figure being referenced is provided.

A

Acid
   from mining, 71–74
   precipitation, 70–71, 74f, 75f
Adirondack Mountains, 71, 75f
Agriculture industry
   consumption of red meat and poultry, 103t
   effect on ground water, 98–102, 101f
Air pollution, 4, 7, 43–65, 56f
   result of waste incineration, 20
   transmitted to water pollution, 74f
   See also Indoor air quality
Air toxics, 52–55, 55f
Aircraft air pollution, 60
Airport emissions, air pollution, 60
Alternative fuels, 57t
   vehicles, 58t, 59–60, 60t
Aluminum
   in municipal solid waste, 21–22
   recycling, 35f
Ancient civilizations, 1
Animal waste, 4, 100–102, 103f(6.16)
Aquatic life. *See* Marine life
Aquifers, 91
Arsenic, 76t
Atlantic Coast Demolition and Recycling Inc. v. Atlantic County (1997), 24–25
Atomic bomb, 116–117
Automobiles and auto industry, 55–60
   alternative fuel vehicles, 58t
   emissions, 62
   scrap automobiles, 39

B

Beaches. *See* Coastal waters
Beef industry, 23

Ben Oehrleins, Inc. v. Hennepin County (1997), 25
Beverage containers, 21–22
Bioaccumulation of pollutants, 68, 68f
Bioremediation, 81, 81t
Birds, effected by marine debris, 77
Boats and boating
   air pollution, 60
   effect of marine debris, 78
Brownfields redevelopment areas, 112–113
Buy-back centers, 31

C

C & A Carbone v. Clarkstown (1994), 24
Cadmium
   in municipal solid waste, 17
   in water pollution, 76t
CAFE. *See* Corporate Average Fuel Efficiency (CAFE) standards
Canada, 14
Carbon dioxide, 62
Carbon monoxide, 44t, 47–48, 49f(4.5), 49f(4.6)
Casks, radioactive material containers, 127
CERCLA. *See* Comprehensive Environmental Response, Compensation, and Liability Act of 1980
Chesapeake Bay, 71
Chevron Oil Company, 114
China, 63
Clarkstown, C & A Carbone v. (1994), 24
Clean Air Act Amendments of 1990, 7, 45, 56, 61
Clean Air Act of 1970, 45, 56, 60–61
Clean Water Act (1972), 74
Cleanup and restoration
   Clean Water Act (1972), 74
   ground water cleanup, 94–95, 104–105
   National Estuary Program, 82–83
   oil spills, 81, 81t
   Superfund sites, 108–112, 111f, 112f
   wetlands, 87
Cleveland, OH, 74
Clothes and textiles reuse, 4
Coastal waters, 69
   beach closing advisories, 72t–73t

Louisiana, 68
marine debris, 77t
medical waste, 79–80
oil spills, 80f, 81
pollutants and sources, 78–79, 78f
Collection programs, recycling and composting, 21
Combustion. *See* Incineration
Commercial waste. *See* Industrial practices
Comparative risk assessment, 135
Composting, 29, 31–33
   rates, 21t–22t
   See also Municipal solid waste; Recycling
Comprehensive Environmental Response, Compensation, and Liability Act of 1980 (CERCLA), 105, 108–109
Comprehensive State Ground Water Protection Programs (CSGWPP), 104f, 105
Compressed natural gas (CNG), 58–59
Consumer society, 5–6, 30
Consumption of resources, 5–6, 5t
Containers. *See* Packaging
Corporate Average Fuel Efficiency (CAFE) standards, 56–57
Court cases
   air pollution standards, 61
   Atlantic Coast Demolition and Recycling Inc. v. Atlantic County (1997), 24–25
   Ben Oehrleins, Inc. v. Hennepin County (1997), 25
   C & A Carbone v. Clarkstown (1994), 24
   environmental justice, 113–114
   environmental policy, 136
   Kennedy Heights Lawsuit (1997), 113–114
Criteria air pollutants, 43–44, 44t, 45t
Curbside recycling programs, 30–31
Cuyahoga River fire (1969), 74

D

DDT (Dichloro-diphenyl-trichloroethane), 98
Decomposition, in landfills, 15
Department of Energy (DOE), 57, 120, 120f, 121t
Deposit programs (recycling), 31